Aims & Scope

European Policy Analysis (EPA) is a double-blind peer-reviewed journal addressing European perspectives on the study of public policy. Published on behalf of the Policy Studies Organization, the journal provides a platform for individually submitted articles and special foci of high quality. Both empirical and theoretical contributions are welcomed, but EPA prefers submissions that present new theoretical or methodological perspectives combined with current data. Likewise, EPA invites overviews of country and regional perspectives on the study of public policy. With a focus on European countries, issues and studies, the journal follows a comparative approach enhancing the cross-continental theoretical understanding of policy research.

Copyright and Photocopying

Disclaimer

Proceedings of the Policy Studies Organization are available online at www.psocommons.org/proceedings.

Editorial Introduction to the Fifth Issue of European Policy Analysis

Nils C. Bandelow and Johanna Hornung

Origins and Aims of EPA

Both the practical "Policy Analysis" and the more academic "Theories of the Policy Process" originated in the United States. American perspectives still are very influential for the development of the field. However, each region and country has specific political and scientific institutions as well as political and scientific traditions, resulting in the existence of several interpretations and adaptations of Policy Studies (Blum & Schubert, 2013; Brans & Aubin, 2017; Halpern, Hassenteufel & Zittoun, 2017; van Nispen & Scholten, 2015; Veselý, Nekola & Hejzlarová, 2016). Very often, the country-specific discussion in the respective native language does only sporadically reach the international state of the art. Consequently, the different perspectives of Policy Analysis and Theories of the Policy Process in several European countries are less divided than in the United States. European scholars adopt theoretical frameworks stemming from the US-American perspective but often face the need to modify the lenses to deal with their respective political environment. Moreover, existing typical perspectives originating in non-American policy analysis have not been systematically included into the international discussion. For example, the French political science has developed the Programmatic Actor Framework (PAF, Genieys, 2010; Hassenteufel, Smyrl, Genieys & Moreno-Fuentes, 2010), which has not yet been included in American textbooks on Theories of the Policy Process (see e.g., Sabatier & Weible, 2014).

We founded *European Policy Analysis (EPA)* to reduce the gap between the international development and the European contributions to the field. Our journal provides a platform to publish high quality articles that apply the established perspectives of the field to European cases, to present new theoretical frameworks originated from European cases or by European scholars, to discuss the state of the art in European countries and regions, and to compare different perspectives of Policy Analysis. Introductions to the earlier issues also outline the general ideas of EPA (Bandelow, Sager & Schubert, 2015a; Bandelow, Sager, Schubert & Biegelbauer, 2015b; Bandelow, Sager & Schubert, 2016; Bandelow et al., 2015a,b).

The Policy Studies Organization established the journal together with the European editorial team starting in 2015 as one of the PSO's online journals. The success of the first issues enabled the cooperation with Wiley, starting in 2017.

doi: 10.1002/epa2.1013

EPA has different sorts of contributions. All articles present fresh theoretical and/or empirical results and undergo a strict double blind peer review process. Some issues comprise a special focus organized by guest editors. Contributions to a special focus also undergo the double blind peer review process. Additionally, EPA provides a platform for shorter essays by leading scholars who discuss recent political and scientific challenges. We also present some selected recent book publications of the field authored by our board members and reviewers, who will give a short summary of their work, to include the development of European policy studies, which is not solely based on journal articles but sometimes takes place in important high quality monographs.

Content of EPA Volumes 2015 and 2016

EPA is very much interested in *theoretical contributions and theoretical developments* of Policy Analysis in European countries also in combination with European case studies. The special focus of the third issue brings together some contributions that generated from a workshop organized by Klaus Schubert in Muenster, Germany. Robert Hoppe and Hal Colebatch (2016) address the disconnection between the academic study of the policy process and many political practices. Strassheim (2016) gives an overview on theories of time in Policy Analysis. Bornemann (2016) presents the perspective of integrative political strategies.

Among the most applied theoretical lenses of public policy are the Multiple Streams Framework (MSF) and the Advocacy Coalition Framework (ACF). While there are systematic reviews of the ACF and its applications in other journals, EPA provides a platform for both overviews on national particularities. European applications and developments of the MSF are presented by de Leeuw, Hoeijmakers and Peters (2016) and Deruelle (2016). Nohrstedt and Olofsson (2016) give an overview over ACF applications in Sweden. Blatter, Bombach and Wiprächtiger (2015) combine the MSF, the ACF, and the Rational Policy Cycle (RPC) to analyze how evidence can be used in gender policy.

EPA presents analyses of recent challenges and developments of specific policy subsystems in European countries, partially compared to other industrialized regions. There are special issues on perspectives on the governance of welfare markets (Klenk, 2015) and on demographic change and health care in Europe (Hunger & Neumann, 2016). A lot of EPA contributions have an *international comparative perspective*. Neil Gilbert (2015) distinguishes three different modes of welfare privatization. Bernhard Ebbinghaus (2015) discusses similarities and variances of welfare state transformation toward marketization and privatization in times of austerity. Klenk and Reiter (2015) compare the governance of hospital market in France and Germany. Neby, Lægreid, Mattei and Feiler (2015) show how different waiting list scandals resulting from similar reforms on hospital financing are handled in Norway and Germany. Rinscheid (2015) explains why Germany has reacted much more on the Fukushima disaster than Japan by focusing on the level of subsystem polarization. Skučiene and Moskvina (2016) provide a meta-analysis of retirement policies in central and eastern European countries.

Other papers focus on *specific national cases,* like Breidahl and Larsen (2015) on Denmark and Benjamin Ewert (2015), Paul and Huber (2015), Hegelich and Shahrezaye (2015), Neumann and Hunger (2016), Gkolfinopoulos (2016) on Germany, Sager, Mavrot and Hadorn (2015), Ingold and Pflieger (2016) on Switzerland, Vecchione and Parkhurst (2015) on Ghana (with a perspective based on European Policy Analysis) and Mondragón Ruiz de Lezana et al. (2016) on Spain.

Apart from country studies, EPA is also interested in contributions on EU policies. Igor Guardiancich (2015) explicates the hurdles toward any efforts for harmonization of pension schemes in the European Union. Wolf and Wenzelburger (2016) analyze problems of the recently founded European Insurance and Occupational Pensions Authority (EIOPA).

Some papers address *general questions* going beyond any specific regional focus. Hinterleitner and Rosser (2015) argue for the use of a sociological perspective to complement the rationalist perspective for understanding the role of credit ration agencies (CRAs) after the 2008 crisis. Schweizer (2015) discusses Law Activation Strategies (LAS) by using illustrations from Swiss cases. Hegelich (2016) presents machine learning techniques, adopts them and discusses applications for Policy Analysis and challenges that come with the applications. Ceccobelli and Cotta (2016) show that apart from leftist and young politicians major political actors do not give environmental issues on facebook a very relevant concern.

Overview Over the Fifth Issue of EPA (1/2017)

This fifth issue of EPA starts with an essay by **Nikolaos Zahariadis** who explains the paradox, that the migration crisis at the same time highlighted and intensified the internal conflicts within the European Union and brought the Member States closer together (Zahariadis, 2017). He thereby ties on the forum debate of previous issues (Beyme, 2016; Forss & Magro, 2016; Hansen, 2016; Hübner, 2016).

A greater political emphasis is to be expected in farm animal policy. **Colette S. Vogeler** compares German, Austrian, and Swiss policies in this field adopting revised versions of partisan theory and the lens of multilevel policies (Vogeler, 2017). Party politics explains large parts of the variance of national policies in Austria and Germany, while in Switzerland the focus on the domestic market leads to a high level of animal welfare policy.

Annette Elisabeth Töller questions the thesis that the "shadow of hierarchy" is a necessary and sufficient condition for voluntary regulation (Töller, 2017). She analyzes why the German pharmaceutical industry adopted the voluntary FSA codex. The case study demonstrates that a combination of rational choice institutionalism and normative institutionalism, which takes normative pressure into account explains both the adoption and the revisions of the codex.

Frans van Nispen and Peter Scholten test the influence of the economic and financial crisis on the use of expert knowledge by analyzing two very different Dutch cases (van Nispen & Scholten, 2017). They did not find evidence that expert knowledge has been used less as a result of the crisis. However, there was evidence for a more political or symbolic use of knowledge.

To what extend do European states use policies to lower emissions (mitigation) and/or to reduce expected climate change impacts (adaptation) as reactions to climate change? **Andreas Fleig, Nicole Schmidt and Jale Tosun** show that all EU states but Hungary have adopted at least one sort of these measures (Fleig, Schmidt & Tosun, 2017). While the literature expected mitigation to be the prevailing strategy, the evidence of the paper gives two strategies similar weight. However, there is no homogenous strategy.

Minna van Gerven and Mikael Nygård investigate work/family reconciliation policies in Finland and the Netherlands since 1995 (van Gerven & Nygård, 2017). They show the stability of policy paradigms over time by tracing the dominant ideas to be found in the coalition programs concerning equal treatment, employment promotion, and social investment.

Instutionalization of new policy subsystems undergoes different phases and ways. In German Policy Studies, this has been a focus for some years (Scheffel, 2016). **Abel Reiberg** uses a combination of field theory and institutional theory to interpret the construction of the subsystem as a form of collective production of understanding by an emerging policy elite (Reiberg, 2017).

European applications of the ACF often focus on the original element of policy oriented learning as a possible trigger of policy change (Bandelow, 2006). **Balázs Babarczy and László Imre** use the ACF in this way to analyze the establishment of a new Hungarian health system after since regime change in 1989–1990 (Babarczy & Imre, 2017). Unlike most applications of the ACF in established democracies, the Eastern European case study presents an example of cross-coalition policy learning.

The analysis of policy instruments belongs to the main interests of both the American and the European Policy Analysis. European case studies have to deal with the very special ("sui generis") system of the EU that has to use soft instruments in most areas to reach its goal (Pollex, 2017). **Jan Pollex** investigates the question how the EU frames and addresses the consumer for its sustainable consumption policy. Looking at central policy documents, he argues that the EU assumes average-rational consumers.

While the contributions to this issue emerged from different theoretical and empirical perspectives, the next issue will have a special focus on "Infrastructure Policy-Making: Between Regional Interests and Societal Goals". This sixth issue of EPA will appear in November 2017. Irrespective of the special focus, EPA is always interested in high quality original papers within the scope of the journal and in proposals for future special issues.

Nils C. Bandelow and Johanna Hornung
on behalf of the editorial team of EPA

References

Babarczy, Balázs, and László Imre. 2017. "Learning Processes in Hungarian Health Policy 1990–2004: A Case Study of Health Resource Allocation." *European Policy Analysis* 3 (1): 168–84.

Bandelow, Nils C. 2006. "Advocacy Coalitions, Policy-Oriented Learning and Long-Term Change in Genetic Engineering Policy: An Interpretist View." *GPS (German Policy Studies)* 3 (4): 743–95.

Bandelow, Nils C., Fritz Sager, and Klaus Schubert. 2015a. "Editorial Introduction to the First Issue of European Policy Analysis." *European Policy Analysis* 1 (1): 2.

———. 2016. "Editorial Introduction to the Third Issue of European Policy Analysis." *European Policy Analysis* 2 (1): 3–5.

Bandelow, Nils C., Fritz Sager, Klaus Schubert, and Peter Biegelbauer. 2015b. "Editorial Introduction to the Second Issue of European Policy Analysis." *European Policy Analysis* 1 (2): 1–4.

Beyme, Klaus von. 2016. "Refugees and Migration in Europe." *European Policy Analysis* 2 (1): 7–17.

Blatter, Joachim, Clara Bombach, and Roman Wiprächtiger. 2015. "Enhancing Gender Equity Through Evidence-Based Policymaking?: Theorizing and Tracing the Use of Systematic Knowledge in Family and Tax Policy Reforms." *European Policy Analysis* 1 (1): 3–34.

Blum, Sonja, and Klaus Schubert, ed. 2013. *Policy Analysis in Germany. International Library of Policy Analysis*. Bristol: Policy Press.

Bornemann, Basil. 2016. "Integrative Political Strategies—Conceptualizing and Analyzing a New Type of Policy Field." *European Policy Analysis* 2 (1): 168–95.

Brans, Marleen, and David Aubin. 2017. *Policy Analysis in Belgium. International Library of Policy Analysis*. Bristol: Policy Press.

Breidahl, Karen N., and Flemming Larsen. 2015. "The Developing Trajectory of the Marketization of Public Employment Services in Denmark—A New Way Forward or the End of Marketization?" *European Policy Analysis* 1 (1): 92–107.

Ceccobelli, Diego, and Benedetta Cotta. 2016. "Leaders' 'Green' Posts. The Environmental Issues Shared by Politicians on Facebook." *European Policy Analysis* 2 (2): 68–93.

de Leeuw, Evelyne, Marjan Hoeijmakers, and Dorothee T. Peters. 2016. "Juggling Multiple Networks in Multiple Streams." *European Policy Analysis* 2 (1): 196–217.

Deruelle, Thibaud. 2016. "Bricolage or Entrepreneurship?: Lessons from the Creation of the European Centre for Disease Prevention and Control." *European Policy Analysis* 2 (2): 43–67.

Ebbinghaus, Bernhard. 2015. "The Privatization and Marketization of Pensions in Europe: A Double Transformation Facing the Crisis." *European Policy Analysis* 1 (1): 56–73.

Ewert, Benjamin. 2015. "Change Agents and Service Providers?: User Organizations in the German Healthcare System." *European Policy Analysis* 1 (1): 149–67.

Fleig, Andreas, Nicole Schmidt, and Jale Tosun. 2017. "Legislative Dynamics of Mitigation and Adaptation Framework Policies in the EU." *European Policy Analysis* 3 (1): 101–24.

Forss, Karin, and Linnea Magro. 2016. "Facts or Feelings, Facts and Feelings?: The Post-Democracy Narrative in the Brexit Debate." *European Policy Analysis* 2 (2): 12–7.

Genieys, William. 2010 *The New Custodians of the State: Programmatic Elites in French Society*. New Brunswick, NJ: Transaction Publishers.

Gilbert, Neil. 2015. "Restructuring the Mixed Economy of Welfare: Three Modes of Privatization." *European Policy Analysis* 1 (1): 41–55.

Gkolfinopoulos, Andreas. 2016. "The Migration of Greek Physicians to Germany: Motivations, Factors and the Role of National Health Sectors." *European Policy Analysis* 2 (2): 136–57.

Guardiancich, Igor. 2015. "Portability of Supplementary Pension Rights in Europe: A Lowest Common Denominator Solution." *European Policy Analysis* 1 (1): 74–91.

Halpern, Charlotte, Patrick Hassenteufel, and Philippe Zittoun. 2017. *Policy Analysis in France. International Library of Policy Analysis*. Bristol: Policy Press.

Hansen, Randall. 2016. "Immigrants, ISIS, the Refugee Crisis, and Integration in Europe." *European Policy Analysis* 2 (1): 14–9.

Hassenteufel, Patrick, Marc Smyrl, William Genieys, and Francisco J. Moreno-Fuentes. 2010. "Programmatic Actors and the Transformation of European Health Care States." *Journal of Health Politics, Policy and Law* 35 (4): 517–38.

Hegelich, Simon. 2016. "Decision Trees and Random Forests: Machine Learning Techniques to Classify Rare Events." *European Policy Analysis* 2 (1): 98–120.

Hegelich, Simon, and Morteza Shahrezaye. 2015. "The Communication Behavior of German MPs on Twitter: Preaching to the Converted and Attacking Opponents." *European Policy Analysis* 1 (2): 155–74.

Hinterleitner, Markus, and Christian Rosser. 2015. "Regulation and the Management of Expectations – Rating Agencies Revisited." *European Policy Analysis* 1 (2): 71–89.

Hoppe, Robert, and Hal Colebatch. 2016. "The Role of Theories in Policy Studies and Policy Work: Selective Affinities between Representation and Performation?" *European Policy Analysis* 2 (1): 121–49.

Hübner, Kurt. 2016. "Understanding Brexit." *European Policy Analysis* 2 (2): 4–11.

Hunger, Uwe, and Marlene Neumann. 2016. "Demographic Change and Migration in the European Care Sector—Introduction to the Special Focus." *European Policy Analysis* 2 (2): 118–9.

Ingold, Karin, and Géraldine Pflieger. 2016. "Two Levels, Two Strategies: Explaining the Gap Between Swiss National and International Responses Toward Climate Change." *European Policy Analysis* 2 (1): 20–38.

Klenk, Tanja. 2015. "Special Issue on 'The Governance of Welfare Markets' Introduction to the Special Issue: The Governance of Welfare Markets – Trends and Challenges." *European Policy Analysis* 1 (1): 35–40.

Klenk, Tanja, and Renate Reiter. 2015. "The Governance of Hospital Markets—Comparing Two Bismarckian Countries." *European Policy Analysis* 1 (1): 108–26.

Mondragón Ruiz de Lezana, Jaione, Alberto de La Peña, Arantxa Elizondo Varona, Juan Luis Lopetegi, Mokoroa Arizkorreta, and Francisco Juaristi Larrinaga. 2016. "State and Regional Administrative Coordination in Spain: A Case Study of the Spanish Sectoral Conferences on Environmental, Health and Educational Policies (2001–2012)." *European Policy Analysis* 2 (2): 94–117.

Neby, Simon, Per Lægreid, Paola Mattei, and Therese Feiler. 2015. "Bending the Rules to Play the Game: Accountability, DRG and Waiting List Scandals in Norway and Germany." *European Policy Analysis* 1 (1): 127–48.

Neumann, Marlene, and Uwe Hunger. 2016. "Circular Migration of Live-ins in Germany—Reinforcing the Segmentation of the Labor Market?" *European Policy Analysis* 2 (2): 120–35.

Nohrstedt, Daniel, and Kristin Olofsson. 2016. "A Review of Applications of the Advocacy Coalition Framework in Swedish Policy Processes." *European Policy Analysis* 2 (2): 18–42.

Paul, Regine, and Michael Huber. 2015. "Risk-based Regulation in Continental Europe?: Explaining the Corporatist Turn to Risk in German Work Safety Policies." *European Policy Analysis* 1 (2): 5–33.

Pollex, Jan. 2017. "Regulating Consumption for Sustainability? Why the European Union Chooses Information Instruments to Foster Sustainable Consumption." *European Policy Analysis* 3 (1): 185–204.

Reiberg, Abel. 2017. "The Construction of a New Policy Domain in Debates on German Internet Policy." *European Policy Analysis* 3 (1): 146–67.

Rinscheid, Adrian. 2015. "Crisis, Policy Discourse, and Major Policy Change: Exploring the Role of Subsystem Polarization in Nuclear Energy Policymaking." *European Policy Analysis* 1 (2): 34–70.

Sabatier, Paul A., and Christopher M. Weible, ed. 2014. *Theories of the Policy Process*, 3rd ed. Boulder CO: Westview Press.

Sager, Fritz, Céline Mavrot, and Susanne Hadorn. 2015. "Addressing Multilevel Program Complexity by Evaluation Design." *European Policy Analysis* 1 (2): 90–110.

Scheffel, Folke. 2016. *Netzpolitik als Policy Subsystem?: Internetregulierung in Deutschland 2005-2011 [ger]*. Band 9 of Policy Analyse. Baden-Baden: Nomos.

Schweizer, Rémi. 2015. "Law Activation Strategies (LAS) in Environmental Policymaking: A Social Mechanism for Re-politicization?" *European Policy Analysis* 1 (2): 132–54.

Skučiene, Daiva, and Julija Moskvina. 2016. "Policy and Decision to Retire in Central and Eastern European Countries." *European Policy Analysis* 2 (1): 67–97.

Strassheim, Holger. 2016. "Knowing the Future: Theories of Time in Policy Analysis." *European Policy Analysis* 2 (1): 150–67.

Töller, Annette E. 2017. "Voluntary Regulation by the Pharmaceutical Industry: Which Role for the Shadow of Hierarchy and Social Pressure?" *European Policy Analysis* 3(1): 48–80.

van Gerven, Minna, and Mikael Nygård. 2017. "Equal Treatment, Labor Promotion or Social Investment? Reconciliation Policy in Finnish and Dutch Coalition Programs 1995–2016." *European Policy Analysis* 3 (1): 125–45.

van Nispen, Frans K. M., and Peter W. A. Scholten. 2015. *Policy Analysis in the Netherlands. International Library of Policy Analysis*. Bristol: Policy Press.

van Nispen, Frans K. M. and Peter W. A. Scholten. 2017. "The Utilization of Expert Knowledge in Times of Crisis: Budgetary Economic and Migration Policies in the Netherlands." *European Policy Analysis* 3 (1): 81—100.

Vecchione, Elisa, and Justin Parkhurst. 2015. "The Use of Evidence Within Policy Evaluation in Health in Ghana Implications for Accountability and Democratic Governance." *European Policy Analysis* 1 (2): 111–31.

Veselý, Arnošt, Martin Nekola, and Eva Hejzlarová. 2016. *Policy Analysis in the Czech Republic. International Library of Policy Analysis*. Bristol: Policy Press.

Vogeler, Colette S. 2017. "Farm Animal Welfare Policy in Comparative Perspective: Determinants of Cross-National Differences in Austria, Germany and Switzerland." *European Policy Analysis* 3 (1): 20–47.

Wolf, Frieder, and Georg Wenzelburger. 2016. "Second Tier, Second Thoughts—Why it Turns out to be so Difficult for EIOPA to Create a Single Market for Private Pensions." *European Policy Analysis* 2 (1): 39–66.

Zahariadis, Nikolaos. 2017. "Migrexit and its Consequences for the European Union." *European Policy Analysis* 3 (1): 11–19.

Migrexit and its Consequences for the European Union

Nikolaos Zahariadis

Does the influx of hundreds of thousands of irregular migrants in recent years spell trouble for the European Union (EU) as we know it? To adapt Winston Churchill's famous phrase, this is not the end or even the beginning of the end but rather the end of the beginning of the EU's transformation. *The migration crisis has brought to the surface fissures tearing the EU apart and at the same time bringing Member States closer together.* To explain this paradox, I will define terms, examine some dimensions of the problem, discuss the EU response, and assess the consequences. I will not focus on the causes of irregular migration—others in this Forum have already done so (von Beume, 2016; Hansen, 2016). Instead, I will look more closely at the response and consequences drawing on examples mainly from Greece and Italy where the issue is felt most acutely.

Definition of Terms

Irregular migration refers to often temporary entry, residence, or work in a country without the necessary authorization or immigration documents; these migrants often fall prey to human smugglers. Some are refugees—those fleeing persecution at home—although most irregular migrants to Europe are economic migrants, in other words, people seeking a better future on European shores. Labels matter because they may be deliberately used to stigmatize new arrivals (Diedring & Dorber, 2015), deny them basic human rights accorded by the Convention Related to the Status of Refugees (Hathaway, 2007), or justify the militarization of response (Wylie, 2016, 170). The Greek former Deputy Minister for Migration Policy, Tasia Christodoulopoulou (2015), put it cynically in an interview to the Greek MEGA television channel: Greeks need to use the term refugees because "if the European Commission hears you talk about migrants and illegal migrants, they will not approve any funding."

Size and Fatality Ratios of Irregular Migration

Irregular migration is not new to Europe; what is new is the sudden increase in numbers. As Kingdon (1995) argues, issues become public problems when sudden changes in indicators capture the attention of policy makers. Although the number of refugees crossing into Europe is small relative to the global refugee number

doi: 10.1002/epa2.1003

even at the height of the crisis in 2015, the number of (legal and irregular) migrants is high. In 2015, there were 21.3 million refugees worldwide—of whom roughly one million crossed into Europe—the majority of whom were hosted in neighboring countries (United Nations High Commissioner for Refugees (UNHCR), 2016). UN data on migration reveal that the number of international migrants relative to population in Europe stood at 10.3 percent in 2015, up from 7.7 percent in 2000 and 6.8 percent in 1990 (United Nations (UN), 2015). In absolute numbers, it is not really a crisis in Europe, especially relative to income and relative to the burden shouldered by other countries in the Middle East (Turkey, Jordan, and Lebanon). But it became a crisis when the floodgates opened.

Table 1 presents data on migrants crossing by sea into Europe in the first two months over a three-year period. It reveals an upward trend in arrivals since 2015 in two routes of the Mediterranean—the Central and Western. The only exception is the Eastern route which saw a spike in 2016, which later diminished. This is despite the fact that the number of estimated total arrivals from all three routes was dramatically higher in 2015, 1,046,599 persons, as opposed to 387,739 persons in 2016 (IOM various years). The number of fatalities—dead and missing—for the same two months over the last three years is very interesting. It went from 1 in 30 in 2015 to 1 in 34 in 2017 after dipping significantly in 2016. This is because the number of migrants crossing into Greece, the safest of all three routes was dramatically higher in January–February 2016 relative to the same period in the previous and following years. But the real story is in Figure 1. The fatality ratios —dead and missing—show an upward trend on an annual basis although the 2017 figures may go down as the weather improves, making the crossing safer. The conclusion is that the spike in migrants through the Eastern route (mainly Greece) saved lives. Although the number of irregular migrants in 2016 plummeted relative to 2015, the death ratio has increased. *Fewer migrants are choosing to come through different routes but comparatively more are drowning in the perilous journey*. Given the fact that the composition of nationalities differs by route, it appears the lives of more persons from Syria, Afghanistan, Iraq, Pakistan, and Iran (top five nationalities during January–December 2016 following the Eastern route) is spared at the expense of Sub-Saharan African migrants from Nigeria, Eritrea, Guinea, Ivory Coast, and Gambia (top five nationalities during January–December 2016 following the Central route) (IOM various years).

Table 1. Sea Arrivals in the Mediterranean, January–February 2015–17

Country of Arrival	January–February 2015	January–February 2016	January–February 2017
Italy (Central route)	7,882	8,981	13,457
Greece (Eastern route)	4,567	116,005	2,318
Spain (Western route)	285	n.a.	1,000
Total	12,821	124,986	16,775
Dead and Missing			
Italy (Central route)	404	97	444
Greece (Eastern route)	9	321	2
Spain (Western route)	15	7	39
Total	428	425	485

Source: IOM (various years) and UNHCR (2017)

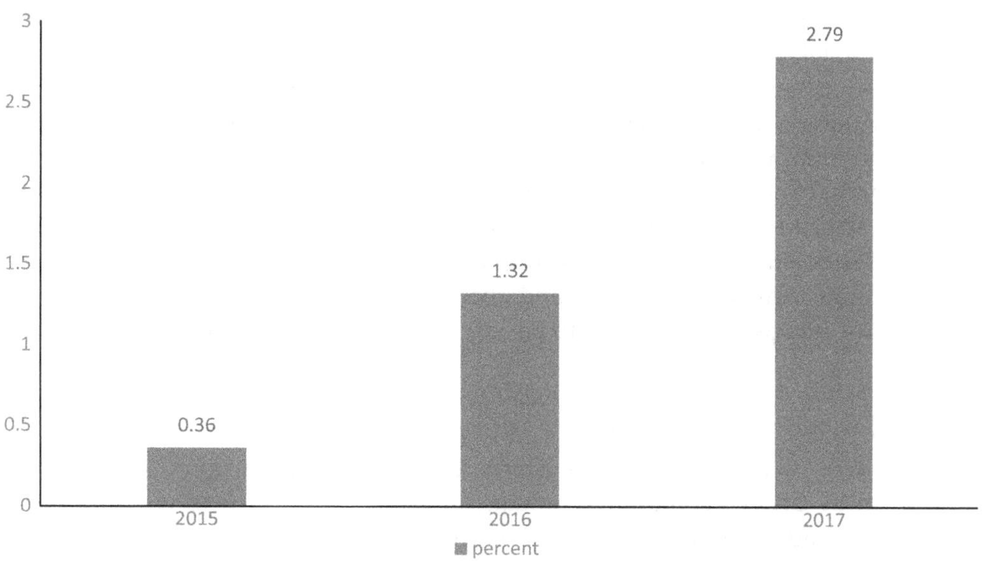

Figure 1. Fatality Ratios in Mediterranean Migration Flows, 2015–17*.
*2017 figures refer to the period January–February.

Source: International Organization for Migration, various years.

The EU Response

The Agenda

Why did migrants shift to more perilous crossings? While each route has its own push-pull dynamics and "clientele," the main reason is the European Agenda on Migration (Agenda hereinafter). Following an emergency meeting of the European Council in April 2015 and similar calls for action by the European parliament a few days later, the Commission proposed the Agenda (COM/2015/0240) as a series of core actions "to restore confidence in our ability to bring together European and national efforts to address migration, to meet our international and ethical obligations and to work together in an effective way, in accordance with the principles of solidarity and shared responsibility." The short-term actions include measures to save lives at sea, confront criminal smuggling networks, relocate asylum-seekers for faster processing, and tackle migration at the regions of origin and transit. The long-term measures rest of four pillars: reducing the incentives for migration, securing the EU's external borders, drafting a new labor mobility package, and creating a common asylum policy.

To stem the rising tide of irregular migrants flooding the Mediterranean (mainly the Aegean Sea in 2015 and early 2016), the EU also concluded an agreement with Turkey in March 2016. The agreement arose from pragmatic concerns and despite having succeeded in reducing numbers through the Eastern route, it has had pernicious side effects. The immediate need to reduce the numbers of irregular migrants to manageable numbers led many EU governments in early 2016 to set aside their reticence and advocate a third-party solution. The aim was to use Turkey as gatekeeper, knowing that the most effective way to stop the flow of migrants is for them not to cross onto European shores. Of course, Turkey's willingness to go along with this scheme came at the cost of €6 billion over three years, €3 billion more than what it was offered in October 2015, easing of EU visa controls, and accelerated negotiations for EU membership. Greece agreed to let NATO forces patrol the Aegean in search of refugee boats, stop prompting migrants to leave for other EU states, and build reception/registration camps ("hotspots") in the islands and relocation camps in the mainland that could provide adequate housing for thousands of refugees who waited to have their cases registered and assessed.

Side Effects

There were two pernicious side effects. First, the agreement produced a storm of criticism by NGOs, some governments, and the UNHCR itself (Collett, 2016). Some NGOs and more spectacularly the UNHCR ceased operations in the Greek islands (but the UNHCR later returned), complaining the agreement did not do enough to protect the rights of refugees while forcible return (as part of the agreement) violated EU and UN principles. Others complained that Turkey did not provide enough safety protection to repatriated individuals while still others thought the agreement did not do enough to address the causes of refugee movements. Second, the migration issue is now caught up in broader EU-Turkey relations, reigniting debates about the European orientation of Turkey, cultural differences, safety concerns, and since the failed coup in July 2016 flagrant human rights violations and a general climate of fear and intimidation of dissent. The agreement has held up so far but more as a matter of political expediency rather than true collaboration to confront the migrant tragedy. By implication, it rests on flimsy foundations with each side accusing the other of dragging its feet and violating the spirit of the agreement.

Consequences

While the migrant tide has decreased significantly since 2015, the number of dead and missing relative to arrivals has climbed dangerously. So *the EU response receives mixed reviews*. I will summarize them in the form of three main consequences for Member States: economic problems, ethical dilemmas, and political confrontations.

Economic Problems

Probably the more immediate and obvious problem is economic. While many Member States face similar issues, they are not all affected equally. Frontline states, primarily Italy and Greece, are bearing an inordinate cost since many states closed their borders in 2015 in retaliation to the huge numbers of migrants streaming through the Eastern route. Greece in particular is facing "a crisis within a crisis" as it struggles to house over 62,000 migrants who are unevenly distributed throughout the country. Apart from the economic crisis that has already sapped more than 25 percent of the country's GDP with no end in sight, the government has to contend with a backlog of applications, lack of capacity to process them efficiently, and new arrivals. Because migrants cannot be relocated until their cases are registered and assessed, the Greek islands where they first arrive are overwhelmed. The government reports 14,371 migrants on Greek islands as of 27 February 2017, in facilities designed to accommodate only 7,450 persons and another 1,564 in hotel rentals under the UNHCR scheme (European Commission 2017, 6). The numbers keep growing albeit not at the pace they did in the last two years. Italy does not face such enormous pressures, but it might as numbers are picking up due to the shift in migration routes.

Ethical Dilemmas

Perhaps the most difficult issue is the ethical dilemma. Migrants have the right to have their case registered and assessed on an individual basis. They can also appeal the verdict, taking time to fully document their case. Unfortunately, various technical issues—lack of interpreters, specialized personnel, the need for security interviews, the frequent lack and need for documentation, and the sheer bureaucracy—increase the time it takes to process applications straining already meager resources. In response, EU authorities plan to build closed hotspots, in other words, first-reception centers with no exit privileges until the case is resolved. While based on pragmatic considerations, they raise serious ethical problems resembling (but not identical to) those raised by the internment of Japanese Americans during World War II. Are the migrants' human rights violated by such camps?

There are even broader concerns. Even though returns from the Greek islands to Turkey are taking place—only 1,487 have returned under the terms of the EU-Turkey agreement since March 2016—the number of persons returned remains much lower than the number of arrivals, adding pressure on the hotspot facilities on the islands. All this despite funding from EU sources—the Commission reports €356.8 million in emergency assistance to Greek authorities to address asylum, migration, and internal security concerns plus another €192 million to provide humanitarian relief through international organizations and NGOs (European Commission 2017, p. 7–8). The problem is that some facilities are still not ready and capacity still lags. It is possible the problem rests with lack of Greek government planning and local pushback to these schemes. Many locals don't want to house more migrants having seen receipts from tourism plummet as a result. But some NGOs, including Amnesty International, point to a more sinister explanation. According to Iverna McGowan, Amnesty International's head of the Office of European Institutions: "Millions of euros have been spent and there is no improvement. Hence the issue is political, not economic. They don't want to help so as not to encourage others to cross into Europe" (*Proto Thema,* 2016). There is no evidence to substantiate the allegation, but the symbolism of its publicity by a major NGO raises uncomfortable questions about the moral hazard. Making life easier for irregular migrants encourages the very crossing EU governments are trying to avoid.

The situation is even graver in Italy. Search and rescue operations save lives, but they also encourage more to come. Desperate migrants might plausibly think: yes, the journey is treacherous, but surely someone will come to the rescue because it is official policy. *By trying to avoid the human tragedy, the EU "invites" more people to cross, creating the requisite conditions that make the tragedy more likely.* And that is what's missing from public discourse: debates to find a way out of this dilemma.

Political Confrontations

The current EU asylum regime under the Dublin II Treaty has proven inadequate to deal with the crisis. The explosion in asylum seekers in Europe coupled with security concerns have led to the *temporary reintroduction of national border controls* in Poland, Hungary, and Slovenia at various times since 2015. The governments of France, Malta, Germany, Austria, Denmark, Sweden, and Norway continue to maintain these controls. Member States are of course responsible for the security of their borders but the reintroduction of such controls, however, temporary or legal under Schengen rules, raises uncomfortable questions about the free flow of persons across national borders. It does not escape notice that the majority of countries reintroducing borders are located in Northern Europe. Whereas they are the main destination for most of the arriving migrants, these countries are also skillfully keeping migrants stuck elsewhere in Europe. *If search and rescue operations avert human tragedy at sea, national border controls reintroduce them through the back door.* Migrants are stuck, at least temporarily, in places they don't want to be and which cannot adequately house them.

As part of the Agenda, Member States pledged in legally binding European Council Decisions in September 2015 to take 160,000 asylum-seekers from Greece and Italy by September 2017 to assist them in dealing with the pressures of the refugee crisis. As of 1 March 2017, only 13,552 have been relocated, amounting to just 8.5 percent (IOM various years). While some countries such as Malta and Finland are likely to meet their obligations, others such as Hungary, Austria, and Poland refuse to even participate. *The lack of progress in the relocation scheme raises significant concerns about the meaning of European solidarity.* The Commission vocally argues there cannot be a fair sharing of responsibility to manage migration challenges without solidarity. The problem is that national governments see migration flows from very different perspectives that not only reflect the ideological/partisan complexion of those in charge but also the varying push and pull factors that make each Member State an appealing (or not) destination for relocation.

Quo Vadis Europa?

Recent migration flows to Europe pose significant challenges for Member States and the EU itself. On the national level they raise three concerns:

First, can Member States manage the consequent rise of xenophobia and racism? The different cultural characteristics of new arrivals raise significant problems of identity and inclusion both among migrants and ordinary citizens. Key variables include the distance between the cultural identity of new arrivals and that of the host country, the host's economic conditions, the social tolerance for diversity and dissent, the political climate, and national electoral cycles.

Second, can Member States adequately address security concerns stemming from irregular migration? While the overwhelming majority of terrorist attacks in Europe in recent years has come from European-born nationals, European publics are concerned with the possibility of violence stemming from new arrivals. Attacks in Germany, confrontations in Sweden and Greece, demonstrations in France over the "Jungle" in Calais, paint a troubling picture of violence, intimidation, and fear among migrants and citizens. To be sure, not everyone shares this picture but such images frequently capture media attention.

Third, can Member States protect and adequately integrate the new arrivals? There are significant problems facing new arrivals not only in terms of language and culture but also in terms of jobs, skills, and housing. As the number of new arrivals increases, strains are put on welfare resources to integrate the migrants, teach them the new language, provide professional skills (if needed), house them, and so on. However, in light of low economic growth and reluctance to raise taxes funding per capita decreases, leading to recriminations of migrants taking jobs or resources away from citizens. To an extent this is true but also temporary. The long-term prospects are actually a rise in welfare spending once migrants come into the work force. Of course, the problem is the benefits are long-term while costs are immediate. Because politics has a short-term electoral horizon the odds are social integration is unlikely or very difficult in most cases. Not only does it involve adjustment to new realities on the part of migrants but also adjustment by citizens.

None of these conditions appear to be met in most EU Member States. A Pew Center poll (Wike, Stokes & Simmons, 2016) found public opinion to be not particularly welcoming of new arrivals either because of poor job prospects for natives (e.g., United Kingdom), or because people feel they have accepted too many new arrivals (e.g., Germany), or because they feel they may increase domestic terrorism (e.g., Hungary), or because they think Muslims don't want to adopt the country's customs and way of life (e.g., Greece). In light of domestic problems, the challenges at the European level are daunting and familiar. They form the main obstacles to collective action:

Can the EU undermine the national risk to free-ride and instead provide collective incentives for solidarity? Because countries are affected differently by the crisis, those affected the most will tend to contribute the most and those hardly affected will tend to free-ride. This does not mean there is a problem with solidarity, for example some governments such as Finland and Malta have contributed their "fair" share in relocation schemes, but that the obstacle is an issue of incentives. If the EU remains unable to impose costs or consequences on those shirking responsibility, why should Member States cooperate even if they have agreed to do so?

Old fissures between North and South continue to plague Europe, while new schisms between East (mostly Visegrad countries plus Austria) and West have opened up. If securing external borders is a national prerogative, then liberal intergovernmentalism (Moravcsik, 1998) suggests collective action is unlikely without national commitment and credibility. The latter are dependent not on EU authorities but on national voters. And here things become more complicated.

The British decision to leave the EU and the election of President Trump in the United States have emboldened populists to "want our country back," whatever this means and at what cost. Upcoming national elections in various European countries will surely reshuffle the balance of political power. At the time of writing (early March 2016), it is unclear how much European solidarity will be affected by national considerations, but it is clear there will be adverse effects. Demands for a more intergovernmental EU will likely grow louder even as policy makers realize they face similar challenges. As long as the issue is framed as a short-term security or cultural concern, the likelihood of zero-sum calculations increases. Nothing good has come out of the culture wars in the United States and the same is expected in Europe as well. Accepting more migrants is a risk that may be worth taking. However, to turn the crisis into a positive-sum scenario, perceptions must change, as prospect theory predicts, from the short-term to the long-term and from possible future gains to certain immediate losses. Whether European leaders are capable of delivering such policies remains to be seen. But in the meantime, *there is no end in sight to the plight of migrants; they keep on coming to countries they cannot leave, they don't want to stay, and they refuse to go back.*

Professor Nikolaos Zahariadis holds the Mertie Buckman Chair in International Studies at Rhodes College, Memphis, TN. He has published widely in comparative public policy and European political economy.

References

von Beume, Klaus. 2016. "Refugees and Migration in Europe." *European Policy Analysis* 2 (1): 7–13.

Christodoulopoulou, Tasia. 2015. "T. Christodoulopoulou: 100,000 Refugees will Enter in 2015" (in Greek) [Online]. Mega TV. http://www.megatv.com/megagegonota/article.asp?catid=27371&subid=2&pubid=34633195. Accessed September 24, 2016.

Collett, Elizabeth. 2016. "The Paradox of the EU-Turkey Refugee Deal" [Online]. *Migration Policy Institute*. March. http://www.migrationpolicy.org/news/paradox-eu-turkey-refugee-deal. Accessed July 19, 2016.

Diedring, Michael, and John Dorber. 2015. *Refugee Crisis: How Language Contributes to the Fate of Refugees* [Online]. 27 October. http://theelders.org/article/refugee-crisis-how-language-contributes-fate-refugees. Accessed October 12, 2016.

European Commission. 2017. *Fifth Report on the Progress Made in the Implementation of the EU-Turkey Statement* [Online]. https://ec.europa.eu/home-affairs/sites/homeaffairs/files/what-we-do/policies/european-agenda-migration/20170302_fifth_report_on_the_progress_made_in_the_implementation_of_the_eu-turkey_statement_en.pdf. Accessed March 5, 2017.

Hansen, Randall. 2016. "Immigrants, ISIS, the Refugee Crisis, and Integration in Europe: A Response to Klaus von Beume." *European Policy Analysis* 2 (1): 14–19.

Hathaway, James C. 2007. "Why Refugee Law Still Matters." *Melbourne Journal of International Law* 8 (1): 89–103.

International Organization for Migration (IOM). Various years. *Migration Flows—Europe* [Online]. http://migration.iom.int/europe/. Accessed March 3, 2017.

Kingdon, John W. 1995. *Agendas, Alternatives, and Public Policies*. New York: Harper Collins.

Moravcsik, Andrew. 1998. *The Choice for Europe*. Ithaca, NY: Cornell University Press.

Proto Thema. 2016. *Amnesty International: Living Conditions of Refugees Remain Intentionally Bad (in Greek)* [Online]. *Proto Thema*. http://www.protothema.gr/greece/article/620592/diethnis-amnistia-oi-sunthikes-diaviosis-ton-prosfugon-stin-ellada-paramenoun-skopima-ashimes/. Accessed March 5, 2017.

UNHCR. 2017. *Mediterranean Arrival Data* [Online]. https://data2.unhcr.org/en/documents/details/53876. Accessed March 3, 2017.

United Nations (UN). 2015. *International Migrant Stock 2015* [Online]. http://www.un.org/en/development/desa/population/migration/data/estimates2/estimates15.shtml. Accessed March 3, 2017.

United Nations High Commissioner for Refugees (UNHCR). 2016. *2015: Forced Displacement Hits Record High* [Online]. http://www.unhcr.org/en-us/global-trends-2015.html. Accessed March 3, 2017.

Wike, Richard, Bruce Stokes, and Katie Simmons. 2016. *Negative Views of Minorities, Refugees Common in EU* [Online]. Pew Research Center. http://www.pewglobal.org/2016/07/11/negative-views-of-minorities-refugees-common-in-eu/. Accessed March 5, 2017.

Wylie, Gillian. 2016. *The International Politics of Human Trafficking*. New York: Palgrave Macmillan.

European Policy Analysis, Vol. 3, No. 1, 2017

Farm Animal Welfare Policy in Comparative Perspective: Determinants of Cross-national Differences in Austria, Germany, and Switzerland

Colette S. Vogeler

Societal concerns for the welfare of animals are increasing: a majority of Europeans believe that farm animals should be better protected. Even so, there is no systematic policy analytic assessment of the development and the determinants of animal welfare policy. This paper addresses these research gaps and contributes to the inclusion of the field of animal welfare in policy analysis. Austria, Germany, and Switzerland share comprehensive legislation in the field of farm animal welfare. However, concrete policies vary considerably between the three countries. Through an international comparison, the paper characterizes diverging policy instruments and identifies possible determinants of farm animal welfare policy derived from established theories of policy analysis. While perspectives focusing on party political difference add to the understanding of farm animal welfare policy in Germany and in Austria, this does not apply to the case of Switzerland. Here, theories focusing on the degree of international economic integration have a greater potential in understanding cross-national differences. The paper thereby presents a first systematic assessment of farm animal welfare from a policy analysis perspective.

KEY WORDS: animal welfare policy, livestock production, agricultural policy, Partisan theory, policy instruments

比较视角下的农场动物福利政策:奥地利、德国和瑞士间出现政策差异的决定因素

社会对动物福利的关注正在不断上升: 大多数欧洲人认为农场动物应受到更好的保护。即使如此, 关于动物福利政策的发展和决定因素还没有进行系统性的分析评估。本文不仅处理了这些研究空白, 还将动物福利领域纳入了政策分析。奥地利、德国和瑞士在农场动物福利方面共用综合性立法, 然而, 三国实际实施的政策却有很大差异。通过进行国际对比, 本文描述了政策工具之间的差异, 并从源自现有政策分析理论的农场动物福利政策中识别了可能的决定因素。尽管研究党派政治差异的观点能促进理解德国和奥地利的农场动物福利政策, 却不能促进理解瑞士的政策。本文中, 聚焦于国际经济一体化程度的理论更有潜能帮助理解跨国差异。由此, 本文从政策分析视角首次呈现了关于农场动物福利的系统评估。

关键词: 动物福利政策, 畜牧生产, 农业政策, 党派理论, 政策工具

Introduction

Farm animal welfare is increasingly moving into the focus of the general public in Western Europe: Studies reveal that the majority of Europeans is concerned

doi: 10.1002/epa2.1015

about animal welfare, 82 percent of EU citizens believe that animals should be better protected (European Commission 2015). The conditions under which animals are kept for food production are especially criticized, scandals around BSE or avian flu redound to the negative image of the prevailing structures in livestock farming (Cornish, Raubenheimer & McGreevy, 2016; Ingenbleek et al., 2013). As a consequence, animal welfare is turning into a challenge for economic actors along the supply chain on one hand and for policymakers on the other. Many countries have passed specific animal protection laws. What is more, market-based initiatives to improve welfare of livestock are gaining relevance (Ingenbleek et al., 2013; Jones, Lensink, Mancini & Tranter, 2017; Lundmark, Berg, Schmid, Behdadi & Röcklinsberg, 2014). Despite the rising social, political, and economic attention, there is no systematic policy analytic approach to the development and the determinants of animal welfare policy. How are animal welfare policies—especially in the field of livestock farming—developing in different countries? Which policy goals are defined and which instruments applied to reach these aims? Finally, which factors may add to the understanding of cross-national policy differences? This paper addresses these research gaps and substantially contributes to the inclusion of the field of animal welfare in policy analysis. Through an international comparison, the paper characterizes diverging policy instruments and identifies determinants of farm animal welfare policy derived from established theories of policy analysis. The paper thereby presents a first systematic exploration of animal welfare from a policy analysis perspective and should serve as the starting point for future research and the integration of this relatively neglected field in policy analysis.

Three European countries with comparatively high animal welfare standards are chosen for the empirical analysis. Austria, Germany, and Switzerland share comprehensive legislation in the field of animal welfare. However, policies vary considerably between the three countries. While Switzerland has the highest legislative standards for farm animals in Europe, regulations in Germany and Austria are still above the European Union's formal requirements (Schmid & Kilchsberger, 2010; Wissenschaftlicher Beirat Agrarpolitik beim BMEL 2015). The comparative analysis shows that policymakers in all three countries apply a combination of regulatory and market-based instruments to obtain improvements in animal welfare in productive livestock. However, the degree to which legislation is preferred over voluntary or incentive schemes differs substantially.

The study fosters the understanding of these cross-national differences by combining hypotheses from comparative policy analysis. Firstly, the empirical analysis reveals that the theoretical perspective of party political difference contributes to the understanding of diverging policies. This finding is especially strong for the case of Germany where animal welfare policy is still a political niche: here animal welfare policies are primarily taken up by smaller parties such as the Greens, while the bigger parties are still very much reluctant in this area. Similar findings are made for the case of Austria: farm animal welfare is primarily addressed by two parties: the Greens and the Team Stronach, both present detailed concepts for the improvement of farm animal welfare, while the other parties do not make mention of the issue at all. However in Switzerland, where animal welfare policies are the most elaborated in Europe, stronger similarities among political parties are found: most parties do not address animal welfare at all. In the past, major improvements in animal welfare were initiated through popular petitions.

Secondly, diverging agricultural production patterns and different degrees of international integration pose unequal challenges to policymakers in the three countries. These patterns most likely add to different perceptions of animal welfare in agricultural production: In Germany, with its export-oriented and agro-industrial structures primarily driven by profit-maximization, animal welfare is often seen as an impediment for international competitiveness and growth. Although the structure of the Austrian livestock sector deviates substantially with predominantly small farms, the dependence on exports is almost as high and accordingly is the concern for international competitiveness. On the other hand, in Switzerland, livestock farming focuses on the domestic market and the production of premium and high-priced products and can thus "afford" higher animal welfare standards.

The contribution begins with the theoretical framework for the empirical analysis contrasted against central hypotheses from comparative policy analysis (Theoretical Framework—Cross-national Policy Differences). Third section presents the research design. The fourth to sixth sections comprise the empirical analysis and the presentation of the research findings for the investigated countries. The analysis starts with an overview of the evolution of animal welfare policy in Austria, Germany, and Switzerland, and then examines the policy instruments applied in each country from a comparative perspective. The fifth and sixth sections present possible theoretical explanations for understanding cross-national variation. The conclusion summarizes theoretical and practical implications and highlights perspectives for future research.

Theoretical Framework—Cross-national Policy Differences

In policy analysis, animal welfare policy is not yet an established policy field (See Farm Animal Welfare Policy in Austria, Germany and Switzerland in Comparative Perspective section). Different approaches exist for the comparative analysis of policymaking in different countries. Some of these frameworks were originally developed for economic or social policies and were consequently applied to numerous other policy fields (For an overview, see Schmidt, Ostheim, Siegel & Zohlnhöfer, 2007). Given the lack of empirical application to the field of animal welfare policy, this paper seeks to combine several theoretical perspectives. While the chosen theories contribute to the understanding of animal welfare policy, the analysis makes no claim to be complete. It presents a first possible approach to the understanding of policies in this specific field for the three countries. Future research should take up these findings and add explanatory variables from other theoretical perspectives to gradually gain insights into the field of animal welfare policy. Actor-centered theoretical approaches could help to gain insights into the process of policymaking for example by using social network analysis (Ingold & Pflieger, 2016).

Theoretical approaches focusing on socio-economic determination would expect that policymaking is a reaction to economic and societal challenges (Ostheim, 2007). With regard to animal welfare policy, the increasing public concern for animals in food production that is picked up by the media and regularly peaks whenever a new food scandal comes up, can be considered a societal pressure on policymakers. Previous research shows that a central driving force for improvements in animal welfare is the societal perception of animal welfare (Cornish et al., 2016). From this perspective, one would expect that in view of the increasing public discontent with current conditions in livestock production (European Commission 2015), policymakers would foster improvements in this area. In Austria, Germany, and Switzerland, public concerns about animal welfare are almost equally high. Nevertheless, current policy efforts for advancing farm animal welfare vary substantially. To understand these differences, empirical analyses taking into account the role of political parties and of different economic and political preconditions are enlightening.

Party Political Difference

Empirical studies analyzing the influence of political parties on policymaking come to different conclusions: among other factors the role of political parties depends on the institutional setting, on the policy field, or on the period under review (Franzese, 2002; Imbeau, Petry & Lamari, 2001). Originally developed for the understanding of varying economic policies, the question whether parties matter has been transferred to a variety of policy fields and countries (Hibbs, 1977; Schmidt, 1996; Wenzelburger, 2015; Zohlnhöfer, 2012). Generally speaking, two reasons are given that make political parties pursue diverging policies: Vote-seeking refers to the satisfaction of potential voters to ensure reelection, while policy-seeking assumes that policymaking reflects the beliefs and values of party members. Depending on the electoral cycle and the intensity of party competition, a combination of policy and vote-seeking motives is common (Wenzelburger, 2015). Empirical studies demonstrate that the impact of political parties varies considerably depending on the policy field. In some policy fields, different policy preferences manifest rather within than across political parties; this was shown for German health policy (Bandelow & Hartmann, 2014).

In view of the rising societal concerns about farm animal welfare in Austria, Germany, and Switzerland, I expect that political parties respond to these demands by including farm animal welfare policies in their party and electoral programs. Hypothesis 1 thus assumes:

> *H1: Farm animal welfare policy is taken up by political parties as a response to the increasing societal concerns.*

In the field of environmental policy, a positive connection has been demonstrated with the participation of green parties in government

(Wenzelburger, 2015). Parties that are not dominated by one of the historical cleavages (e.g., capital-labor) are more likely to address such issues. The focus on environmental policy reflects changing cleavages with regard to post-material values (Inglehart, 1977; Niedermayer, 2009). Animal welfare is related to these concerns. Hence, I expect a connection between "green" or environmental parties and an emphasis on animal welfare. Accordingly hypothesis 2 reads:

H2: Parties that are not connected to the traditional cleavages but instead stress environmental concerns will place the strongest emphasis on animal welfare.

These two hypotheses will be explored in sixth section for the cases of Austria, Germany, and Switzerland. The analysis takes into account the different role of political parties in the three countries: In Switzerland, the existence of strong participatory elements confines the standing of parties in the policymaking process and makes it more likely that societal demands are expressed through popular petitions (Krumm, 2013; Vatter, 2016).

International Hypothesis

A second theoretical perspective that contributes to the understanding of policy differences is the international hypothesis, which presupposes that national policymaking depends on the international political and economic integration. The international integration of markets puts pressure on national governments to create a competitive environment and limits the capacity of national governments. This does not solely apply to economic policy but is likely to affect other policy subsystems such as social or environmental policy (Scharpf & Schmidt, 2005; Zohlnhöfer, 2005). Livestock production patterns in Germany, Austria, and Switzerland vary substantially: While Germany is a net exporter of meat and other animal products and the sector is dominated by large-scale farms, Swiss farmers focus mainly on the domestic market. The Austrian livestock sector situates somewhere between the German and the Swiss model but is still highly dependent on exports (see International Integration of the Livestock Sector and the Impact on Farm Animal Welfare section). It is expected that the degree of international economic integration affects the development of farm animal welfare policies. Countries with export-oriented livestock farming will tend to adopt lower animal welfare standards arguing with the risk to competiveness. Instead, business models such as in Switzerland with a focus on the domestic market and on high quality might be able to afford higher animal welfare standards. Hence, hypothesis 3 reads:

Hypothesis 3: The greater the international integration of the livestock sector, the more animal welfare is seen as a competitive disadvantage. As a consequence, higher international integration leads to poorer animal welfare standards.

Hypothesis 3 is explored by analyzing the international integration and dependence on export markets of the livestock sector in the three countries. With regard to the political dimension of international integration, I further expect that EU membership is likely to influence farm animal welfare policies. However, the effect EU regulations have on national policy-making varies depending on the policy field. The influence of EU membership may have either a positive or a negative impact on farm animal welfare. In the case of veterinary drugs, it was shown that Germany and Austria even adopted policies above the EU level (Sager, Thomann, Zollinger & Mavrot, 2014; Thomann, 2015). In Southern and Eastern European countries, farm animal welfare conditions tend to be worse than in Northern Europe (Wissenschaftlicher Beirat Agrarpolitik beim BMEL 2015). In these cases, EU membership may have a positive effect on animal welfare, if at least minimum European requirements are translated into national regulations. In Northern Europe, I assume that EU membership may instead lead to lower regulation to maintain competitiveness with neighboring countries.

Research Design

The empirical analysis starts with a comparative overview of the current status quo in farm animal welfare policy in Austria, Germany, and Switzerland. For each country, the development of animal welfare policies and the range of legal regulations are depicted. Based on the existing legal framework, the section leads into a compilation of major differences in animal welfare regulation in the three countries (see Table 1). In a second step, specific policy instruments to achieve improvements in farm animal welfare for each of the three countries are compiled. I find that in addition to legal regulation, incentive systems for farmers, with or without state involvement, and retail initiatives play a major role in the improvement of farm animal welfare (see Figure 1).

Building on these findings, I look at possible determinants for understanding cross-national policy differences. The analysis takes into account the theoretical perspectives of party political difference and the international hypothesis. To analyze party political differences with regard to animal welfare policy, the positions of all political parties that are currently participating in the federal government of each country were analyzed. The analysis included party programs and electoral programs from the last elections on the federal level (Germany 2013, Switzerland 2015, and Austria 2013) as well as policy and position papers published by the parties. Future analyses could enrich these findings by analyzing the voting behavior of politicians from different political parties in concrete animal welfare legislative processes. To address the second theoretical strand, the influence of different degrees of international integration on animal welfare policies, livestock production data are compared.

Farm Animal Welfare Policy in Austria, Germany, and Switzerland in Comparative Perspective

With a view to the absence of a systematic policy analysis approach to animal welfare policy, this section gives a short summary on what animal welfare is in general and its significance for policymaking. In social sciences, the field of Human-Animal-Studies has emerged only recently (Buschka, Gutjahr & Sebastian, 2012). Economic sciences are beginning to explore the economic dimension of animal welfare with regard to market-based instruments and consumer research (Harvey & Hubbard, 2013; Lusk & Norwood, 2011). Within political science, animal welfare is studied in the fields of political philosophy, political theory, and ethics (Ahlhaus & Niesen, 2015; Donaldson & Kymlicka, 2013; Niesen, 2014; Saretzki, 2015; Singer, 1975). Recent research addresses animal welfare in EU agricultural policy especially regarding improvements in the welfare of livestock (Bennett, Anderson & Blaney, 2002; Blokhuis, Miele, Veissier & Jones, 2013; Grethe, 2007; Jones et al., 2017; Veissier, Butterworth, Bock & Roe, 2008). A major challenge is seen in diverging national regulations that result in huge differences in the conditions of raising farmed animals and thereby affect the welfare of animals (Grethe, 2007; Schmid & Kilchsberger, 2010). Another area where animal welfare plays an important role is the field of regulating veterinary drugs that is closely connected to food safety, a field that is only recently being explored (Sager et al., 2014). Regulation of veterinary drugs can make a contribution to the welfare of animals; one element of animal welfare is the freedom of injuries and diseases (see the five freedoms by Brambell in this section).

In policymaking, animal welfare is relevant in different fields. Due to different challenges, it can be distinguished between the fields of animal experiments, livestock farming, companion animals, and wild animals. This separation is reflected in national animal protection laws in the three countries with specific regulations for each of the named fields. The field where the largest number of animals is directly affected by human intervention is livestock farming. Within this field, a challenge for policymakers is the trade-off between the welfare of farm animals and economic interests (Grethe, 2007). In Germany alone, 200 million animals are being farmed with a significant share of exports to other European and third countries. On a global level, livestock farming is among the fastest growing agricultural sectors due to population growth and changing consumer patterns (Wissenschaftlicher Beirat Agrarpolitik beim BMEL 2015). Nonetheless, the implications for policymaking with regard to the welfare of farm animals, is still only a niche in the scientific debate (Gall, 2016).

The lack of a globally accepted definition or shared understanding of animal welfare (Blokhuis et al., 2013; Broom, 1991; Cornish et al., 2016; Lundmark et al., 2014; Ohl & van der Staay, 2012; Yeates & Main, 2008) makes this policy field especially challenging to study, "(...) every definition of animal welfare is influenced by the moral or ethical standards of society. (...) The political relevance of animal welfare science is strongly (...) based on societal concerns about how animals are treated." (Ohl & van der Staay, 2012, p. 13). Often a distinction between animal welfare—how the animal experiences its own situation—and animal protection—what people do to protect animals—is made (Ingenbleek et al., 2013). In many European countries, laws to prevent cruelty against animals were already passed in the nineteenth century. The idea of animal welfare grew stronger after the Second World War when livestock production underwent major changes toward industrialization and intensification. The Brambell report that was released in 1965 presented a milestone for farm animal welfare policies. The report is the result of a commission that was mandated by the British government to investigate the welfare of intensively farmed animals (Brambell Committee, 1965). The report increased the awareness among political and societal actors about the conditions in which farm animals were kept and their widespread suffering in modern intensive farming. The Brambell committee proposed five freedoms that decisively influenced animal welfare legislation in Great Britain and other European countries (Ohl & van der Staay, 2012; Veissier et al., 2008). According to the report, animal welfare requires the farm animal to be free from (1) hunger, thirst, or inadequate food; (2) thermal and physical discomfort; (3) injuries or diseases; (4) fear and chronic stress; and (5) is free to display normal, species-specific behavioral patterns. Despite this early definition that is commonly used to evaluate farm animal welfare, the empirical analysis shows that current animal welfare policies often do not even achieve these aims. The five freedoms are also reflected at the European level where work on animal protection policies began in the 1960s and 1970s. Conventions were drafted for areas such as the transport of farm animals and for slaughter with the aim to increase animal welfare (for an overview see Veissier et al., 2008). An important step for European animal welfare policy was the Treaty of Amsterdam that included a protocol on animal welfare (European Communities 1997). Animals were legally recognized as "sentient beings," thereby highlighting the ethical dimension (Ingenbleek et al., 2013). Since then directives were passed for many farm animals, and animal welfare is now regulated within the "European Convention for the Protection of Animals Kept for Farming Purposes" (Council of Europe 1976). One important motive of the initiative was the avoidance of national disparities that could hamper competition in livestock production (Veissier et al., 2008). The rising societal concerns are reflected in a number of policy initiatives such as the "Action plan on animal welfare" in 2006 (European Commission 2006). However legislation to improve farm animal welfare varies considerably among member states. Generally, south and eastern European countries have the lowest standards and merely fulfill the EU's minimum requirements, while animal welfare policies in northern Europe usually exceed the EU's targets (Veissier et al., 2008; Wissenschaftlicher Beirat Agrarpolitik beim BMEL 2015, pp. 106–9). Due to the above-EU level animal welfare regulations, in the three case studies, detailed regulations on the European level are not discussed in this paper. Future studies should take up existing research and address questions regarding the impact of EU animal welfare regulation on national legislation in comparative perspective and regarding the process of animal welfare policymaking on the EU level (see for example Bennett & Appleby, 2010; Grethe, 2007; Jones et al., 2017). In the following, an overview of the development and the specifics of farm animal welfare policy for Germany, Austria, and Switzerland is presented.

Farm Animal Welfare Policy in Germany

At a formal level, Germany has comparatively extensive animal welfare legal regulations. It was the first country within the European Union to include the protection of animals as a national state objective in the constitution in 2002 (Bundesregierung, GG Artikel 20a). State regulation was formalized in 1933 with the "Reichstierschutzgesetz" (Reich law on animal welfare). The "Reichstierschutzgesetz" was basically transferred into the Federal Republic of Germany and partially included in the new "Tierschutzgesetz" that was passed in 1972 (Gall, 2016; Hirt, Maisack & Moritz, 2016). Since then animal welfare is part of the concurrent legislation. This means that the federal government and the states share legislative responsibility. On the federal level, the ministry of agriculture (BMEL) is in charge of farm animal welfare policies. In the field of concurrent legislation, the general imperative is that the federal government should only assume responsibility when it is necessary for the creation of equal living conditions or economic unity (Bundesregierung, GG Artikel 74 Absatz 1, No 20). One outcome of the concurrent legislation is the divergent farm animal welfare policies in the federal states and a lack of a national strategy for livestock production (Meyer, 2017). The German "Tierschutzgesetz" is based on the ethical premise of animals as fellow creatures and stresses the responsibility of humans to protect animals from pain, damage, and suffering (Hirt et al., 2016). Originally stemming from the "Reichstierschutzgesetz" is the controversial premise of the "good or reasonable cause." The wording that no person may harm an animal without a reasonable cause is often interpreted as a concession to economic interests (Gall, 2016). A recent case that illustrates the policy implications of this wording was a judgment concerning the slaying of male day-old chicks, which is a common practice in poultry farming. The court decision in favor of the slaying of millions of chicks was highly disputed in the media and in the public. Court ruled that raising these male chicks would be so expensive that it would economically endanger the existence of poultry farming, thereby identifying a reasonable cause (Oberverwaltungsgericht für das Land Nordrhein-Westfalen 2016). This superiority of economic interests over animal welfare is reflected in a number of past and current policy decisions. A policy option that is increasingly used in Germany and likewise in Switzerland and Austria to circumvent these tensions is a mix of economic incentives for animal welfare instead of legislation (see Figure 1). Compared to the financial resources that are spent on agri-environmental measures, state spending for animal welfare is extremely low on a European level as well as on the German national level (Wissenschaftlicher Beirat Agrarpolitik beim BMEL 2015). While in 2014 Germany spent only 100 Million Euro on animal welfare programs, over four billion was spent for environmental purposes in agriculture. A comparison of selected animal welfare-related regulations with the situations in Austria and Switzerland is presented in Table 1.

Farm Animal Welfare Policy in Austria

Since 2005, animal welfare legislation has been concentrated at the federal level in the Austrian "Tierschutzgesetz" (Animal Protection Act). Prior to this, animal welfare legislation was the responsibility of the federal states, which resulted in highly diverging regulations in the states. A petition for a referendum in 1996 was the starting point for a nationwide animal welfare legislation (Parlament der Republik Österreich 1996) that was passed in 2004. The enforcement of animal welfare regulations remains on the local level (Bundeskanzleramt Österreich 2017). Despite the centralization of legislation, the federal states still play an important part in the field of farm animal welfare: The enforcement of animal welfare regulations remains on the local level. In addition, each federal state aside from Vienna commands over the Austrian "Animal Health Services" that control and support livestock farming (Österreichischer Tiergesundheitsdienst 2017). Similar as in the German case, the decentralization of the enforcement of animal welfare in livestock production leads to regional differences in the keeping and health conditions.

From an ethical point of view, Austrian animal welfare policy shares a similar basis with the German Tierschutz: It is likewise based on the ethical premise of fellow creatures and derived from this the responsibility of humans toward animals. In contrast to the German Tierschutzgesetz that stresses the imperative of protection from negative influences, the Austrian wording goes beyond this by adding the commitment to foster the well-being of animals. Concerning farm animals, the Austrian Tierschutzgesetz comprises detailed regulations on the conditions under which different livestock species should be kept, as well as regulations on transportation and slaughter (Ministerium für Gesundheit und Frauen). On the institutional level, the Ministry of Health (BMG) is in charge of animal welfare. In the field of the protection and welfare of farm animals, the BMG cooperates with the Ministry of Agriculture and Environment (BMLFUW) that is responsible for the livestock sector (Bundesministerium für Land- und Forstwirtschaft, Umwelt- und Wasserwirtschaft).

Farm Animal Welfare Policy in Switzerland

In global comparison, animal welfare standards in livestock production in Switzerland are among the highest and generally exceed the levels reached in Austria and Germany (see Table 1). Legal regulations for the protection of animals were already passed in the nineteenth century on a cantonal level. A nationwide comprehensive animal welfare act came into force in 1981 and was amplified in 2008 by, among other things, including regulations for horses, sheep, goats, and fish. By stressing the dignity of animals, Switzerland has the strongest ethical commitment in animal welfare policies compared to most other countries: The Tierschutzgesetz aims at "protecting the well-being and the dignity of animals" (Der Bundesrat Schweiz 2017). In the development of animal welfare policies in Switzerland popular petitions played an important part. The revision of animal

Table 1. Major Differences in Farm Animal Welfare Regulation in Comparison

	Austria	Germany	Switzerland
Animal protection in constitution	Yes	Yes	Yes
Castration of piglets without anesthesia	Allowed	Allowed (from 2019 onwards forbidden)	Forbidden
Farrowing crates for sows	10 days for insemination, 5 days before and during farrowing, legal improvements in 2033	4 weeks for insemination, 1 week before and during farrowing	Maximum 10 days for insemination
Limit of transportation times	EU regulations, 8 hours but longer transportation times possible with adapted vehicles	EU regulations, 8 hours but longer transportation times possible with adapted vehicles	Maximum 6 hours
Slaughtering of male day-old chicks	Allowed	Allowed	Allowed
Beak-clipping for poultry	Allowed	Allowed Voluntary agreement since January 2017 between poultry association and federal government (only for hens, not for turkey)	Forbidden
Tail-docking for piglets	Allowed if necessary to protect the animal from other injuries	Allowed if necessary to protect the animal from other injuries	Forbidden
Teeth clipping or grinding for piglets	Allowed	Allowed	Forbidden
Battery-cages for chicken	Enriched cages	Enriched cages	Forbidden
State license for barns/stalls	No	No Announced for the current legislative period, part of coalition agreement	Yes
State animal welfare label for meat	No	Plans presented in 2017	Retail labels based on state programs "RAUS" and "BTS"

Source: own compilation based on animal welfare acts in Austria, Germany, and Switzerland

welfare regulations in 2008 was initiated by the "Tierschutz- Ja!" petition in 2002 (Schweizer Tierschutz 2013). Strong participatory elements make it more likely that societal demands are taken up in the policymaking process. Earlier than most other countries, strict rules on the conditions for different livestock species were passed, for example, the prohibition of cage-rearing for poultry was passed in 1981 with a transitional period until 1992. The advance attracted international attention. Germany and Austria would follow only a decade later. Another example for the pioneering role of Swiss animal welfare policies were detailed regulations on the raising of farm rabbits already in 1990. In Germany, such regulations were only passed in 2014 and in Austria shortly before that. In addition to legal regulations, voluntary incentive-based programs are an important part of Swiss animal welfare policy. The state provides financial incentives to encourage farmers to foster animal welfare standards even above the legal level. The programs "BTS" and "RAUS" financially reward farmers who invest in either above-average animal friendly barns (BTS) or grant free-range (RAUS) to their livestock. RAUS

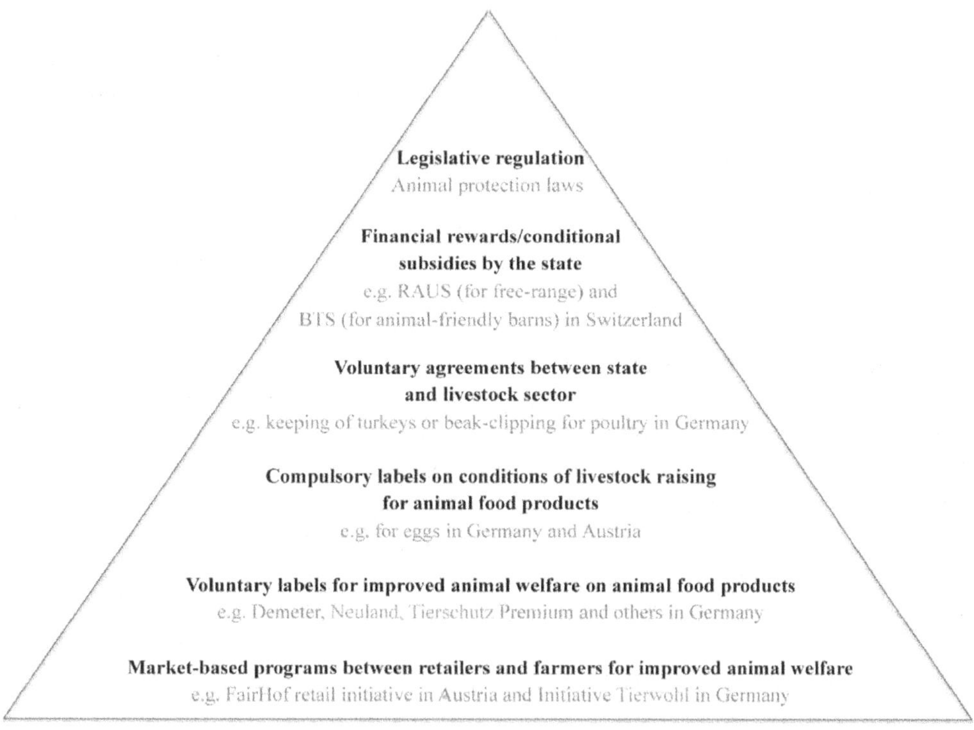

Figure 1. Policy Instruments Applied in the Field of Farm Animal Welfare Regarding the Level of State Intervention.
Source: Own Compilation Based on the Case Studies.

was already established more than two decades ago in 1993, BTS followed in 1996 (Bundesamt für Landwirtschaft). In an international comparison, financial compensation for specific animal welfare measures are high and almost as high as the financial incentives granted for agri-environmental improvements (OECD 2015).

Comparison of Farm Animal Welfare Policies in Austria, Germany, and Switzerland

What concrete differences exist in current animal welfare policy between the three countries? To respond to the challenge of the lack of a consistent scientific definition of farm animal welfare (Blokhuis et al., 2013; Cornish et al., 2016; Lundmark et al., 2014; Ohl & van der Staay, 2012; Yeates & Main, 2008), I will refer to the five freedoms (Brambell 1965), assuming that guaranteeing those freedoms will lead to improved animal welfare. Conditions that enable the animal to "be free to display normal, species-specific behavioral patterns" will accordingly improve animal welfare. Referring to concrete legislation, I assume that the allowance of permanent fixation or stables that do not allow the animal to turn around, such as farrowing crates, harm the animal's welfare. Another aspect that is relevant in current farm animal welfare regulation affects the "freedom of injuries and fear." Legislation that allows castration without anesthesia or teeth clipping can accordingly be seen as a restriction to the welfare of the animal (Brambell

Committee, 1965, see Table 1). Due to the high regulatory density of farm animal welfare policies in Austria, Germany, and Switzerland, the comparative assessment will highlight areas where substantial differences are apparent. Table 1 summarizes animal welfare-related issues and the diverging legal regulation in the three countries. The selection is the result of prior qualitative content analyses of current political and media debates. Thus, the compilation gives an overview of major differences, making no claim to be complete. The findings illustrate the comprehensive consideration of animal welfare regulations in Switzerland compared to Germany and Austria.

Improved farm animal welfare can be achieved by legal regulation on one hand. Further available policy instruments are incentive-based measures by the state, voluntary agreements, or market-based instruments in cooperation with the retail sector. Ingenbleek et al., 2013 distinguished between three types of animal welfare policies: government-based, market-based, and farmer-based (e.g., investment tax reduction or subsidies when complying to higher welfare standards). Blandford & Harvey (2014) argued that a mix of market-based and regulatory instruments may best reach the goal to improve animal welfare in livestock. A common critique on market-based instruments is that they rather reinforce differences: mostly farmers who already have relatively high animal welfare standards will participate in such measures. A second challenge is that poor animal welfare is seldom apparent to the customer, the reach of market-based instruments is thus limited (Jones et al., 2017). In policy analysis, there is up to now no systematic and holistic evaluation of policy instruments for the field farm animal welfare. Insights can be gained from the field of environmental policy, the complexity requires a mix of policy instruments (Schweizer, 2015). In the course of the research for this paper, a wide spectrum of policy instruments that go beyond the proposed divisions was found. Figure 1 shows a compilation of the identified policy instruments distinguished by the degree of state intervention that are applied in the three countries and gives examples for each measure.

In addition to the strictest legal regulation, Swiss farm animal welfare policy also offers the most extensive financial incentive system. The Swiss state initiated programs "RAUS" and "BTS" are accessed by a high percentage of farmers. "RAUS" provides financial rewards for granting free-range to farm animals. "BTS" stands for "Besonders Tierfreundliche Ställe" and rewards particularly animal friendly barns. Criteria include prohibition of fixation, existence of different barn areas to satisfy species-appropriate behavior, day-light, and manipulable material. Depending on the species, currently 50–80 percent of Swiss farm animals benefit from these programs (Bundesamt für Landwirtschaft; Landwirtschaftlicher Informationsdienst, 2017). Thereby the incentive-based instruments succeed in providing farming conditions above the legal requirements for a significant share of total livestock in Switzerland. In Germany, comparable state financial incentives are up until now only granted on a federal states level: The federal state of Lower Saxony financially rewards the renunciation of noncurative operations such as tail-docking and beak-clipping with so-called animal welfare premiums (Niedersächsisches Ministerium für Ernährung, Landwirschaft und

Verbraucherschutz). In Austria, comparable state-financed incentives to date do not exist. In Germany and in Austria, an increase in market-based initiatives is found, such as the recently initiated Austrian "FairHof" label and the "Für mehr Tierschutz" label in Germany. Within these programs, retailers, farmers, and in some cases animal protection organizations cooperate to improve farm animal welfare as a reaction to changing consumer demands. For example, "FairHof" animals are provided with 100 percent more space than the legal requirements, have open-air areas, straw bedding, and organic manipulable material, and tail-docking is prohibited (Hofer, 2017). In the Austrian market for meat, several other voluntary labels exist that advertise animal welfare above the legal requirements (Homolka, 2016). Similar requirements apply for the German retail-based programs Demeter, Naturland, Bioland, Neuland, Für mehr Tierschutz Premium, and Tierschutz kontrolliert (Bundesministerium für Ernährung und Landwirtschaft). In Switzerland, comparable programs—partly in cooperation with animal welfare associations—have existed since 1970s for eggs and since 1980s for meat and are common to most retailers (Huber, 2016). These demands seem to be partially adopted by the state: In Germany, the ministry of agriculture recently suggested a state-run but voluntary label for meat in addition to the existing and legally binding label on nonprocessed eggs (Bundesministerium für Ernährung und Landwirtschaft 2017). While animal welfare labels are just beginning to gain relevance in the German and Austrian market, in Switzerland, labels for eggs were already initiated in the 1970s by a cooperation of retail and animal protection associations. Labels for meat followed in the 1980s. Since the introduction of the state-directed incentive systems RAUS and BTS, many of these labels are based on RAUS and BTS, which further increased their market share. Another instrument particularly popular in current German farm animal welfare policy is voluntary agreements between state and farmers or farmer associations. These agreements are often applied instead of legal regulation and are standing under the shadow of hierarchy. Examples are found in the poultry sector: In the absence of legal requirements for rearing turkeys, a voluntary agreement between the German poultry association and the government exists. Another example is the voluntary agreement regarding beak-clipping for hens. The ministry of agriculture and the association of poultry farmers confirmed that beak-clipping will not be practiced on hens from January 2017 onwards (turkeys are excepted from this regulation, allegedly because of the lack of scientific research on the avoidance of cannibalism) (Bundesministerium für Ernährung und Landwirtschaft 2015).

The explained measures are exemplary for the scope of policy instruments applied in the field of farm animal welfare. The three countries apply different strategies to achieve higher animal welfare standards on one hand. On the other hand, the emphasis on improving farm animal welfare differs considerably, with Switzerland having the most elaborated and financially supported programs. How can theories of policy analysis yield a better understanding of these differences? The following section focuses on party political difference as a potential explanatory variable for cross-national differences. While this theoretical perspective is especially common in economic and social policy, it has not been systematically applied in the field of farm animal welfare. Sixth section looks at the different degree of international embedment of the livestock sector as a further explanatory variable. I expect that a combination of theoretical perspectives is fruitful to the understanding of farm animal welfare policies.

Party Political Differences with regard to Farm Animal Welfare Policies

The leading question of this section is, whether political parties matter for farm animal welfare. The analysis is structured along two hypotheses: Firstly, I assume that the increasing public concerns especially in the field of livestock production will lead politicians to take up these societal demands and address animal welfare in their policy programs. Secondly, I expect that especially green parties will stress animal welfare policies.

Therefore, in a first step the party and electoral programs of all political parties that are currently represented in government or parliament on a federal level are analyzed for each country. The programs are scanned regarding farm animal welfare-related issues. Do the parties address the field at all? What is the position of the parties toward farm animal welfare? Do they identify specific problems or challenges in the field and if so, do they suggest measures to tackle the named challenges? Or, on the other hand, do they identify improvements in farm animal welfare as a competitive disadvantage and advocate less regulation? Tables 2, 3, and 4 present the findings of this analysis for the three countries.

Table 2. German Political Parties and Farm Animal Welfare

	Grüne	CDU/CSU	SPD	FDP	DIE LINKE;
Specific section for animal welfare	X				
Establishment of an animal protection delegate on the federal level	X				
End keeping on fully slatted floors	X				
End cage-rearing of poultry	X				
End cage-rearing of rabbits	X				
Stop of intensive livestock farming	X				
End of mutilations (e.g., beak-clipping or tail-docking)	X				
Elimination of construction privileges for industrial livestock farming	X				
Elimination of export guarantees for foreign stables	X				
Labeling of rearing conditions	X	X	X		
New animal protection law for species-appropriate keeping	X				
Improvements in slaughtering conditions and more state controls	X				
Improvements in transportation conditions and more state controls	X	X			X
Strengthening of state controls in animal welfare	X		X	X	X
The right of animal welfare associations to initiate proceedings	X		X		X
Water access for water fowl	X				
Mandatory outdoor access	X				
Subsidies for biological and vegan products in public canteens	X				
Reduce the use of antibiotics in livestock farming	X	X	X		X
Improve general livestock raising conditions	X	X	X	X	X

Source: own compilation based on party and electoral programs (see appendix)

Table 3. Austrian Political Parties and Farm Animal Welfare

	SPÖ	ÖVP	FPÖ	GRÜNE	TS	NEOS
Specific section for animal welfare				X	X	
Environmental and animal protection are part of the solidaric society	X					
Appropriate conditions for livestock raising in pig and cattle farming				X		
Farrowing crates for sows: earlier termination and end of subsidies				X		
Limitation of transportation time to maximum 8 hours EU wide				X	X	
Inclusion of animal protection as a national objective in the constitution				X		
Termination of intensive livestock rearing				X		
State licensing and monitoring of livestock housing				X		
Linking agricultural subsidies to species-appropriate keeping conditions				X		
End of mutilations and operations without pain elimination				X		
Strengthening of controls in industrial livestock farming				X		
EU-wide labeling of animal products related to rearing and feeding conditions				X		
Elimination of export subsidies for animal transports				X		
Treat livestock as living creatures capable of suffering with dignity					X	
Animal protection laws that ensures species-appropriate livestock farming					X	
Prohibition of permanent animal cages and animal prisons in livestock farming					X	
EU-wide animal welfare standards at least on the Austrian level					X	
Recognition of animals as living beings instead of as object in the law					X	
No foreign animal transport through Austria					X	
Labeling of the national origin of meat products					X	

Source: own compilation based on party and electoral programs (see appendix)

Table 4. Swiss Political Parties and Farm Animal Welfare

	SVP	SP	FDP	CVP	GPS	glp	BDP	EVP	EDU
Specific section for animal welfare									
Against new animal welfare regulation	X								
Against exaggerated animal and environmental protection			X						
Respect for the well-being of animals in food production			X						
Enforcement of animal protection law in livestock farming					X				
Engagement for exemplary animal protection in livestock farming						X			
Species-appropriate conditions raising livestock						X			
Animal friendly production								X	
Charges on imported products with low animal welfare standards								X	
Prohibition of imports from cage-rearing or animal factories					X				
Equal animal welfare standards for imported and for Swiss products									X

Source: own compilation based on party and electoral programs (see appendix)

Comments on the Parties: **Bündnis 90/Die Grünen** (the Greens): emerging from communist, feminist, and environmental movements in West Germany that merged with anticommunist movements in Eastern Germany; **CDU** Christlich Demokratische Union Deutschlands (Christian Democratic Union): party of the current chancellor Angela Merkel; **CSU** Christlich-Soziale Union in Bayern (Christian Social Union in Bavaria): sister party of the CDU, only in the federal state of Bavaria; **SPD** Sozialdemokratische Partei Deutschlands (Social Democrats): emerged from the labor movement, coalition partner of the current Merkel government; **FDP** Freie Demokratische Party (Free Democratic Party): liberal party and in the previous decades repeated coalition partner of the CDU; **DIE LINKE** (the Left): mergence of left parties from East and West Germany (party political programs; Niedermayer, 2009).

Comments on the Parties: **SPÖ** Sozialdemokratische Partei Österreichs (Social Democratic Party): party of the current chancellor Christian Kern, emerged from the labor movement; **ÖVP** Österreichische Volkspartei (Austrian People's Party): coalition partner of the current Kern government, historically the more conservative and catholic party; **FPÖ** Freiheitliche Partei Österreichs = (Freedom Party of Austria): right-wing party; **GRÜNE** (the Greens): stemming from the postmaterial, environmental movement in the 1970s; **TS** Team Stronach: new political party founded by the entrepreneur Frank Stronach in 2012, critical against established party system and the EU, many previous nonvoters; **NEOS** Das Neue Österreich und Liberales Forum (New Austria and Liberal Forum): new political party founded in 2012, economically liberal positions, many previous voters of the greens, many female voters (party political programs; Onken, 2013; Kritzinger, Müller & Schönbach, 2014; Filzmaier, Perlot & Zandonella, 2014).

Comments on the Parties: **SVP** Schweizerische Volkspartei (Swiss People's Party): conservative, right-wing party, originally emerging from the agrarian party; **SP** Sozialdemokratische Partei der Schweiz (Social Democratic Party): emerged from the labor movement; **FDP** Freisinnig-Demokratische Partei der Schweiz (Liberal Party): liberal, bourgeoisie party; **CVP** Christlichdemokratische Volkspartei (Christian Democratic People's Party): stemming from the religious-secular cleavage; **GPS** Grüne Partei der Schweiz (Green Party): stemming from the postmaterial, environmental movement in the 1970s; **glp** Grünliberale Partei (Green Liberal Party); **BDP** Bürgerlich-demokratische Partei (Conservative Democratic Party): splinter group of the SVP; **EVP** Evangelische Volkspartei (Evangelical People's Party): stemming from the religious-secular cleavage; **EDU** Eidgenössisch-demokratische Union (Federal Democratic Union): Christian and national-conservative party (party political programs; Krumm, 2013 and Vatter, 2016).

In the case of Germany, major differences are found in the commitment of political parties to animal welfare. While all parties agree that in general conditions for rearing livestock should be improved, CDU, CSU, FDP, and SPD comment only very briefly and rather superficially on farm animal welfare. These parties apparently do not assign importance to the field of farm animal welfare. However, the Greens dedicate a particular section to animal welfare. They identify major problems in the prevailing conditions of rearing farm animals in Germany and present detailed policy proposals to improve animal welfare. These proposals include legislative changes such as the prohibition of cage-rearing of poultry and rabbits, of noncurative operations and of full-gap floors. Furthermore, they advocate increased outdoor access of farm animals, better conditions for transport and slaughter and an increase in state controls. More frequent state control is also stipulated by the SPD, FDP, and the Left Party. With CDU and CSU, the Greens share the idea of introducing a label on meat products regarding rearing conditions and the reduction of antibiotics in farming. The latter is also mentioned by the Left Party.

Similar conclusions are drawn for Austria: The Greens, in particular, focus on animal welfare-related issues with the dedication of a specific section for animal welfare. They advocate the inclusion of animal protection in the constitution as a state objective. In addition, the Greens make detailed proposals on policy changes: the prohibition of farrowing crates for sows, the limitation of transportation times, the prohibition of operations without anesthesia, and the labeling of meat products. A second political party in Austria that emphasizes farm animal welfare is a party that was founded only a few years ago, the "Team Stronach." As with the Greens, "Team Stronach" dedicates a section to animal welfare in their party program and demand legal adaptations. They claim to recognize animals as living beings instead of things in the legal framework. In addition, they want specific improvements in rearing conditions such as a prohibition of cages and "animal prisons." They also advocate improvements on the European level. The SPÖ, ÖVP, FPÖ, as well as the NEOS do not mention farm animal welfare at all; the SPÖ states only very generally that animal protection is part of solidarity.

In the cases of Germany and Austria, hypothesis 2 is thus confirmed: Green parties place a stronger emphasis on farm animal welfare than other parties. For hypothesis 1, which propounds that political parties address growing societal concerns, the results are mixed: In Germany, all parties make at least some reference to farm animal welfare policy. However, aside from the Greens, the field is only touched upon very superficially. In Austria, the bigger political parties do not address farm animal welfare at all, only the Greens and Team Stronach advocate improvements.

However, in Switzerland, I find greater similarities in the positions of political parties toward animal welfare: Party positions do not seem to vary as much as in Germany or Austria. While most parties make some reference to farm animal welfare, it is mostly on a very general level, and claims for specific improvements, as they are found in the cases of Austria and Germany, are not common. The already high levels of farm animal welfare may add to the understanding why animal welfare does not seem to be a topic of party competition. Another explanation might be the different role of parties in the political system of Switzerland. For the case of Switzerland, I conclude that theories dealing with party political difference are not effective in understanding farm animal welfare policy—at least with regard to current day policymaking. A concern that is addressed by several parties in Switzerland is the handling of imported animal products that do not comply with Swiss animal welfare standards. The suggestions extend from charges on imported products that do not meet Swiss animal welfare standards up to the prohibition of such imports.

For the cases of Austria and Germany, the findings reveal major differences regarding the emphasis of farm animal welfare between the political parties. Here theoretical perspectives on party political differences foster the understanding of variation in policymaking. Future studies should pick up these findings and analyze the role of the parties in legislative processes and other relevant policy output.

International Integration of the Livestock Sector and the Impact on Farm Animal Welfare

The second theoretical perspective applied to the understanding of cross-national differences in farm animal welfare policy is the degree of international integration. Hypothesis 3 assumes that the greater the international integration of the livestock sector, the more animal welfare is seen as a competitive disadvantage. I expect that higher levels of international integration of the livestock sector will lead to poorer farm animal welfare standards. Numbers of livestock and export volumes are contrasted to measure international economic entrenchment and a short overview of the characteristics of the livestock sector for each country is given. The data presented in Figures 2–5 focus on the three species that represent the biggest share in livestock production: poultry, pigs, and cows. Other species such as goat, sheep, or rabbit will be excluded from the analysis as they do not play a major role in all three countries. The data are derived from government and farmers associations' statistics and represent the year 2015/2016. Due to the high degree of international

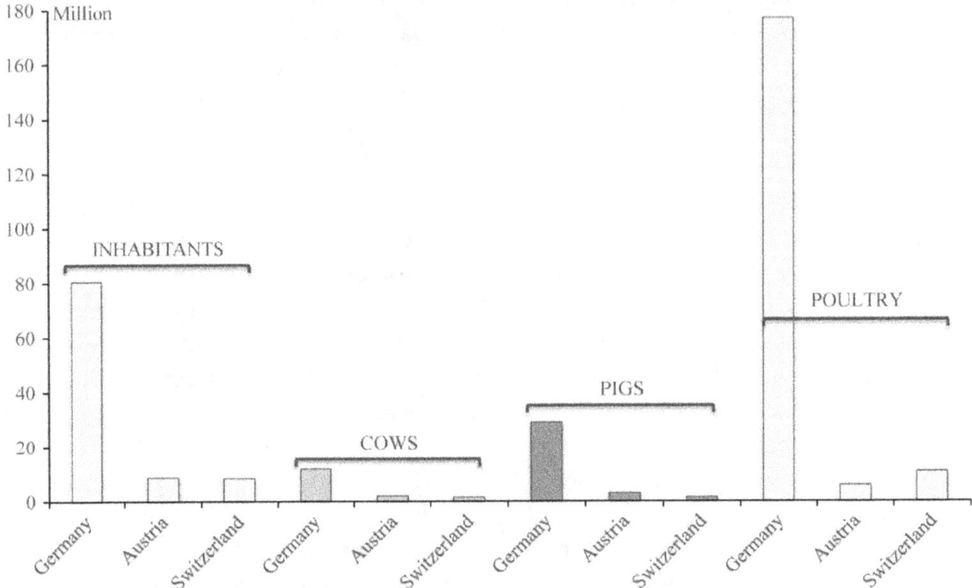

Figure 2. Number of Farm Animals Compared to the Number of Inhabitants.
Source: Own Compilation Derived from Government and Farmer Associations' Data (See Appendix).

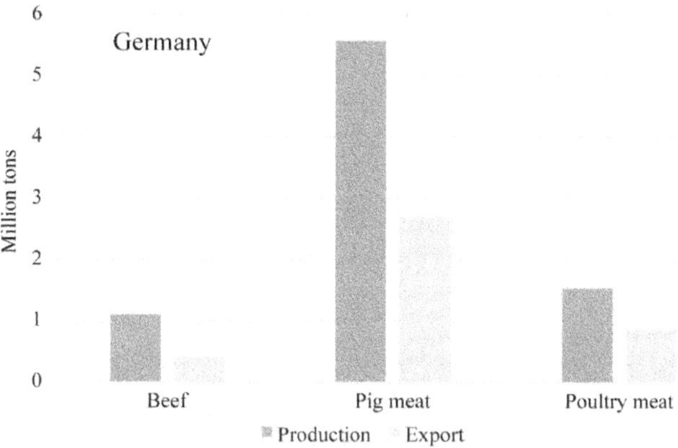

Figure 3. Meat Production and Meat Exports by Species in Germany.

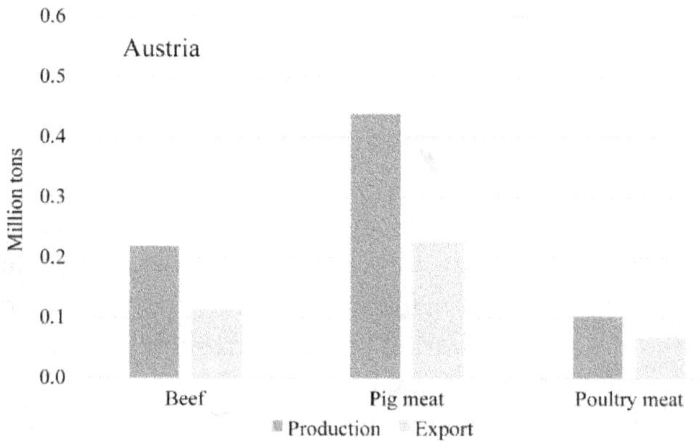

Figure 4. Meat Production and Meat Exports by Species in Austria.

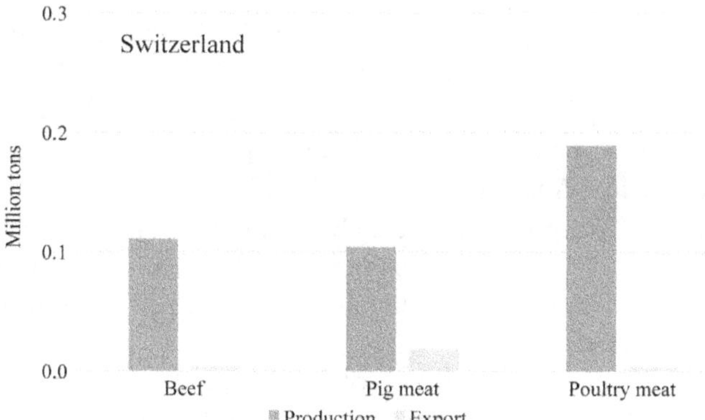

Figure 5. Meat Production and Meat Exports by Species in Switzerland.
Source: Own Compilation Derived from Government and Farmer Associations' Data (See Appendix).

entrenchment of the livestock sector especially in Germany, the slaughter data deviate from number of livestock data. Rearing and slaughtering as specialized production steps are often done in different countries, for example, a pig slaughtered in Germany was not necessarily raised in Germany, accordingly the Germany animal welfare regulations only apply to the production step of slaughtering. At the same time, the data do not allow conclusions regarding domestic consumption, because animal products are imported as well. The data compiled in Figures 2–5 illustrate the great differences in size and in the degree of international integration of the livestock sector in the three countries.

Germany has been a net exporter of meat since 2007; about half of all meat of domestic slaughter is exported. Livestock production is further expanding: Within the European Union, Germany is the biggest supplier of pork and milk and has the second largest export share in beef and poultry. In egg production, Germany still ranks third within Europe. Animal products represent around one quarter of total agriculture exports in Germany, but agriculture exports account for around 6 percent of total exports (Bundesministerium für Ernährung und Landwirtschaft, 2016). German livestock farming has not achieved a major differentiation by quality but focuses on cost leadership. Cost advantages in animal farming can be achieved by economy of scale or at the expense of either working conditions for farm workers or animal welfare standards (Spiller & Schulze, 2008). The strong international integration of the German livestock sector combined with its large-scale and cost-oriented business model contributes to the perception of animal welfare as a threat to competiveness. Looking at recent policy initiatives (e.g., beak-clipping agreements with the poultry association, voluntary labeling on meat products), a strong preference of market-based instruments or of voluntary agreements to the improvement of farm animal welfare is found.

Similar findings can be drawn for the Austrian livestock sector, where exports within the European Union are an important element of livestock farming. About two-thirds of the agriculture production value stems from animal production, of which the most important products are milk and other products derived from cows and then pigs. Milk is the most important export good in livestock production, with domestic production at 150 percent of self-sufficiency and beef self-sufficiency exceeding 140 percent (Bundesministerium für Land- und Forstwirtschaft, Umwelt- und Wasserwirtschaft, 2016). Unlike Germany, Austrian farms are small, especially in the production of beef and milk products, and animal farming presents a major source of income for many farmers in the Alpine areas (Bundesanstalt für Agrarwirtschaft, 2016). International competitiveness is thus a major concern for farmers and stricter animal welfare regulation may pose an economic threat to the individual farmer. Therefore, binding legislative requirements or obligatory animal welfare labels are probably even more difficult to implement than in Germany.

An important peculiarity in the case of Switzerland is that it is not a member of the European Union. EU regulations for livestock farming thus do not apply to the Swiss farming sector, thereby creating a unique situation for policymakers. Swiss livestock primarily focuses on the production of high-quality products for its domestic market. Exports play a minor role. In the area of milk products, for example, the major share of its exports stems from processed goods, in this case cheese. Agricultural production accounts for less than 1 percent of GDP, of which half of the production value stems from the livestock sector. A combination of legal regulations and incentive-based instruments leads to above-average animal welfare standards in this sector. As production capacity does not meet the national demand, a large share of animal products is imported. But even these imports often conform to the Swiss animal welfare standards. As a reaction to societal demands, retailers increasingly use labels to guarantee higher animal welfare and ensure that animal products that are imported meet the same standards as Swiss products (Huber, 2016). The outlined diverging agricultural production patterns, and especially the different degrees of international integration of the livestock sector, pose unequal challenges to policymakers in the three countries. These patterns most likely add to different perceptions of animal welfare in agricultural production: Animal welfare is either seen as an impediment for international competitiveness and growth or as indispensable for producing high-quality products and meeting societal concerns.

Discussion

The field of farm animal welfare is only recently beginning to be explored. This paper presented a first systematic policy analytic and comparative assessment of this relatively neglected policy field. In view of changing socio-economic demands in Western Europe and rising societal concerns for farm animal welfare, a greater political emphasis is to be expected in the coming years. At present, policies vary considerably between Austria, Germany, and Switzerland. The comparative analysis showed that a combination of regulatory and market-based instruments to obtain improvements for farm animals is applied. The degree to which legislation is preferred over voluntary or market-based instruments differs substantially. Switzerland takes a pioneering role: It imposes the strictest regulations and provides the most comprehensive financial incentive programs to improve the welfare of farm animals. This double-tracked strategy could serve as an inspiration for policymakers in other countries. In Germany, voluntary agreements between farmer associations and the state are preferred over legal regulations and financial incentives are up until now only granted at the federal states level; for Austria, similar conclusions can be drawn.

The combination of different perspectives of policy analysis added to the understanding of these cross-national policy differences. The determinants of farm animal welfare policy diverge in the three countries: While I find great differences with regard to farm animal welfare between political parties in Germany and in Austria, this does not apply to the case of Switzerland—at least with regard to present-day positions of political parties. The greater similarities in party political positions in Switzerland might on one hand be attributed to the weaker role of parties compared to the role of direct democratic elements in the Swiss political system. Likewise, the already very high standards in livestock production and the ample legal regulations contribute to an explanation of the findings. Here theories focusing on the degree of international political and economic entrenchment have a greater potential to understand cross-national differences. The relatively domestic-oriented livestock sector in Switzerland is less subject to concerns that higher animal welfare standards will harm competiveness than the export-oriented German livestock industry or the Austrian livestock industry that still has a considerable export share, especially in milk products. German policymakers in particular will have to deal with challenges in farm animal welfare due to the leading international position of the livestock sector. Social demands for improvements in the conditions for rearing livestock are increasing. At the same time, policymakers have to weigh up the international competitiveness of their livestock sector. The current German business model based on cost leadership might have to be amended by putting a stronger emphasis on quality and premium products as in other German economic sectors. Though the Austrian livestock sector is smaller than the German, the degree of international integration is similar and the challenges are comparable. In both countries, especially the Green parties stress the importance of improved farm animal welfare. The mid-term development of farm animal welfare policies in Germany and Austria may thus be connected to future government constellations. I expect a greater emphasis when these parties assume government power.

The aim of the paper was an exploration of farm animal welfare policy in a comparative perspective and the integration of this field in policy analysis. Future research should contribute to the research agenda by transferring the findings to other countries and by complementing further theoretical approaches. Studies of other European countries would be enlightening, especially for Southern and Eastern Europe where animal welfare regulations are less elaborated compared to Austria, Germany, and Switzerland. This could help to identify challenges in the field of farm animal welfare policies in these countries and to find a common European agenda. Theoretical perspectives dealing with political–institutional characteristics, path-dependency, or interest groups could be systematically integrated in future studies to deepen the understanding of cross-national differences in farm animal welfare policies.

Colette S. Vogeler is a postdoctoral researcher at the Chair of Comparative Politics and Public Policy at the University of Braunschweig. Her research interests include economic and agrarian policy with a focus on farm animal welfare policy.

References

Ahlhaus, Svenja, and Peter Niesen. 2015. "What is Animal Politics? Outline of a New Research Agenda." *Historical Social Research* 40 (4): 7–31.

Bandelow, Nils C., and Anja Hartmann. 2014. "Health Policy Prior to the German Federal Election of 2013: The Party Political Marginalisation of a Previously Central Topic in Election Campaigns." *German Politics* 23 (4): 371–85.

Bennett, Richard, J. Anderson, and Ralph Blaney. 2002. "Social Consensus, Moral Intensity and Willingness to Pay Concerning Farm Animal Welfare Issues and the Implications for Agricultural Policy." *Journal of Agricultural and Environmental Ethics* 15 (2): 187–202.

Bennett, Richard, and Michael Appleby. 2010. "Animal Welfare Policy in the European Union." In *EU Policy for Agriculture, Food and Rural Areas*, ed. Arie Oskam, Gerrit Meester, and Huib J. Silvis. Wageningen: Wageningen Academic Publ, 243–52.

Blandford, David, and David Harvey. 2014. "Economics of Animal Welfare Standards: Transatlantic Perspectives." *Euro Choices* 13 (3): 35–40.

Blokhuis, Harry, Mara Miele, Isabelle Veissier, and Bryan Jones, ed. 2013. *Improving Aarm Animal Welfare: Science and Society Working Together: The Welfare Quality Approach*. Wageningen: Wageningen Academic Publishers.

Brambell Committee. 1965. *Report of the Technical Committee to Enquire into the Welfare of Animals kept under Intensive Livestock Husbandry Systems: The Brambell Report*. London: HMSO.

Broom, Donald M. 1991. "Animal Welfare: Concepts and Measurement." *Journal of Animal Sciences* 69 (10): 4167–4175.

Bundesamt für Landwirtschaft. *Tierwohlbeiträge BTS/RAUS*.

Bundesanstalt für Agrarwirtschaft. 2016. Agrarstruktur in Österreich [Online]. http://www.agraroekonomik.at/index.php?id=780. Accessed March 8, 2017.

Bundeskanzleramt Österreich. 2017. *Gesamte Rechtsvorschrift für Tierschutzgesetz*.

Bundesministerium für Ernährung und Landwirtschaft. 2015. *Verzicht auf Schnabelkürzen bei Legehennen und Puten*.

———. 2016. Agrarexporte verstehen: Fakten und Hintergründe [Online]. http://www.bmel.de/SharedDocs/Downloads/Broschueren/Agrarexporte-verstehen.pdf?__blob=publicationFile. Accessed March 8, 2017.

———. 2017. *Schmidt: Das staatliche Label sorgt für mehr Tierwohl in den Ställen, gleichzeitig profitieren die Landwirte*. Berlin [Online]. http://www.bmel.de/DE/Tier/Tierwohl/_texte/Tierwohllabel-Vorstellung-IGW.html. Accessed March 8, 2017.

Bundesministerium für Ernährung und Landwirtschaft. *Label für mehr Tierwohl* [Online]. http://www.tierwohl-staerken.de/einkaufshilfen/tierwohl-label/. Accessed March 8, 2017.

Bundesministerium für Land- und Forstwirtschaft, Umwelt und Wasserwirtschaft. *Tierische Produktion*.

Bundesministerium für Land- und Forstwirtschaft, Umwelt- und Wasserwirtschaft Österreich, ed. 2002. *Grundgesetz für die Bundesrepublik Deutschland Art 20a*.

———. 2016. *Tierische Produktion 2016—Tabellensammlung*. Wien: BMLFUW.

Bundesregierung. *GG Artikel 74 Absatz 1, Nummer 20*.

Buschka, Sonja, Julia Gutjahr, and Marcel Sebastian. 2012. "Tiere—Grundlagen und Perspektiven der Human-Animal Studies." *Aus Politik und Zeitgeschichte* 62: 20–27.

Cornish, Amelia, David Raubenheimer, and Paul McGreevy. 2016. "What We Know about the Public's Level of Concern for Farm Animal Welfare in Food Production in Developed Countries." *Animals* 6 (11): 1–15.

Council of Europe. 1976. European Convention for the Protection of Animals kept for Farming Purposes. Treaty No. 087.

Der Bundesrat Schweiz. 2017. *Tierschutzgesetz: TSchG*.

Donaldson, Sue, and Will Kymlicka. 2013 *Zoopolis: Eine politische Theorie der Tierrechte*. Berlin: Suhrkamp.

European Commission. 2006. *Action Plan on Animal Welfare 2006–2010* [Online]. http://eur-lex.europa.eu/legal-content/EN/TXT/?uri=URISERV%3Af82003. Accessed March 8, 2017.

———. 2015. "Special Eurobarometer 442. Report. Attitudes of Europeans towards Animal Welfare."

European Communities. 1997. *Treaty of Amsterdam* [Online]. http://www.europarl.europa.eu/topics/treaty/pdf/amst-en.pdf. Accessed March 8, 2017.

Filzmaier, Peter, Flooh Perlot, and Martina Zandonella. 2014. "Das Wahljahr 2013: Wahlverhalten, Wählerwanderung und neue Parteien." *SWS-Rundschau* 54 (2): 108–32. http://nbn-resolving.de/urn:nbn:de:0168-ssoar-48047-8. Accessed March 8, 2017.

Franzese, Robert J. 2002. "Electoral and Partisan Cycles in Economic Policies and Outcomes." *Annual Review of Political Science* 5 (1): 369–421.

Gall, Philipp V. 2016. *Tierschutz als Agrarpolitik: Wie das deutsche Tierschutzgesetz der industriellen Tierhaltung den Weg bereitete. Human-animal studies.* Bielefeld: Transcript.

Grethe, Harald. 2007. "High Animal Welfare Standards in the EU and International Trade—How to prevent potential 'low Animal Welfare Havens'?" *Food Policy* 32 (3): 315–33.

Harvey, David, and Carmen Hubbard. 2013. "Reconsidering the Political Economy of Farm Animal Welfare: An Anatomy of Market Failure." *Food Policy* 38: 105–14.

Hibbs, Douglas A. 1977. "Political Parties and Macroeconomic Policy." *American Political Science Review* 71 (04): 1467–87.

Hirt, Almuth, Christoph Maisack, and Johanna Moritz, ed. 2016 *Tierschutzgesetz: Mit TierSchHundeV, TierSchNutztV, TierSchVersV, TierSchTrV, EU-Tiertransport-VO, TierSchlV, EU-Tierschlacht-VO: Kommentar,* 3rd ed. München: Verlag Franz Vahlen.

Hofer. 2017. Fairhof [Online]. https://www.blw.admin.ch/blw/de/home/instrumente/direktzahlungen/produktionssystembeitraege/tierwohlbeitraege.html. Accessed March 8, 2017.

Homolka, Gabriele. 2016. Labels für Fleischprodukte—Status Quo in Österreich [Online]. http://www.tieranwalt.at/fxdata/tieranwalt/prod/media/dieumweltberatung_Labels-Fleischprodukte.pdf. Accessed March 8, 2017.

Huber, Hansuli. 2016. *Tierwohl im Detailhandel: 2015/6.* Schweizer Tierschutz STS.

Imbeau, Louis M., Francois Petry, and Moktar Lamari. 2001. "Left-right Party Ideology and Government Policies: A meta-analysis." *European Journal of Political Research* 40 (1): 1–29.

Ingenbleek, Paul, David Harvey, Vlatko Ilieski, Victor Immink, Kees de Roest, Otto Schmid, Paul T. M. Ingenbleek, and Victor M. Immink. 2013. "The European Market for Animal-Friendly Products in a Societal Context." *Animals* 3 (3): 808–29.

Inglehart, Ronald. 1977. *The silent revolution: Changing Values and Political Styles among Western Publics [eng]. Princeton Legacy Library.* New Jersey: Princeton University Press.

Ingold, Karin, and Géraldine Pflieger. 2016. "Two Levels, Two Strategies: Explaining the Gap Between Swiss National and International Responses Toward Climate Change." *European Policy Analysis* 2 (1): 20–38.

Jones, Philip, Joop Lensink, Maria C. Mancini, and Richard Tranter. 2017. "Designing an Institutional Network for Improving Farm Animal Welfare in the EU." *JCMS. Journal of Common Market Studies* 69 (10): 1–13.

Kritzinger, Sylvia, Wolfgang C. Müller, and Klaus Schönbach, ed. 2014. *Die Nationalratswahl 2013.* Köln/Wien: Böhlau Verlag.

Krumm, Thomas. 2013 *Das politische System der Schweiz: Ein internationaler Vergleich.* München: Oldenbourg.

Landwirtschaftlicher Informationsdienst. 2017. Steter Zuwachs bei Tierwohlprogrammen. February 8 [Online]. https://www.lid.ch/medien/mediendienst/grafiken/interaktive-grafiken/tierwohl-programme/. Accessed March 8, 2017.

Lundmark, Frida, C. Berg, O. Schmid, D. Behdadi, and H. Röcklinsberg. 2014. "Intentions and Values in Animal Welfare Legislation and Standards." *Journal of Agricultural and Environmental Ethics* 27 (6): 991–1017.

Lusk, J. L., and F. B. Norwood. 2011. "Animal Welfare Economics." *Applied Economic Perspectives and Policy* 33 (4): 463–83.

Meyer, Christian. 2017. *Wir brauchen eine gemeinsame nationale Nutztierstrategie von Bund und Ländern.* Hannover [Online]. http://www.ml.niedersachsen.de/aktuelles/pressemitteilungen/wir-brauchen-eine-gemeinsame-nationale-nutztierstrategie-von-bund-und-laendern-150156.html. Accessed March 8, 2017.

Ministerium für Gesundheit und Frauen. *Das österreichische Tierschutzgesetz.*

Niedermayer, Oskar. 2009. "Gesellschaftliche und parteipolitische Konfliktlinien." In *Wähler in Deutschland: Sozialer und politischer Wandel, Gender und Wahlverhalten*, 1st ed., ed. Bettina Westle, Steffen Kühnel, and Oskar Niedermayer. Wiesbaden: VS Verlag für Sozialwissenschaften/GWV Fachverlage GmbH Wiesbaden, 30–67.

Niedersächsisches Ministerium für Ernährung, Landwirtschaft und Verbraucherschutz. *Tierschutzplan Niedersachsen.*

Niesen, Peter. 2014. "Kooperation und Unterwerfung. Vorüberlegungen zur politischen Theorie des Mensch/Nutztier-Verhältnisses." *Mittelweg 36* 23 (5): 45–58.

Oberverwaltungsgericht für das Land Nordrhein-Westfalen. 2016. Töten von Eintagsküken ist mit dem Tierschutzgesetz vereinbar. May 20. [Online]. http://www.ovg.nrw.de/behoerde/presse/pressemitteilungen/01_archiv/2016/19_160520/index.php. Accessed March 8, 2017.

OECD. 2015 *OECD-Studie zur Agrarpolitik: Schweiz 2015*. Paris: OECD Publishing.

Ohl, F., and van der Staay F. J. 2012. "Animal Welfare: At the Interface between Science and Society." *Veterinary journal (London, England: 1997)* 192 (1): 13–19.

Onken, Holger. 2013. "Analyse des Parteiensystems in Österreich." In *Parteiensysteme im Wandel: Deutschland, Großbritannien, die Niederlande und Österreich im Vergleich.* Vol. 7 of Bürgerbewusstsein, ed. Holger Onken. Wiesbaden: Springer, 283–330.

Österreichischer Tiergesundheitsdienst. 2017. [Online]. http://www.tgd.at. Accessed March 8, 2017.

Ostheim, Tobias. 2007 "Die Internationale Hypothese." In *Der Wohlfahrtsstaat: Eine Einführung in den historischen und internationalen Vergleich*, ed. Manfred G. Schmidt, Tobias Ostheim, Nico A. Siegel, and Reimut Zohlnhöfer. Wiesbaden: Springer VS, 75–84.

Parlament der Republik Österreich. 1996. *Volksbegehren zur Schaffung eines Bundes-Tierschutgesetzes.*

Sager, Fritz, Eva Thomann, Christine Zollinger, and Céline Mavrot. 2014. "Confronting Theories of European Integration: A Comparative Congruence Analysis of Veterinary Drug Regulations in Five Countries." *Journal of Comparative Policy Analysis: Research and Practice* 16 (5): 457–74.

Saretzki, Thomas. 2015. "Taking Animals Seriously: Interpreting and Institutionalizing Human-Animal Relations in Modern Democracies." *Historical Social Research* 40 (4): 47–54.

Scharpf, Fritz W., and Vivien A. Schmidt. 2005. *From Vulnerability to Competitiveness*, ed. Fritz W. Scharpf; Vol. 1 of Welfare and Work in the Open Economy. Oxford: University Press.

Schmid, Otto, and Rahel Kilchsberger. 2010. Overview of Animal Welfare Standards and Initiatives in Selected EU and Third Countries. [Online]. http://www.econwelfare.eu/publications/econwelfared1.2report_update_nov2010.pdf. Accessed March 8, 2017.

Schmidt, Manfred G. 1996. "When parties matter: A Review of the Possibilities and Limits of Partisan Influence on Public Policy." *European Journal of Political Research* 30 (2): 155–83.

Schmidt, Manfred G., Tobias Ostheim, Nico A. Siegel, and Reimut Zohlnhöfer, ed. 2007. *Der Wohlfahrtsstaat: Eine Einführung in den historischen und internationalen Vergleich.* Wiesbaden: Springer VS.

Schweizer, Rémi. 2015. "Law Activation Strategies (LAS) in Environmental Policymaking: A Social Mechanism for Re-politicization?" *European Policy Analysis* 1 (2): 132–54.

Schweizer Tierschutz STS. 2013. Tierschutz und Landwirtschaft. [Online]. http://www.tierschutz.com/publikationen/nutztiere/index.html. Accessed March 8, 2017.

Singer, Peter. 1975 *Animal liberation: The Definitive Classic of the Animal Movement*, 1st ed. New York, NY: Ecco Book/Harper Perennial.

Spiller, Achim, and Birgit Schulze. 2008 *Zukunftsperspektiven der Fleischwirtschaft: Verbraucher, Märkte, Geschäftsbeziehungen.* Göttingen: Universitätsverlag Göttingen.

Thomann, Eva. 2015. "Customizing Europe: Transposition as bottom-up implementation." *Journal of European Public Policy* 22 (10): 1368–87.

Vatter, Adrian. 2016. *Das politische System der Schweiz*, 2nd ed. *UTB Politikwissenschaft*. Baden-Baden: Nomos.

Veissier, Isabelle, Andrew Butterworth, Bettina Bock, and Emma Roe. 2008. "European Approaches to Ensure Good Animal Welfare." *Applied Animal Behaviour Science* 113 (4): 279–97.

Wenzelburger, Georg. 2015 "Parteien." In *Handbuch Policy-Forschung*, ed. Georg Wenzelburger, and Reimut Zohlnhöfer. Wiesbaden: Springer VS, 81–112.

Wissenschaftlicher Beirat Agrarpolitik beim BMEL. 2015. *Wege zu einer gesellschaftlich akzeptierten Nutztierhaltung. Gutachten*. Berlin: BMEL.

Yeates, James W., and David C. J. Main. 2008. "Assessment of Positive Welfare: A Review." *Veterinary journal (London, England: 1997)* 175 (3): 293–300.

Zohlnhöfer, Reimut. 2005. "Globalisierung der Wirtschaft und nationalstaatliche Anpassungsreaktionen. Theoretische Überlegungen." *Zeitschrift für internationale Beziehungen* 12 (1): 41–75.

———. 2012. "Machen Parteiensysteme einen Unterschied? Die Struktur des Parteienwettbewerbs und die Kürzung von Sozialausgaben in Westeuropa." *Der moderne Staat* 5 (2): 341–60.

Appendix

Table 2 Germany (Accessed March 8, 2017):

https://www.gruene.de/fileadmin/user_upload/Dokumente/Gruenes-Bundestagswahlprogramm-2013.pdf;

https://www.cdu.de/sites/default/files/media/dokumente/regierungsprogramm-2013-2017-langfassung-20130911.pdf;

https://www3.spd.de/linkableblob/96686/data/20130415_regierungsprogramm_2013_2017.pdf;

https://www.fdp.de/files/408/B_rgerprogramm_A5_Online_2013-07-23.pdf;

https://www.die-linke.de/fileadmin/download/wahlen2013/bundestagswahlprogramm/bundestagswahlprogramm2013_langfassung.pdf;

Table 3 Austria (Accessed March 8, 2017):

https://spoe.at/sites/default/files/spoe_wahlprogramm13.pdf;

https://spoe.at/sites/default/files/das_spoe_parteiprogramm.pdf;

www.oevp.at/down.load?file=Wahlprogramm_Ansicht_WEB.pdf&so=download;

https://www.oevp.at/down.load?file=Grundsatzprogramm.pdf&so=download

https://www.fpoe.at/fileadmin/user_upload/www.fpoe.at/dokumente/2015/2011_graz_parteiprogramm_web.pdf;

https://www.gruene.at/themen/demokratie-verfassung/das-gruene-wahlprogramm-2013;

http://www.teamstronach.at/themen/parteiprogramm-pdf;

https://neuwal.com/wp-content/uploads/2013/08/plaene-fuer-ein-neues-oesterreich.pdf

Table 4 Switzerland (Accessed March 8, 2017):

https://www.svp.ch/de/assets/File/Parteiprogramm_2015-d.pdf;
http://www.sp-ps.ch/de/kampagnen/wahlen-2015/wahlplattform;
https://www.sp-ps.ch/de/partei/wir-sind-die-sp/unser-programm;
http://www.fdp.ch/images/stories/Dokumente/Factsheets/20150724_FAC_Agrarpolitik_d.pdf;
http://www.fdp.sg/wp-content/uploads/2015/07/20140329_MED_Zukunftsstrategie_d.pdf;
https://www.cvp.ch/sites/default/files/CVP-Wahlprogramm-DE.pdf;
http://www.gruene.ch/gruene/de/die_gruenen/gruene_programme.html;
http://www.grunliberale.ch/unsere-positionen/positionspapiere/mainContent/05/collapsableContentSection/0/download_website/Link%20auf%20unsere%20vollständigen%20Leitlinien.pdf;
http://www.bdp.info/data/uploads/schweiz/deutsch-unterlagen/verschiedenes/parteiprogramm/programm-bdb-schweiz_september_2015.pdf;
https://www.evppev.ch/politik/programme/parteiprogramm/?noMobile=1;
http://www.edu-schweiz.ch/fileadmin/user_upload/_Allgemein/Doku-EDU/Aktionsprogramm_EDU_CH_2015-2019.pdf

Sources for Figures 2–5 (Accessed March 8, 2017):

http://www.agrarbericht.ch/de/markt/tierische-produkte/fleisch-und-eier;
http://www.bmel-statistik.de//fileadmin/user_upload/monatsberichte/AHT-0040040-2015.pdf;
http://www.bmel.de/SharedDocs/Downloads/Broschueren/Agrarexporte-verstehen.pdf?__blob=publicationFile;
https://www.bfs.admin.ch/bfs/de/home/statistiken/land-forstwirtschaft.assetdetail.1880327.html;
https://www.destatis.de/DE/ZahlenFakten/Wirtschaftsbereiche/LandForstwirtschaftFischerei/TiereundtierischeErzeugung/AktuellSchlachtungen.html
http://www.bmel.de/SharedDocs/Downloads/Broschueren/Landwirtschaft-verstehen.pdf?__blob=publicationFile;
https://www.sbv-usp.ch/fileadmin/sbvuspch/07_Preise/archiv%20Mista/Mista_2014.pdf;
http://milchindustrie.de/marktdaten/aussenhandel/;
Tierische Produktion 2016, Bundesministerium für Land- und Forstwirtschaft, Umwelt- und Wasserwirtschaft Österreich

European Policy Analysis, Vol. 3, No. 1, 2017

Voluntary Regulation by the Pharmaceutical Industry—Which Role for the Shadow of Hierarchy and Social Pressure?

Annette Elisabeth Töller

In 2004, the voluntary FSA Codex was adopted by part of the German pharmaceutical industry and was revised several times in the subsequent 10 years. The codex—as many others in OECD countries do—addresses the delicate relationship between the pharmaceutical industry and physicians. This article presents a case study of the FSA Codex and addresses the question of why this voluntary regulation was adopted and revised. In doing so, the article challenges a strong position in the literature, that voluntary regulation is dependent on the shadow of hierarchy. In addition, it addresses the question how social pressure can trigger voluntary regulation. For this case, rational-choice institutionalism and normative institutionalism in combination prove useful for identifying the driving forces and causal mechanisms of voluntary regulation.

KEY WORDS: health policy, corruption, voluntary regulation, pharmaceutical industry, shadow of hierarchy, social pressure, institutional theories

制药产业的自愿监管—科层阴影和社会压力各扮演哪些角色?

2004年, 部分德国制药业采用了"制药业自愿自律" (*Freiwillige Selbstkontrolle für die Arzneimittelindustrie*, 简称*FSA*)法典, 该法典在接下来的十年里经历了好几次修订。和许多经合组织国家使用的法典一样, 该法典用于处理制药业和医生之间脆弱的关系。本文对*FSA*法典进行案例分析, 处理了"为何自愿监管会被采纳和修订"这一问题。为此, 本文质疑了文献的强有力观点, 即自愿监管取决于科层阴影。此外, 本文还处理了社会压力如何能引发自愿监管的问题。在该案例中, 理性选择制度主义和规范制度主义通过结合的方式能有效识别出自愿监管的驱动力和因果机制。

关键词: 卫生政策, 腐败, 自愿监管, 制药产业, 科层阴影, 社会压力, 制度理论

Introduction

Traditionally, regulation has been seen as "synonymous with government intervention and, indeed with all the efforts of the state, by whatever means, to control and guide economy and society" (Levi-Faur, 2010, p. 5). In light of such a Weberian conception of regulation, *voluntary regulation* provokes puzzlement. Here there are no binding rules, no role for the courts, no forcible implementation by the state and sometimes no public agency at all; yet we call it

doi: 10.1002/epa2.1006

"regulation" and it obviously succeeds in obtaining desired outcomes, in enhancing public welfare, correcting market failures and reducing social risks, albeit certainly to different degrees (Gunningham & Rees, 1997, p. 363, 386; Levi-Faur, 2010, p. 20). Voluntary regulation can be defined as 'rule structures [...] that seek to persuade firms to incur nontrivial costs of producing positive externalities beyond what the law requires of them' (Potoski & Prakash, 2009c, p. ix).[1] The term "voluntary" expresses the fact that companies (individually or with the help of associations or committees) adopt rules and (at last ideally) comply with them even though these rules are not compulsory in a legal sense.

Part of the abundant literature on voluntary regulation has either described or systematized the occurrence of voluntary regulation (e.g., Bell & Hindmoor, 2011; Cummins, 2004; Marx, 2011; Marx & Cuypers, 2010) or analyzed its design and effects, or the conditions affecting the efficacy of voluntary regulation (e.g., Croci, 2005; Berliner & Prakash, 2014; Potoski & Prakash, 2009a,b). Furthermore, the role of voluntary regulation in value chains and the interaction of voluntary regulations with each other and with the law have been discussed (Eberlein, Abbott, Black, Meidinger & Wood, 2014; Turcotte, Reinecke & den Hond, 2014; Wahl & Bull, 2014). An increasing number of studies has also addressed the question of *why* such voluntary forms of regulation emerge or *why* they are being adopted at all, aiming at a theory-driven causal explanation of the phenomenon (see e.g., Bartley, 2003, 2007; Büthe, 2010; Gulbrandsen, 2010; Gunningham & Rees, 1997; Héritier & Eckert, 2008; Koop, 2014; Marx, 2008; Töller, 2011, 2013; Turcotte et al., 2014). Among these, many publications focus on the *shadow of hierarchy* as *the* driving force of voluntary regulation. The core argument is that voluntary regulation will only be adopted if government can threaten credibly to intervene hierarchically (e.g., Börzel, 2008, p. 118; Gunningham & Rees, 1997, p. 400; Héritier & Eckert, 2008; Newman & Bach, 2004, p. 398; Potoski & Prakash, 2009b, p. 37). However, as some analyses have shown, the shadow-of-hierarchy hypothesis is more a metaphor than a theory and needs some reconsideration (e.g., Börzel, 2008; Koop, 2014; Meyer, 2013; Töller, 2008). In addition, most studies suggest that social pressure plays a role in voluntary regulation, but the mechanism through which social pressure translates into voluntary regulation is not clear, and neither is how this can be conceptualized in theoretical terms (e.g., Bartley, 2003, p. 442–45; Gunningham & Rees, 1997, p. 379; Haufler, 2009). With this article, the author wants to contribute to our understanding of *why industries or businesses adopt voluntary regulation* by applying institutional theories. While applying rational-choice institutionalism allows for addressing the shadow of hierarchy as one driving force in a more reflected way, normative institutionalism can help reveal the causal mechanisms through which social pressure can trigger voluntary regulation.

The article investigates a case of voluntary regulation in health policy. The codex of the "voluntary self-regulation of the pharmaceutical industry" (*Freiwillige Selbstkontrolle für die Arzneimittelindustrie,* FSA) was adopted by the major part of the German pharmaceutical industry in 2004 and addresses in particular the delicate relationship between the pharmaceutical industry and physicians. Over the last 16 years, approximately, voluntary schemes have been adopted by the pharmaceutical industry in many OECD countries. US voluntary regulation in this field even began in the early 1990s and continues until today (Francer et al., 2014, p. 5; Grande, 2009; Hemphill, 2006; Katz, Caplan & Merz, 2010).[2]

Pharmaceuticals are a unique kind of product. Approval of such a product and application requires the highest standards of professional knowledge and care. Equally relevant is the fact that health insurance companies pay a large proportion of the cost of pharmaceuticals.[3] For example, whereas health expenditures as a share of GDP in Germany increased only moderately and expenses were reduced on a few items, the share attributable to the cost of pharmaceuticals continued to rise.[4] The two major reasons for this were that, up until 2004, the pharmaceutical industry could demand any price for so-called "innovate medicines," and secondly, that these medicines were prescribed comparatively often. Heavy marketing strategies carried out by the pharmaceutical industry play a role here: The close relationship between the pharmaceutical industry and physicians was a central part of these marketing activities (Francer et al., 2014, p. 9–10; Hemphill, 2006, p. 187; Wiesner & Lieb, 2011, p. 163). In most countries, this relationship used to be shaped by gifts for the doctors in return for a friendly attitude toward specific firms and their products. More recently, there has been much debate on "what should be considered as appropriate business practices" (Hemphill, 2006, p. 187). The United States has adopted strict legislative measures,[5] while in many European states at least part of regulation of "appropriate practice" still relies on voluntary regulation.

Among other reasons, the case of pharmaceutical voluntary regulation is interesting because so far, no studies with an explanatory purpose have been presented for this field. This is in contrast to the many studies on voluntary regulation e.g., in the fields of agriculture, forestry and in the apparel industry (Büthe, 2010; Wahl & Bull, 2014, p. 590). Whereas voluntary regulation has a long history in Germany in general, and in German health policy in particular (Töller, 2012, p. 83–4; Gerlinger, 2009), the FSA Codex belongs to a *new type* of voluntary regulation. This new type differs from other, more traditional, types of voluntary regulation due to its much stronger institutional foundation: It contains a law-like, refined rule system and rules of procedure; it includes a secretariat; it has been continuously revised; it includes a body of arbitration with two instances; and it entails sanctions (fines). With regard to this stronger institutionalization, the code is typical of other more recent codes in Germany, such as the German Corporate Governance Codex adopted in 2002.[6] The case is also exemplary in that most national codes of practice regulating the pharmaceutical industry display similar characteristics (Francer et al., 2014, p. 10). Even more important for case selection is that this case is particularly suitable to show the usefulness of my theoretical argument: First, as with many other cases, the shadow of hierarchy did play a role in the emergence of the codex in 2004 and its revisions since 2011, as analyzed below. When the codex was adopted in 2004, the shadow of hierarchy was, however, less credible than the shadow-of-hierarchy hypothesis would have us expect. Furthermore, said hypothesis cannot explain the major revisions that were adopted in 2005 and 2008. Instead, the dramatic change in the public and professional perceptions of what an appropriate relationship between physicians and the pharmaceutical industry is has been reflected in heated public debates and challenged the pharmaceutical industry's role in society at large.

In terms of methods, this is a single case study in which causality is established by the theory-driven qualitative interpretation of mainly primary data. Qualitative-guided interviews with relevant actors[7] were conducted at an early stage of research and served in particular for understanding the changing social norms of the field, for identifying relevant actors and for developing working hypotheses rather than for fact finding. The case study as such is based on three sources: (1) a qualitative content analysis of all newspaper and journal articles on the issue covered in the press databases, Lexisnexis and WISO, between 2000 to 2014, including daily newspapers and professional journals, such as the "Ärzteblatt," "Arzt und Wirtschaft" and others[8] ; (2) the analysis of primary documents, such as legislative proposals, various versions of the FSA Codex, court decisions or reports published by different organizations; and (3) the analysis of secondary publications on the issue, many of which deal with the U.S. codes (Francer et al., 2014; Grande, 2009; Hemphill, 2006; Katz et al., 2010). On the FSA Codex, in particular, there are publications by law scholars (e.g., Dieners, 2007; Kuhlen, 2010; Rübenstahl, 2011) and practitioners (Grusa, 2011; Volz, 2008) that certainly present the case in a biased way. In terms of theoretical concepts, surely a broader range of literature on voluntary regulation and regulation in general is of relevance (e.g., Gunningham & Rees, 1997; Levi-Faur, 2010; Marx, 2008).

The article proceeds as follows: The first section addresses the question if and how institutional theories can help explain the adoption and the regulatory substance of voluntary regulation. It starts with the shadow-of-hierarchy hypothesis and reviews other explanations that focus on the market and on social pressure. In a second step, rational-choice institutionalism is presented as a context within which to integrate explanations such as the shadow-of-hierarchy hypothesis. Normative institutionalism is proposed as a complementary approach that is particularly useful for understanding how social pressure can trigger voluntary regulation. In the next section, the FSA Codex is presented. First, I briefly sketch the problems that are addressed by the codex and then describe the emergence of the codex and the development of the regulatory substance in the course of a decade. The next section contains a theory-driven explanation of its emergence and development that starts with rational-choice institutionalism and then continues into normative institutionalism. The results of the analysis are presented in Figure 1. The article ends with a conclusion. The overall aim of the paper is to present a case study on voluntary regulation in the pharmaceutical sector and answer the question of why voluntary regulation was adopted here. In doing so, the article aims to address two theoretical puzzles: the role of first the shadow of hierarchy and second of social pressure for the emergence of such voluntary regulation.[9] While concentrating on these two most important explanatory factors, for reasons of space and stringency the article does not address a number of other explanatory factors which might also have had an impact on the FSA Codex, though arguably more limited. Such factors are e.g., developments in the European law, European voluntary codices (such as the EFPIA code[10]), the fact that pharmaceutical industry as such is highly globalized, or the recent critical situation of the pharmaceutical sector due to major problems in the production of ever more medical innovations. Neither does the article deal with questions of enforcement or compliance of the FSA Codex or with the extent to which the codex succeeded to change the problematic practices, which would be an interesting question to address.

Theories and Theoretical Arguments for Explaining Voluntary Regulation

The section title refers theories and *theoretical arguments* because not all relevant arguments have the quality of a full-fledged and consistent theory. Rather, some of them are bits and pieces that need to be assigned to certain theories or families of theories.

The "Shadow of Hierarchy": More a Metaphor than a Theory

This paragraph aims at addressing the problems that come with applying the shadow of hierarchy metaphor to cases of voluntary regulation. There is a strong agreement among researchers working in this field that voluntary regulation of business actors is dependent on the shadow of hierarchy (e.g., Gunningham & Rees, 1997, p. 400; Newman & Bach, 2004, p. 398; Börzel, 2008, p. 118; Héritier & Eckert, 2008; Potoski & Prakash, 2009b, p. 37). The shadow of hierarchy refers to the possibility of any hierarchical intervention by the state or any other public organization, in particular by adopting new regulation, having already-existing regulation interpreted by courts, or enforcing already-existing regulation, including by the application of force (Gunningham & Rees, 1997, p. 400–401).

This means that voluntary regulation *only occurs* if the state (or a functional equivalent) credibly threatens to use its traditional means of control. The credibility of this threat depends in particular on the costs that the regulation associated with it would impose on those subject to it and the probability of the measure actually being adopted. However, both aspects cannot be maximized simultaneously: Due to the logic of the political process, the stricter a measure is, the less likely it is to be adopted (Maxwell & Lyon, 2004, p. 192; Paris & Sofsky, 1998; Töller, 2008). As a reaction to this shadow of hierarchy, the addressees of the suggested regulation propose the voluntary regulation, and if agreement can be reached, it is established.[11]

More precisely, the idea of the shadow-of-hierarchy hypothesis is as follows. Firstly, only if a government presents a credible threat will then business offer to regulate voluntarily to avert the hierarchical intervention and to create security about the regulatory future. That is, the shadow of hierarchy is a necessary condition and relevant causal driving force for the *emergence* of voluntary regulation (Büthe, 2010, p. 12; Croci, 2005, p. 12; Héritier & Eckert, 2008, p. 114; Mayntz & Scharpf, 1995, p. 29; Maxwell & Lyon, 2004, p. 193; Newman & Bach, 2004,

p. 398; Töller, 2008, p. 283). Secondly, only if the threat is credible will the regulatory *content* of the voluntary measure go beyond "business as usual" (Héritier & Eckert, 2008, p. 117; Maxwell & Lyon, 2004, p. 180, 193). Therefore, the shadow of hierarchy is considered to have an impact on the *regulatory substance* of voluntary regulation. Thirdly, enforcement can only be successful if the shadow of hierarchy can be upheld. This is because the shadow of hierarchy should help addressees to overcome the free-rider problem typical of voluntary regulation because it facilitates associations or other bodies in charge of enforcing the voluntary rule to put pressure on their members (e.g., Börzel, 2008, p. 118; Büthe, 2010, p. 19; Gunningham & Rees, 1997, p. 391). Thus, the shadow of hierarchy enables the *enforcement* of voluntary regulation, because if societal actors do not comply with the voluntary regulation, "the state can step in at any time" (Offe, 1987).[12]

However, the shadow-of-hierarchy hypothesis, even if spelled out as above, is obviously more a metaphor than a consistent theory, since its assumptions are rather simple, not wholly coherent and, to some extent, even contradictory. Furthermore, it is based in part on doubtful assumptions, and in addition, the conditions under which it would apply have not been defined. Finally (and most important for our purpose), empirical analysis shows that sometimes the shadow of hierarchy plays a rather limited role and yet voluntary regulation still emerges.

In conceptual terms, it seems paradoxical that, on the one hand, governments do accept such forms of voluntary regulation *because* the state has experienced many restrictions to its ability to regulate hierarchically (e.g., Black, 2001; Mayntz & Scharpf, 1995), while on the other hand, the shadow-of-hierarchy metaphor presupposes an almost almighty state that could intervene hierarchically at any time. To put it another way: If the state were able to act at any time, it would not need to get involved in voluntary regulation (Börzel, 2008, p. 128; Töller, 2008, p. 284). What is more, the welfare-economic strand of the shadow-of-hierarchy hypothesis, in particular, seems fairly blind with regard to the institutional context in which the shadow of hierarchy is evoked. For example, its role would differ markedly depending on whether the context is a parliamentary or a presidential system, or also depending on the regulatory tradition.

In empirical terms, Meyer observed, in a case study on European standardization in the field of transport policy, that a shadow of hierarchy created by the European Commission did not spur voluntary regulation (as would be expected), but caused its failure instead (Meyer, 2013, p. 761). Based on this case study, Meyer's critique is that the shadow-of-hierarchy hypothesis assumes a homogeneity in the interests and preferences of business actors that does not always correspond to reality. As a consequence of this doubtful assumption, "the shadow-of-hierarchy literature tends to overemphasize industry's desire to prevent regulatory interventions by adopting self-regulatory measures" (Meyer, 2013, p. 768). In her study on voluntary environmental agreements in Germany, this author finds that often a moderate shadow of hierarchy produces uncertainty and can thus be enough to make business adopt voluntary regulation. Yet the lack of a very credible threat impedes the adoption of meaningful regulatory substance (Töller, 2008, 2012). In her study on the adoption of forms of voluntary accountability by Dutch independent executive agencies, Koop suggests that the intention to preempt legislative threats might not be sufficient, as a causal mechanism, to explain the adoption of such voluntary accountability. She argues that organizations may also adopt voluntary accountability because it is considered appropriate (Koop, 2014, p. 567–68). Since such causal mechanisms are difficult to test empirically (Peters, 2005, p. 164), Koop treats them as possible mechanisms underlying several dependent variables (such as issue salience, competences or source of funding), which she then tests. Thus, in the end, both mechanisms can be neither verified nor falsified, but remain plausible assumptions.

Especially (but not only) when trying to explain voluntary regulation beyond the nation state, explanatory factors beyond the shadow of hierarchy are badly needed, because there is no state, and if there are any institutions that could produce a shadow of hierarchy, they are usually weak.[13] Some authors point to the market as a driving force and argue that business players fear losing market shares and that therefore they need to improve their image and would participate in voluntary regulation (Bartley, 2003, p. 442; Gunningham & Rees, 1997, p. 391–92; Marx, 2008). In their volume on (US) voluntary programs and the conditions of their effectiveness, Potoski and Prakash also touch upon the question of why businesses participate in voluntary programs at all. Obviously, pressure from stakeholders or social activists can play a role, especially when firms fear that their brand may be seriously affected (Marx, 2008; Potoski & Prakash, 2009a, p. 5; Potoski & Prakash, 2009b, p. 32). However, descriptions of the causal mechanism that may link such pressure to the willingness to participate in voluntary regulation remain vague.

In a welfare-economic contribution to the same volume, Baron argues that it is social pressure that motivates firms to participate in voluntary regulation, because they can expect consumers to pay a higher price for their products with "credence attributes" (Baron, 2009). This explanation does not really help our case for two reasons, one of which is specific for the pharmaceuticals sector, while the other is of general relevance: In the pharmaceuticals sector, at least in Germany, most of the products are not sold in a free market. The market does not determine prices, and consumers (in this case patients) do not choose the products. However, in many other cases and sectors, social pressure is fundamental and does not simply affect the price of products but can also radically challenge the practices and the operation of entire industries.[14]

To sum up, the shadow-of-hierarchy hypothesis needs to be handled with more care and, in particular, the empirical role and effect of the shadow has to be analyzed. Moreover, social pressure should be expected to play a role, but we need to understand better the causal mechanism that transforms social pressure into the willingness of business to engage in voluntary regulation.

Institutional Theories as a Means for Addressing our Theoretical Puzzles

I will now present two sketches of institutional theories in order to address the theoretical puzzles brought up above. It is certainly more adequate to speak of various institutional theories that differ with respect to many fundamental aspects (e.g., what an institution is and how it affects agency) instead of one institutional theory. However, all varieties of institutional theory have one thing in common: the assumption that institutions are more important than anything else when it comes to explaining the course of action and its outcomes (Peters, 2005, p. 164).

I will first introduce the basic assumptions of rational-choice institutionalism and then apply it to systematize a number of arguments that are relevant for the explanation of voluntary regulation. Then, I will argue that rational-choice institutionalism might not be sufficient to fully explain the adoption of voluntary regulation, and that normative institutionalism could be a useful complement. This is, however, not a totally new idea. Several other authors have suggested similar approaches (Gulbrandsen, 2010; Gunningham & Rees, 1997, p. 364; Koop, 2014; Turcotte et al., 2014); Whereas the theoretical portion of Koop's paper is rather brief, the theoretical chapter in Gulbrandsen's book on the certifications of forests and fisheries—a book that aims to "shed light on the causal mechanisms that help to explain institutional formation. . . ." (Gulbrandsen, 2010, p. 17)—focuses deeply on institutions in the international context, given the transnational nature of the certification systems he examines. The same holds true for Bartley's publications.[15] Turcotte et al. (2014) have a slightly different focus when applying three institutionalist perspectives (economic, ideationalist, and political institutionalism) in order to explain different patterns of multiplicity of voluntary standards in different sectors.

The core idea of rational-choice institutionalism is that institutions are "a collection of rules and incentives" (Peters, 2005, p. 48) under which rational, utility-maximizing actors calculate the actions and strategies that serve them best. Accordingly, the establishment of voluntary regulation is understood as a consequence of there being specific institutional structures in which it appears rational for business actors to engage in voluntary regulation. The shadow-of-hierarchy hypothesis is clearly based on such a rational-choice institutionalist argumentation (see Héritier & Eckert, 2008, p. 114): The credible regulatory threat derived from a hierarchical institutional structure motivates rational business actors to offer voluntary measures to preempt the proposed new regulation or the enforcement or interpretation of already-existing regulation. The more costly a suggested measure is and the more probable its adoption appears to be, the higher is the business actor's motivation to engage in credible voluntary regulation. Furthermore, depending on branch structure, voluntary regulation, including control and sanctions, allows for the individual firm to control the behavior of its competitors (Gulbrandsen, 2010, p. 21). In addition, it also appears rational for state actors to accept such a voluntary measure, because they save transaction costs and can demonstrate that they are doing something to solve a problem.[16] However, the results of the conceptual criticism presented above are, first, that the shadow of hierarchy does not necessarily have to be as "big" as it has been suggested so far in order for it to have an effect, and second, that the shadow of hierarchy can be a major driving force in some cases, but not in others.[17]

However, many studies suggest that even business players not only calculate the costs of either legislative or voluntary regulation, but that there is "something else." This "something else" is either framed in terms of market needs or is attributed to NGOs leading campaigns against firms or branches and thus creating social pressure, as mentioned above—without suggesting how exactly social pressure could make enterprises or branches adopt voluntary regulation, however (e.g., Bartley, 2003, p. 441; Büthe, 2010, p. 12; Gunningham & Rees, 1997, p. 364, 391; Héritier & Eckert, 2008, p. 116).

As other authors have done before (Gulbrandsen, 2010; Gunningham & Rees, 1997, p. 364; Koop, 2014), I want to suggest that a normative institutionalist approach, as represented by the "logic of appropriateness," developed by March and Olsen, would be useful to understand the full range of causal mechanisms that can bring voluntary regulation into being. The core idea of this well-established concept is that "action is often based more on identifying the normatively appropriate behaviors than on calculating the return expected from alternative choices" (March & Olsen, 1989, p. 22). While the latter idea is the conceptual base of rational-choice institutionalism and is called the "logic of consequentiality," the former has been labeled as the "logic of appropriateness." March and Olsen favor the notion that it is the logic of appropriateness that drives actors' behavior in the first place. "Actors seek to fulfill the obligations encapsulated in a role, an identity, a membership in a political community or group, and the ethos, practices, and expectations of its institutions. Rules are followed because they are seen as natural, rightful, expected, and legitimate" (March & Olsen, 2009, p. 2). From this perspective, institutions are not only formal, but also social rules embedded both in structures of resources and of meaning. In addition, institutions are not external to preferences (as rational-choice institutionalism suggests), but they can shape and change preferences.

The reason why the logic of appropriateness also applies to the agency of business actors is that acting according to the logic of appropriateness does not mean to act in an altruistic manner. Rather, March and Olsen construct the logic of appropriateness as a contract: "The conformity to rules can be viewed as contractual, an implicit agreement to act appropriately in return for being treated appropriately, and to some extent there certainly is such a contract" (March & Olsen, 1989, p. 22–3; March & Olsen, 2009, p. 12). Thus, I was interested in the role that social pressure, as exerted e.g., by different sorts of NGOs and the general or media public, plays to make business actors engage in voluntary regulation. The idea derived from March and Olsen is that when the social notion of what is "natural, rightful, expected, and legitimate" changes greatly,[18] some of the business practices are no longer considered appropriate action, and thus the contract, according to which an industry is treated appropriately in return for acting appropriately, could be seriously challenged. This challenge may come from different parts of society: customers who decide no longer to buy a certain product resulting from environmentally or socially problematic practices (as was the case with timber wood or as was feared in the case of diamonds and apparel) and therefore from the market, in the strict sense. It may also come from shareholders (individual or institutional) who are no longer willing to buy or hold shares of businesses that behave unethically, or from stock markets that refrain from registering firms that do not voluntarily comply with certain rules (e.g., Cadbury, 2006). In a professional context, challenges could as well come from the job market (qualified professionals no longer wishing to work for a branch). Certainly, these challenges do not simply "exist," but need to be reconstructed and felt (March & Olsen, 2009, p. 9). In a similar theoretical vein (based on the concept of the organizational field), Gunningham and Rees argue that industrial voluntary regulation should be viewed as "a common meaning system at the industry level" that reacts to "major changes in society" and changes "normative expectations" (Gunningham & Rees, 1997, p. 373).

Against this backdrop, trying to adapt to what society now considers to be appropriate behavior by voluntarily creating rules, controlling compliance and improving credibility obviously does not have to do with altruism, but neither with merely calculating the costs and benefits of a specific measure, or with the shadow of hierarchy. If certain branches run the risk of their business activity as a whole being seen as problematic due to specific business practices that have become subject to societal criticism, they need to define and fight problematic practices themselves in order to re-establish societal trust in the core of their activities. Below, I will analyze the ways in which and the extent to which this applies to the pharmaceutical industry in Germany in the 2000s.

Theories for social science research must be consistent and able to cover a broad range of causal factors and mechanisms. While neither institutional theories as such nor their application to explaining the emergence of voluntary regulation is something entirely new, I want to argue that by applying the two institutionalisms,[19] we are able to cover and conceptualize the most relevant factors and causal mechanisms that can cause voluntary regulation and at the same time can solve the two theoretical puzzles addressed above. We can cover those driving forces that stem from the rational-choice-like reaction of business to institutional stimuli (in particular the shadow of hierarchy) *and* those driving forces that result from a broader orientation of business toward its role in society at large (which certainly in the end again touches its rational interest to continue its activity). Clearly, the shadow of hierarchy and social pressure are two distinct causal factors. Yet they do not operate fully independent from each other. On the one hand, since governments have to be responsive to their electorates, social pressure should encourage the government to envisage adopting new or enforcing already-existing regulation (and thus increase the shadow of hierarchy), while also having a direct and independent impact on voluntary regulation. On the other hand, a lack of or a weak shadow of hierarchy could make media and NGOs put more pressure on a particular sector with perceived problematic practices.

The Phenomenon: Emergence and Substance of the FSA Codex

In this section, I describe the empirical phenomenon that requires explanation. First, I briefly sketch the social practices between physicians and the pharmaceutical industry that were common before 2004 and have been perceived as problematic from a certain point on. Second, I present the construction of the FSA Codex and its regulatory substance as it has developed over time.

The Problem

The problem in this field, as mentioned in the introduction, is the relationship between the pharmaceutical industry and physicians. Most generally, we can say that pharmaceutical firms have been investing major resources in this area in order to make doctors prescribe "innovative" (and thus very expensive) medicines, instead of long-established, much less expensive ones, since this is the sector where they can make most money.[20] In the early 2000s, according to different sources, there were between 16,000 and 20,000 pharmaceutical representatives in Germany whose task was not only to inform physicians about their products, but also to foster good relationships with them. While most observers agree that the contact between pharmaceutical representatives and physicians does fulfill relevant functions in the context of pharmacovigilance, pharma representatives' actions to influence doctors' prescription behavior[21] have been considered increasingly inappropriate (e.g., Dieners, 2007, p. 81–113; Grusa, 2011; Wiesner & Lieb, 2011). The following practices were common before FSA regulation[22] :

- Presenting gifts (ranging from pens and papers to medical text books, Italian coffee machines or cuckoo clocks, just to give some examples).
- Extending invitations to seminars and conferences to five-star holiday-like places, even abroad, often with major portions of leisure time, and frequently including the physician's partner[23] : According to a newspaper article, in 2005, 90 percent of professional trainings for physicians in Germany were financed by the pharmaceutical industry.
- Providing benefits directly (money, technical equipment or journeys) in return for the prescription of particular drugs, or providing them disguised as honoraria;
- Carrying out so-called post-marketing surveillance studies (PMSS), in which doctors are paid money for filling in some forms on the application of a particular (innovative) medicine: Critics say that these studies lack scientific substance and only serve the purpose of making the doctor prescribe the product more often.
- Presenting products promotions that over-emphasize positive scientific evidence and conceal negative evidence with regard to both the intended effects and the side effects.
- Distributing unrequested product samples.

- Providing computer programs for organizing work in residence with an in-built bias in favor of the prescription of one particular medicine, if only the substance is entered.

Certainly, it is difficult to tell what effects such practices have on physicians' behavior. A number of surveys carried out in the United States show that a large majority of physicians were involved in such marketing activities with pharmaceutical companies. While most of them were convinced that these did not influence their behavior, they thought their colleagues were indeed being influenced (Campbell et al., 2007; Grande, 2009). Similar studies have been presented for Germany as well (Wiesner & Lieb, 2011, p. 164–67). While all physicians I talked to rejected the idea of being influenced in such a way, there are a number of studies that show that a physician's prescription behavior can indeed be influenced by such marketing instruments (Hemphill, 2006; Wiesner & Lieb, 2011, p. 166–67).

Emergence and Development of the FSA Codex

The FSA Codex had *three predecessors* and one relevant counterpart, presented by physicians. As is often the case in public policy, the emergence of pharmaceutical voluntary regulation was initially driven by crises and scandals that brought the practices mentioned above, which had been known to insiders before, into the awareness of a broader public. In the so-called "cardiac valve scandal" ("*Herzklappenskandal*") in the mid-1990s, 1800 clinicians were prosecuted for having been paid for making their hospitals order overpriced artificial cardiac valves. Even though the medical device industry and pharmaceutical industry are clearly distinct branches, after this, routines and practices between pharmaceutical firms and doctors were also looked at more critically (Dieners, 2007; Kuhlen, 2010, p. 876). Between 1997 and 2003, three codes were developed (Kuhlen, 2010, p. 880–81). Finally, the association of the research-based pharmaceutical companies (*Verband der forschenden Arzneimittelindustrie*, VfA) founded the Voluntary Self-Control of Pharmaceutical Industry (Freiwillige Selbstkontrolle der Arzneimittelindustrie—FSA) as an organization in early 2004.[24] At the same time, the FSA Codex was adopted. Initially, the codex was supposed to be supported by two more pharmaceutical associations,[25] but in the end only the VfA was left. In addition, health insurance companies had participated in the beginning, but they left because they found the rules were not strict enough (Handelsblatt February 17, 2004).

The codex features three characteristics that its predecessors did not have: First, its stipulations have the character of binding rules for its members, while the predecessors were only guidelines and recommendations. Second, there is a rule of procedure, based on which the compliance with the code is supervised. At the core of this is a board of arbitration including two instances. Third, sanctions can be imposed (today, these are a maximum of 200,000 euros for the first instance, and 400,000 euros for the second).

Between its establishment in 2004 and 2014, the codex was revised six times: in 2005 (with changes coming into effect in 2006), in 2008 (with changes coming into effect in 2008), in 2009 (with changes coming into effect in 2010), in 2011 (with changes coming into effect in 2012), in 2012 (with changes coming into effect in 2013) and in 2013 (with changes coming into effect in 2014).[26] Two additional codes were established in 2008 and 2013 (see below).

Within the 10 years of codex history, we can identify three phases:

- The first phase (2004–2005) was characterized by the establishment of the codex, with the regulatory substance restricted to mainly one problem field: invitations to conferences.
- The second phase (2005–2010) was characterized by two major revisions of the codex (which came into effect in 2006 and 2008, respectively), and the establishment of a distinct code on relations with patients' organizations and one revision without major substantial changes, both of which came into effect in 2010.
- The third phase began in 2011 and covers further revisions in 2012 and 2013 that led to a relevant sharpening of the codex, not only in terms of substance but also in terms of sanctions. Furthermore, the Transparency Code was adopted in late 2013 and came into force in the summer of 2014.

If we take a first look at the codex's development in terms of sheer numbers, we see that the chapter(s) with substantial regulations tripled within 10 years: the 2004 codex contained 10 paragraphs, the 2006 codex had 18 such paragraphs, the 2008 and 2009 versions contained 20, and the one adopted in 2013 includes 30 paragraphs. The codex is organized in several chapters. The first chapter has to do with the scope of application and (later) the applicable rules of interpretation. The codex states that, as a general principle, doctors may not be influenced in a dishonest way in their decisions on therapies, prescriptions, and procurement. A first set of rules (§ 4, FSA 2004) claims that any kind of collaboration has to be based on written contracts, remuneration may only be in the form of money, and the sum should be based on the relevant medical fee schedule (Gebührenordnung für Ärzte, GOÄ). Doctors may not be given money or other things for the application or prescription of particular medicines. Rules on post-marketing surveillance studies (§ 5) at that time were rather general and referred to guidelines published by the Federal Institute for Pharmaceutical Products (Bundesinstitut für Arzneimittel und Medizinprodukte, BfArM). The rules regarding invitations to professional training events (§ 6) represented a major topic in this first codex version. From then on, firms were allowed to pay only for *adequate* travel and accommodation costs for such professional training events and then only if the *professional cause* was central to the event. No entertainment could be financed. Accommodation and catering was not allowed to exceed a justifiable dimension and no costs could be paid for a doctor's companion. Finally, gifts to doctors could be presented only for exceptional events, such as anniversaries (§ 7).

The codex version adopted in 2005 (FSA 2006) added a number of chapters and paragraphs, introducing some issues for the first time and sharpening the rules for others that had been introduced before. Most importantly, a paragraph

(§ 5) and a full chapter (chapter 3) on product promotion[27] were added. It stipulated that product promotion should support a sensitive use of pharmaceuticals and that therefore information for promotion should be true, fair, balanced, and complete. Now, promotion could not be misleading; it had to be based on scientific evidence and could not contradict such evidence. Second, new rules covered the distribution of samples: Only the smallest available size could be given to physicians and only after they had sent a written request (§ 15). Third, the chapter on invitations to professional, scientific trainings (§ 20) was extended to cover conferences and seminars abroad, which were now allowed only under certain conditions (§ 20 par. 8–9).

Two relevant changes were adopted in the 2008 version (FSA 2008): First, rules on cooperation with doctors became much more detailed. Second, the rules on post-marketing surveillance studies (§ 19) were extended. In particular, it was now stipulated that such studies had to pursue scientific aims, fulfill scientific standards and be organized by the medical department of the company (instead of the marketing department). The doctor's decision to prescribe a particular product had to be separated from the decision to participate in such a study. Doctors' remuneration has to be commensurate to the doctors' activity. Third parties had to do the evaluation of the studies. The code also emphasized the legal duty of notifying several institutions of these studies.

In 2008, the FSA organization saw the need to establish a distinct "code of cooperation with patient organizations," while the actual codex was called the "code of cooperation with healthcare professionals."[28] In the version of the FSA Codex adopted in 2009, no substantial changes are traceable.

In 2011 however, relevant revisions were adopted (that came into force in 2012), in particular regarding the chapter on product promotion (FSA 2012). The chapter on unacceptably importunate promotion (§ 13) was tightened. In § 15, the distribution of samples was further restricted. The rules on PMSS were adapted to some legislative changes. Furthermore, the types of event that pharmaceutical firms were allowed to hold were restricted to training seminars ("Weiterbildung"), and in the field of formal professional qualification as a specialist ("Fortbildung") they were no longer allowed to be active (§ 20). These substantial changes were complemented by changes of procedure: Whereas in the past the names of companies that were found guilty of seriously violating the codex were made public only in particularly serious cases, now the "naming and shaming" of any company seriously violating the codex was fixed as a rule and not as an option (§ 15 par. 3). In terms of sanctions, they could range from 5,000 to 50,000 euros in the first instance and reach a maximum of 250,000 euros in the second instance. Since the 2011 revision, fines have a 200,000 euro maximum in the first instance (§ 20 FSA Rules of Procedure 2012) and a 400,000 maximum in the second instance (§ 24). The 2012 codex version added § 18a on the transparency of clinical studies and strengthened disclosure duties with regard to post-marketing surveillance studies (FSA 2013). Finally, the 2013 revision added that gifts from pharmaceutical firms to medical doctors are no longer allowed (§ 21, FSA 2014). In late 2013, a new Transparency Codex was introduced that came into force in the summer of

2014. According to § 5 of the codex, from 2015 on member companies have to publish every type of benefit of monetary value that they give to doctors, disclosing the name of the recipient and the amount of the benefit.[29]

A question that always comes up with voluntary regulation is how far codes repeat effective statutory regulation and to what extent they go beyond what is required by law. Indeed, the FSA Codex creates new rules as much as it summarizes existing legal obligations and—what is important—it concretizes them, i.e., it gives clear guidance to practitioners as to what is and what is not legal and it provides information on unproblematic forms of action. On some points, the FSA Codex goes clearly beyond what is required by law.

With regard to the binding force of the codex, at first glance it is little more than a gentlemen's agreement that is only morally binding those who want to be bound by it: its members. However, there are two relevant qualifications to this statement: First, civil courts apply the codex's rules when they have to decide on cases involving the law on unfair competition (*Unlauterer Wettbewerbs-Gesetz*, UWG) with regard to pharmaceutical firms. In several cases so far, courts applied the codex's rules as an indication of what the standards of fair or unfair competition in this branch could be (Volz, 2008, p. 23). Second, the FSA as an association is not only entitled to create rules and implement them with their members, but it is also allowed to act as an association to guard against unfair practices ("*Abmahnverein*"). In this function, it can bring firms that are *not members* of the FSA to civil court when it determines that they have participated in unfair practice (§§ 3 and 4 UWG). Therefore, even though, strictly speaking, the FSA Codex's rules apply only to FSA members, the FSA can impose its rules on non-members too, albeit indirectly, if they can bring them to court for violating norms of the UWG, and courts then apply the codex in order to interpret what may or may not constitute unfair practice in this branch.

To sum up this section, there are several things which require explanation: First, the adoption of the FSA Codex in 2004; second, major substantial revisions of the codex in 2005 (in force 2006) and 2008 (in force 2008); and third, a relevant tightening up in terms of substance and procedure adopted in 2011 (in force in 2012) and two further revisions in 2012 (in force 2013) and 2013 (in force 2014).

Explanation with the Help of Institutional Theories

In this paragraph, I will apply the two theoretical perspectives developed above in order to explain why the FSA Codex was adopted at all and why its regulatory substance was strengthened step by step. I will first apply the rational-choice institutionalist perspective and then the normative institutionalist perspective.

Rational-Choice Institutionalism: Which Role for the Shadow of Hierarchy?

To what extent can the shadow of hierarchy, i.e., the state's credible threat to intervene hierarchically by either adopting new regulation or by enforcing or interpreting already-existing regulation, explain the adoption of the FSA Codex in 2004 and its subsequent revisions?

If we look at the shadow of hierarchy for this case, it is important to note that, in spite of a long tradition of corporatism, since the 1990s the German government has increased its autonomy to intervene hierarchically in the health system (Gerlinger, 2009, p. 33; Hartmann, 2010, p. 340). Possibly due to the legalist German tradition, the debate on problematic practices between the pharmaceutical industry and physicians has focused strongly on labeling such practices as "corruption" (whereas, legally, many of these activities were *not* covered by the penal provisions on corruption, as will be shown below). After some of the scandals mentioned already revealed a broad variety of unsavory—if not downright illegal—behaviors, the red-green government (in the context of a broader initiative for reforming the German health system) proposed three fierce measures in 2003: First, all statutory health insurers and associations of statutory health insurers would have to establish appointees to monitor corruption. Second, the government would introduce a "commissioner for corruption" within the Federal Ministry of Health. This commissioner would have the task of investigating any kind of irregularity or illegal use of resources in the context of the operations of health insurers. He or she would have a number of powers and duties, among others, the duty to inform the public prosecutor of any case of an initial suspicion of a criminal offense (§ 274b, par. 1), and to report to the Ministry on a regular basis and in special cases. Third, within the realm of physicians' formal professional qualification as specialists ("Fortbildung") pharmaceutical firms would no longer be allowed to sponsor events (parliamentary print, BT-Drs. 15/1170, p. 13, 34, 36 and 18). This appeared as an effective shadow of hierarchy: physicians and pharmaceutical firms were appalled by these projects. As a reaction, doctors adopted major changes in their (self-regulatory) professional code in 2003.[30] As mentioned above, the pharmaceutical industry had already adopted some guidelines before, but it was aware that, without sanctions, these guidelines would lack credibility. Thus, the pharmaceutical industry offered to adopt a voluntary scheme, including sanctions, if the project to establish a commissioner to fight corruption was dropped. The Ministry agreed, and the project was removed from the proposal (Ärzte Zeitung February 18, 2004; Deutsches Ärzteblatt February 27, 2004; Arzt und Wirtschaft 3/2004; der Spiegel August 8, 2005).

However, drawing on my considerations on the problematic nature of the shadow-of-hierarchy hypothesis, one has to ask what would have been the legal foundation of the work of such a commissioner for corruption? There were two major problems at that time with regard to the penal norms on corruption, which had been sharpened after the cardiac valve scandal in 1997 (Kuhlen, 2010, p. 878; Erices, Frewer & Grumz, 2013, p. 104). According to German Penal Code before 1997 (§ 331 and § 333 StGB), corruption occurred when a person holding an office accepted a benefit for an activity in this office. Thus, the connection between the benefit and the activity had to be clear—and needed to be proven. The revision of 1997 was meant to make the prosecution of corruption easier, and therefore loosened the necessary connection between the benefit and the activity. Then, benefits with the general aim of creating a friendly atmosphere could also be considered to be corruption. Hence, Kuhlen, a legal expert, in an article on the relationship between physicians and the pharmaceutical industry, emphasizes that, particularly for this relationship, the revision adopted in 1997 created uncertainty about what was or was not allowed (Kuhlen, 2010, p. 879). The second—and very important—point is that at that time there was consensus among lawyers that the application of the norms on corruption (§ 331 and § 333 StGB) was restricted to persons holding an office and that they were not applicable to doctors in residence (Dieners, 2007, p. 12–20). In addition, another paragraph (§ 299 StGB), which deals with the competition aspect of corruption in business relations, was considered applicable only to physicians working in hospitals. Coming back to the idea of appointing a commissioner to fight corruption, as proposed by the government in 2003, this position would obviously have had little legal clout, and therefore it would have been doomed to be ineffectual. In this way, the commissioner for corruption shed an unpleasant light on the pharmaceutical industry and its practices, but was no serious *legal* threat. Thus, the shadow of hierarchy was present, but its magnitude was limited.

Only from 2010 onward, the shadow of hierarchy increased stepwise. At that time, the legal situation regarding the applicability of corruption law to doctors in residence, mentioned above, became the major focus of the legal debate. In 2010, the Higher Regional Court of Braunschweig (*Oberlandesgericht Braunschweig*) reasoned that at least § 299 *StrafGesetzBuch* is applicable to doctors in residence who are seen as commissioned by the health insurers (OLG Braunschweig ZStZ 2010, p. 392; Erices et al., 2013, p. 105). In May 2011, the Federal Court of Justice (*Bundesgerichtshof*) suggested that §§ 331 and 333 might also be applicable to doctors in residence (Rübenstahl, 2011). This would mean that a number of practices between doctors in residence and pharmaceutical firms, such as post-marketing surveillance studies, could fall under the prohibitions in the Penal Code (Schneider & Strauß, 2011). In 2012, the Berlin Administrative Court decided that pharmaceutical firms had to publish data on PMSS after Transparency International had referred to the Freedom of Information Act, based on the European Freedom of Information Directive (VG Berlin 2 K 177.11 June 2012; Ärztezeitung June 5, 2012). In spring 2012, however, the Federal Court of Justice took an unexpected route: Contrary to what had been suggested before, the court decided that the penal norms on corruption were *not* applicable to doctors in residence. The court emphasized, however, that it was only able to apply the existing legal norms, whereas it was the task of the legislator to better regulate questions of corruption in the health system (BGH HRRS Br. 612). This decision gave rise to a major political debate on corruption in the health system from 2012 onward. In March 2012, the German Bundestag held a public hearing on "fighting corruption in the health system" which was brought up by the Social Democrats in the Parliament, who at that time were part of the parliamentary opposition (see BT-Drs. 17/3685). In the summer of 2013, the conservative-liberal majority in the Bundestag adopted a law according to which corruptive behavior would be illegal and could be prosecuted more easily, even though—surprisingly—these norms were to be situated in the Social Code instead of the Penal

Code (BT-Drs. 17/14575). However, the law was not supported by the Federal Chamber (*Bundesrat*), because the majority of social democratic *Länder* governments wanted to have corruption regulated in the Penal Code. The Bundesrat was not entitled to reject the law, but delayed its adoption until the legislative period was over (Deutsches Ärzteblatt September 20, 2013). In spring 2016 the Big Coalition[31] finally adopted a new law on "corruption in the health system" making all members of the health system subject to clear rules on corruptibility and corruption (Bundesrat 2016; Deutsches Ärzteblatt October 14, 2016).

While the impact of the "shadow of hierarchy" on the FSA Codex, as just pointed out, is reported in many primary and secondary sources, there is another factor that was arguably a relevant threat and that, progressively, became regulatory reality in parallel to the development of the FSA Codex. As mentioned above, the major reason for the high costs of pharmaceuticals for the health system was the fact that, for a long time, the pharmaceutical industry had been able to demand any price for so-called "innovate medicines" and that these medicines were prescribed comparatively often. Arguably, this was also the case due to the marketing activities that the FSA Codex was now meant to regulate. Critics said that some of these medicines were pseudo-innovations for which high prices were not justified (e.g., FAZ February 2, 2004), whereas pharmaceutical industry insisted that innovations are real and that high prices are necessary to refund enormous costs for research and development. In line with a growing general willingness to intervene more strongly in the health system, in 2001 the red-green government started to propose a number of regulations that increasingly restricted the prescription and also the pricing of innovative medicines (see Bandelow & Hartmann, 2015; Hartmann, 2010; Rosenbrock & Gerlinger, 2014): In 2001, they stipulated that, as a rule, pharmacists could offer the cheapest product to the patient provided that the doctor had not explicitly excluded the substitution of the originally prescribed product by a cheaper one with equal active ingredients (aut idem) (The *Arzneimittelausgaben-Begrenzungsgesetz,* AABG). In 2003, it was determined that insurers could negotiate directly with pharmaceutical firms over rebates for medicines (*Gesundheitsmodernisierungsgesetz,* GMG). In addition, two organizations were established in order to adopt regulations on medicines (the *Gemeinsamer Bundesausschuss,* G-BA, and the *Institut für Qualität und Wirtschaftlichkeit im Gesundheitswesen,* IQWIG). Furthermore, from that point on, the medical benefit of innovative medicines would have to be demonstrated. In 2007, the IQWIG was commissioned to develop a methodology not only to examine the use of the innovative medicines but also to carry out a cost–benefit analysis (*GKV-Wettbewerbstärkungsgesetz*). In 2011, this cost–benefit analysis was made obligatory for newly introduced innovations (*Arzneimittelmarktneuordnungsetz,* AMNOG).

Certainly, the regulation of prescription and pricing is closely related to the criticized marketing activities that the FSA Codex regulates, since these were meant to make physicians prescribe the expensive medicines more often. In fact, the pharmaceutical industry might fear a regulation of prescription and pricing much more than a strict legal norm on corruption. However, the concept of the shadow of hierarchy is restricted to regulatory threats that are *substantially* related to the voluntary regulation, in that the voluntary code aims at preempting the statutory regulation. Thus, the development of the regulation of prescription and pricing is not seen as a shadow of hierarchy for the FSA Codex in a stricter sense, since the FSA Codex does not (and cannot) deal with prescription and pricing, but only with the relationship between the pharmaceutical industry and physicians. Therefore, this development of regulation is seen as a relevant "background threat."

Concluding my findings on the shadow of hierarchy (also see Figure 1), we see that the threat of the government's appointment of the commissioner for corruption was what caused the establishment of the FSA Codex. Yet our theoretical considerations made us look more closely at the legal clout of this proposed commissioner, which showed it was problematic. Consequently, we have a typical situation, in which a rather limited shadow of hierarchy led to the adoption of a codex, but one that was meager in terms of regulatory substance at that time. For the revisions of the rule system adopted in 2005 and 2008, no relevant shadow of hierarchy could be identified that could have been a significant driving force. Only since 2010 has a new shadow of hierarchy emerged, with several courts deciding on the applicability of penal norms on corruption and on the duty to publish data on PMSS, due in part to the Physician Payments Sunshine Act, then about to be implemented in the United States.[32] In particular, the Federal Court

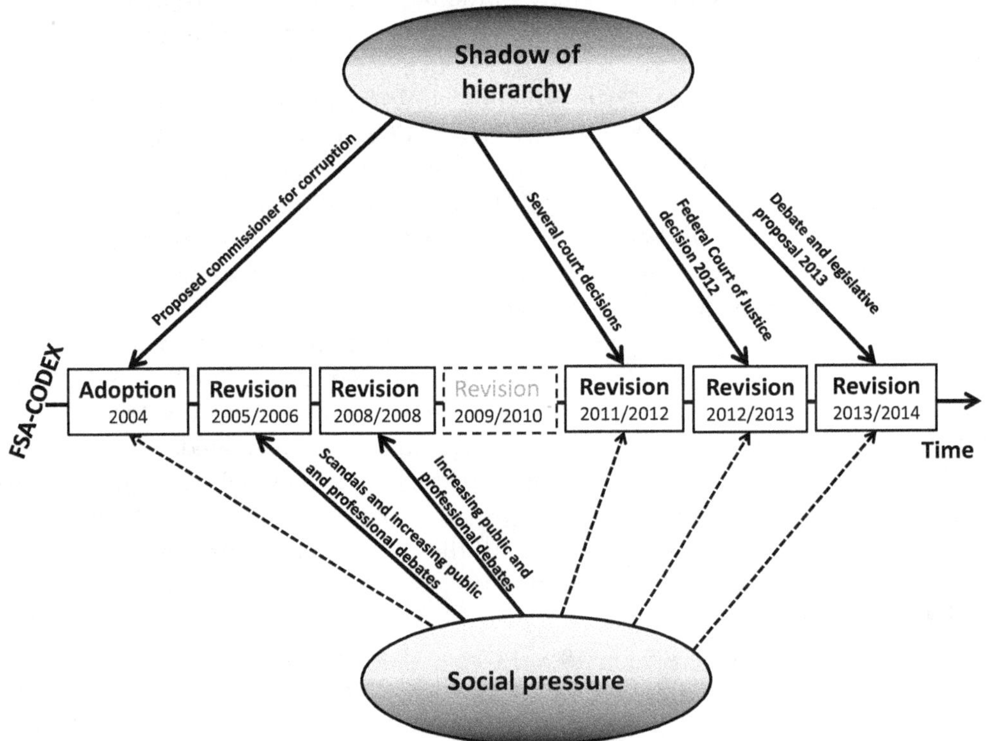

Figure 1. Causal Relationships on Several Stages of the Development of the FSA Codex.

decision in 2012 and the subsequent political debates and legislative projects (proposed in 2013 and 2016) caused major changes in the substance and procedures of the FSA Codex, adopted in 2011, 2012, and 2013 (Ärzte-Zeitung February 19, 2013). Pharmaceutical companies also feared the increasing regulation of prescription and pricing that occurred parallel to the development of the FSA Codex. However, for reasons given above, this was not seen as a shadow of hierarchy in the strictest sense, but rather as a background threat.

Normative Institutionalism: Which Logic of Appropriateness?

The shadow of hierarchy was relevant for the initial establishment of the codex in 2004 and for the more recent developments since 2011, but not for the major changes introduced between 2005 and 2008. What were the driving forces for the latter? According to normative institutionalism one can argue that the social norms determining what was appropriate behavior between physicians and the pharmaceutical industry changed dramatically starting in 2005. As March and Olsen point out, "rules of appropriateness develop and change through a myriad of disjointed processes and experiences in a variety of places and situations...." (March & Olsen, 2009, p. 17). Below is an outline of the manifestations of such changes in our field of analysis, and an explanation of how they may have caused the revision of the FSA Codex, particularly in 2005 and 2008.

During most of the 1990s, most actors inside the health system perceived the practices between the pharmaceutical industry and physicians, mentioned above (in particular gifts, invitations to professional training seminars and conferences, direct provisions and disguised honoraria) as being appropriate, while actors outside the health system seemed little aware of them. This started to change with the cardiac valve scandal in the mid-1990s, but changed the most starting in the mid-2000s. A condition contributing to this change is that at that time the actor constellation in German health policy had changed considerably. Among other things, this led to a pluralization of doctors' organizations and an enormous strengthening of health insurers and their association (the *GKV-Spitzenverband*) as political actors (Döhler, 2002, p. 37; Gerlinger, 2009, p. 42). Under these changed conditions, the numerous scandals were able to lead to an increase and change of the definitions of what is appropriate, especially in terms of professional behavior.

Since the mid-1990s, and more forcefully since about 2005, physicians and their organizations, other actors in the health system and the general public have become more critical toward these practices (Volz, 2008, p. 24). They organized themselves and criticized these practices publicly and influenced media, the general public and politics. The most relevant groups are physicians themselves, in various organizations, health insurers and their association, consumer protection agencies and Transparency International, the well-known international NGO fighting corruption in all fields. Now, not only "outsiders" (like Transparency International, MEZIS, IQTG and others) criticized the behavior of pharmaceutical companies and physicians. Also "insiders" like the Federal Physicians' Chamber (Bundesärztekammer) and the Association of Statutory Health Insurance

Physicians (Kassenärztliche Bundesvereinigung) began to do so, though with a different focus and intensity.

Transparency International (TI) started with its first report on a lack of transparence in the health system in 2000. In 2001, TI organized a conference on "corruption and fraud in the German health system." In 2002, they sent questionnaires to the Länder Health Ministries, asking about the extent to which they exercise their rights of oversight with regard to the medical professions. The organization soon started to become a relevant player that gained media attention, and it was also received positively in the major physicians' professional journal, the *Ärzteblatt* (Deutsches Ärzteblatt May 3, 2000; Deutsches Ärzteblatt October 12, 2001). In 2006, TI published a yearbook with a focus on the health system, stating that in the German health system about 20 billion euros each year are lost on corruption. Another report on corruption in the health system was published in 2008. Already, the explicit framing of what was going on as "corruption" offered a changed understanding of what was normatively adequate. Only shortly after the FSA was founded, TI published its first critique of the codex: the (then marginal) rules on post-marketing surveillance studies were seen as dubious. On the issue of professional training, TI suggested that the Länder physicians' chambers (*Landesärztekammern*) should not accept training events that are financed by pharmaceutical companies. In addition, the rules on "socially acceptable" gifts were criticized fiercely. In 2009, TI published a fundamental criticism of the FSA Codex on cooperation with patient groups, stating that there is nothing good about the code except its good intentions. In 2010, TI attacked post-marketing surveillance studies, characterizing them as "legalized corruption." TI demanded that the studies be prohibited altogether. In May 2012, TI published a survey they had conducted, according to which doctors continue to accept gifts from the pharmaceutical industry (Transparency International 2004, 2006, 2008, 2009, 2010, 2012). Even though TI's positions and demands are usually somewhat fundamental in nature, especially with insisting on the term "corruption," they managed to influence the public perception of the problem to quite some extent.

Other actors became active starting in 2005. In that year, a number of scientific and political organizations held conferences on "fighting corruption in the health system" (e.g., Kahle, 2006; Der Spiegel August 8, 2005). In 2006, two scholars at the University of Bremen published a paper revealing the strategies that the pharmaceutical industry applies to bypass the prohibition of direct product promotion, by influencing patient organizations (Schubert & Glaeske, 2006). The authors suggest that patient groups adopt rules of "Good Sponsoring Practice" and that health insurers establish a monitoring agency for this. In addition, since 2006 a number of popular books, and even crime thrillers (Gøtsche, 2014; Grill, 2007; Schorlau, 2011; Walter & Koblynski, 2010; Weiß, 2008), have been published accusing the pharmaceutical industry of improper practices, corruption, and greed.

Moreover, even insiders started debating "conflicts of interest in medicine" (Lieb et al., 2011), and a number of (public and private) hospitals adopted internal guidelines to prevent such conflicts. As an institute specialized on independent information in the health system, the Institute for Quality and Transparency in the Health System (IQTG) started to publish data on pharmaceutical sponsoring of patients' organizations in 2011.[33] A variety of physician's organizations have begun to criticize the pharmaceutical industry, their practices and physicians. In 2003, the Federal Physicians' Chamber (*Bundesärztekammer*), as the self-organizing governmental body representing physicians, revised the professional regulations for physicians by introducing § 34, which states that physicians may not accept any kind of remuneration for the prescription of a medicine and may not accept gifts if this could influence their professional independence. Paragraph 33 demanded that for every remuneration physicians have to provide an adequate benefit. In 2011, this regulation was extended to stipulate that physicians in any kind of relation with third parties or organizations have to maintain their independence for the treatment of their patients (§ 30 *Berufsordnung*), and that they may not accept any kind of remuneration for the prescription of a medicine. Invitations to professional training events are still allowed, but the invitation may only cover adequate travel and accommodation. Sponsoring is restricted to scientific events and the sponsoring must be disclosed (§ 32). In the case of post-marketing surveillance studies, the remuneration must be proportional to the service provided. This relationship has to be based on a contract that must be submitted to the physician's chamber (§ 33).[34] The Federal Physicians' Chamber has a refined structure, with commissions to deal with a variety of issues. The Pharmaceutical Commission of German Physicians (*Arzneimittelkommission der deutschen Ärzteschaft*) analyzed the FSA Codex in May 2008. They saw a need to set standards for cooperation between the pharmaceutical industry and physicians and found that a code could serve this purpose in general. However, they argued that, so far, the codex's implementation has not achieved a relevant change in the problematic customs. Enforcement is a point for criticism, as are the insufficient clarity and stringency of a number of rules. In particular, the codex does not oblige FSA members explicitly to publish all information they have on their products (BÄK AK 2008a, p. 1). To verify the scientific use of post-surveillance marketing studies, an ethics commission should be involved. The pharmaceutical industry's involvement in professional training should not be regulated, but should be abandoned altogether.[35] If the rules would not become more stringent and their implementation more transparent, the committee should request the legislators to pass binding legislation to fight questionable practices (BÄK AK, 2008a, p. 7). In August 2008, the same commission published a comment on the Codex on Cooperation with Patient Organizations. While the commission found that the codex could become a useful means to regulate dubious practices in this field, it criticized the codex for having a far too limited approach to regulation and demanded a more transparent implementation (BÄK AK 2008b).

The Association of Statutory Health Insurance Physicians (Kassenärztliche Bundesvereinigung), the corporatist federal organization of doctors in residence, has been attacking post-marketing surveillances specifically since 2009, emphasizing that paid remuneration was far too high and the medical benefit was doubtful (FAZ October 2, 2009). A different organization, completely outside the German health corporatism, is MEZIS (*"mein Essen zahl' ich selbst"*—the English phrase is "no free lunch"), which was founded in 2007 as an organization of physicians who strictly reject *any* support from the pharmaceutical industry. Even though they do not have many members so far, the organization and their far-reaching claims are mentioned in the media on a regular basis (Deutsches Ärzteblatt January 26, 2007; see www.mezis.de). For example, in 2008, at the central German congress of psychiatrists and neurologists, organized by their professional organization (*Deutsche Gesellschaft für Psychiatrie und Psychotherapie, Psychosomatik und Nervenheilkunde,* DGPPN), an entire panel critically addressed the question of the relations between the pharmaceutical industry and physicians (Die Zeit, October 11, 2008). The *health insurers* and their associations, in particular the association of the health insurers (*GKV-Spitzenverband)*, have always been critical about the pharmaceutical industrie's practices and the FSA Codex. When it was adopted in 2004, they criticized the code for not being sufficiently strict and for only aiming to improve the industry's tarnished image and not seriously changing problematic conduct (FAZ, February 18, 2004). Later on, they also focused on attacking postmarketing surveillances (FAZ October 2, 2009).

To clarify, the normative changes displayed here, started with two developments: A long-term development was the above mentioned change in the actor constellation of the German health system. This change implied a pluralization especially of doctors' organizations and of hospital operators and a strengthening of health insurers. This, in turn, created a changed situation in which a considerable number of "scandals," cases of improper conduct between pharmaceutical firms and medical doctors that occurred from 2000 onward and especially since 2005, were exposed by Transparency International. Actors within the health system reacted to these scandals by increasingly reflecting on the practices that before had been taken for granted and by establishing voluntary regulation on their part.

At the same time, the scandals and their amplification by TI and daily newspapers created a growing public awareness and criticism that did not primarily focus on particular practices but challenged pharmaceutical industry as a whole. These factors interacted and created increasing social pressure on the pharmaceutical industry in Germany. Whereas before the German pharmaceutical industry had always had a good image, now its greed (second only to that of politicians) was blamed for the financial problems of the German health system (Horizont August 18, 2005). Furthermore, the pharmaceutical industry was accused of corrupting physicians' professional integrity—while physicians themselves were held responsible to a much lesser degree. This public debate reflected, and also changed, society's understanding of what constitutes appropriate or inappropriate conduct in the interaction between the pharmaceutical industry and physicians. Not only were the specific practices criticized, but also the role and legitimacy of the pharmaceutical industry as a whole and in the health system, and its benefits for society, were being challenged, amplified in part by international product scandals (e.g., on Vioxx, see Horizont April 15, 2004). Trust in the pharmaceutical industry in general was at risk, or, to draw on the contractual metaphor by March and Olson, the "implicit agreement to act appropriately in return for being treated appropriately" was being denounced. Compared to other sectors and other countries, the trust in the pharmaceutical industry was now low, in particular among the "German opinion elites" (Edelman Trust barometer 2008).

This loss of trust would hit the pharmaceutical industry particularly hard because, in the changing, pluralized German health system, the image management and legitimacy among the general public had become increasingly important (Gerlinger, 2009, p. 48). What specific problems could result from such a profound and continued loss of trust, what could it mean no longer to be treated "appropriately" and why would it matter? As opposed to the case in the chemical industry in the 1980s, there would not be a risk of plant closure, nor would consumers tend not to buy the industry's products anymore, as with wood, apparel or diamonds. However, physicians and their professional associations might distance themselves further from their former allies. Skilled personnel would no longer want to work for the pharmaceutical industry. Health insurers and their association would gain even more power when negotiating over prices or the general use of pharmaceuticals in the Common Federal Commission (*Gemeinsamer Bundesausschuss*, G-BA). Furthermore, declining trust could have a negative impact on stock prices or it could make institutional investors reluctant to invest in pharmaceuticals. While the examples mentioned so far relate to society, an impact on the state and its organizations would also be likely. Courts would have the negative image in mind when deciding on single cases of potential corruption, and ultimately, the government would introduce a cost–benefit analysis for innovative medicines (which it did indeed in 2011).

The fact that the VfA started a vast image enhancement campaign for the pharmaceutical industry in 2004, which was to last 3 years and allegedly cost 30 million Euros, while at the same time establishing FSA as an organization and adopting the FSA Codex, suggests that fear of losing trust, along with all the consequences mentioned, was a major driving force for its adoption of the FSA Codex and its revisions. One area of focus of the campaign were the benefits for society resulting from innovative pharmaceutical research, and promises of a more transparent and honest way to communicate about pharmaceutical products, in order to regain trust (FAZ February 16, 2004; Horizont August 18, 2005). However, it becomes obvious that the idea behind voluntary regulation is not only that industry does "something" to regain trust, but rather that it defines *improper* behavior on its own. It can do so, for example, by characterizing certain practices as being deplorable, but exceptional, behavior (e.g., Deutsches Ärzteblatt Feb. 27, 2004; pharma marketing journal 4/2008), or by openly denouncing one practice (e.g., invitations to five-star-hotels) while continuing to engage discreetly in others (e.g., directly addressing patient's organizations) (Ostthüringer Zeitung November 24, 2004). The underlying aim is to reestablish the public image of their business as being socially acceptable *in general* while changing their practices just as much as necessary to reach this aim.

In summary (see Figure 1), the adoption of the FSA Codex in 2004 was primarily a reaction to the shadow of hierarchy, i.e., changes in the law that were proposed in 2003. These proposals were at least in part also a consequence of a growing public debate at that time, triggered mainly by the activities of Transparency International (here, as pointed out above, the shadow of hierarchy and social pressure are no fully independent factors, but social pressure leads to government's growing willingness to intervene and thus can strengthen the shadow of hierarchy). The two major revisions adopted in 2005 and 2008, cannot have been caused by a relevant shadow of hierarchy, since at that time there was no such shadow. Even though it is difficult to locate the changed professional and societal perception of what is proper behavior exactly in time, it is unquestionable that the social pressure gained momentum from 2005 onward and can thus explain the relevant increase in the rigor of the codex in 2005 and 2008. Its major revisions adopted in 2011, 2012, and 2013 were caused mainly by a new shadow of hierarchy, starting to come up with the reception of the just adopted Physicians Payment Sunshine act in the United States, and which was followed by a series of German court decisions between 2010 and 2012. These court decisions in turn nurtured a new political debate, which generated new proposals regarding stricter corruption laws in 2013 and 2016. Here, social pressure remained stable and had an impact on the tightening of the voluntary regulation, and arguably on the shadow of hierarchy.

While the shadow of hierarchy and social pressure in conceptual terms are two clearly distinct forces, empirically they did not operate independently from each other (a fact that cannot be displayed in Figure 1). On the one hand, it was the initial lack of compulsory regulation in the wake of several scandals that nourished the social feeling that something of the interaction between the pharmaceutical industry and physicians was wrong, which helped social pressure emerge. Later on, it was the court rulings that fostered the public debate on what is or is not socially acceptable. On the other hand, such growing social pressure to some extent also makes government regulate the field more strictly.

Conclusion

This article explored the question of *why* the voluntary FSA Codex *was adopted* by the German pharmaceutical industry in 2004 and revised several times in the subsequent 9 years. The article presents a case study demonstrating that a combination of *rational-choice institutionalism* and *normative institutionalism* can help to identify the major driving forces and causal mechanisms of voluntary regulation.

In the theoretical section, the article challenged a strong position in the literature, that voluntary regulation is dependent on the shadow of hierarchy. It did so for conceptual and empirical reasons. The shadow of hierarchy is more a metaphor than a theory and needs to be examined empirically and making use of a theoretical underpinning. Empirically, the shadow-of-hierarchy hypothesis has to be handled more carefully and, in particular, the empirical magnitude and real effect of the shadow must be analyzed. What is more, many authors suggest that changed social norms and resulting social pressure play a role in triggering voluntary regulation, but it has been all but clear via which social mechanisms this should happen. Combining two strands of institutional theory, rational-choice institutionalism allowed for critically addressing the shadow-of-hierarchy hypothesis while normative institutionalism promised to reveal the causal mechanisms through which in this case social pressure resulted in voluntary regulation. Next, I presented the phenomenon that required explanation: the adoption and subsequent revisions of the FSA Codex in the course of 10 years. There were three aspects that required explanation in particular: First, that the codex was adopted at all in 2004; second, that in 2005 and 2008 major revisions of the regulatory substance were made; and third, that in 2011 a relevant increase of rigor in terms of substance and procedure was introduced and that in 2012 and 2013 further revisions were made.

The theory-driven empirical analysis brought about two major results: First, I found that the adoption of the codex in 2004 and the major revisions starting from 2011 on were indeed caused by a shadow of hierarchy. Rational business actors calculated the consequences of hierarchical intervention and succeeded in preempting this by offering voluntary regulation, including controls and sanctions. In 2003, the government had threatened to establish—among other things—a commissioner for corruption that would watch over the relationship between the pharmaceutical industry and physicians. This suggestion shed an unpleasant light on the two and made the pharmaceutical industry adopt the FSA Codex. However, a closer look at German corruption law revealed that this commissioner would have been ineffectual—which may explain why the initial codex was meager in its regulatory substance. Furthermore, the change in regulatory substance and procedure (increase of the fines, etc.) from 2011 onward can be explained by the new shadow of hierarchy that has started to emerge since the adoption of the Physicians' Payment Sunshine Act in the United States in 2009 and has increased, incrementally, with several German courts' rulings in Germany since 2010. Even though the Federal Court decided in 2012 that corruption law was *not* applicable to doctors in residence, this created a new shadow of hierarchy by kicking off a new political debate and legislative projects for tightening this legal framework, as was finalized by a new legal act in spring 2016. This can explain why, starting in 2011 major changes were made to the substance and procedure of the FSA Codex, in 2011, 2012, and 2013. The increasing regulation of prescription and pricing—though important and feared by the pharmaceutical industry—was not seen as a shadow-of-hierarchy phenomenon in a stricter sense because the FSA Codex and the regulations dealt with different issues substantially.

Second, the substantial revisions of the codex that came about in 2005 and 2008 cannot be explained by a shadow of hierarchy, since there was none at that time. Here, an analysis based on the "logic of appropriateness" revealed, particularly from 2005 on, a changed professional and public perception of what constitutes an appropriate relationship between the pharmaceutical industry and physicians. This changed perception, facilitated by groups like Transparency International and others and amplified by media coverage of scandals and practices, threatened the pharmaceutical industry's role in German society at large. They had to react to the criticism, both with regard to their practices and with regard to the substance of their voluntary regulation. This helps explain in great measure the first substantial revisions of the FSA Codex in 2005 and 2008. The analysis also addressed a number of interrelations between social pressure and the shadow of hierarchy. Combining the two institutionalisms allowed me to explain the entire development whereas certainly an analysis that would focus on either rational interests or normative aspects alone would miss to explain some parts of the policy development.

Of course, a single case study can make few general theoretical claims that go beyond the case. Nevertheless, the study demonstrated how the two institutional theories can be applied, complementing each other, in order to address open questions in our theoretical understanding of the emergence and further development of cases of voluntary regulation. The shadow of hierarchy and social pressure are the two driving forces that would probably play a role in all cases of voluntary regulation, yet in different mixtures and at different times.

Annette Elisabeth Töller is professor for Public Policy at the FernUniversität in Hagen. Her research interests include public policies in general and voluntary regulation in particular.

Notes

I would like to thank Michael Boecher, Kathrin Loer, Renate Reiter, and Sarang D. Thakkar for many fruitful discussions on the issue and for helpful comments on earlier versions of this paper. I am grateful also to the two anonymous reviewers and to my interview partners in various organizations. Furthermore, I thank Nesrin Günes for her research assistance for this article.

1. I prefer the term "voluntary regulation" to other terms (see e.g., Büthe, 2010; Gunningham & Rees, 1997; Levi-Faur, 2010, p. 25; Wahl & Bull, 2014) because it is the more encompassing concept in terms of the actors involved.
2. Francer et al. (2014, p. 6–7) list 43 codes worldwide.
3. For example, 74 percent in Germany (BMG 2011, p. 131).
4. Between 1995 and 2005, there was 54 percent increase in the amount spent for pharmaceuticals (DESTATIS 2012, p. 17). Between 2000 and 2005, the proportion spent on pharmaceuticals relative to total expenditure rose from 15.4 percent to 18.3 percent (BMG, 2011, p. 138).
5. In particular, the Physicians Payment Sunshine act, adopted in 2009 (Grande, 2009)
6. See Töller (2009). While early voluntary agreements in Germany were little more than gentlemen agreements, more recent agreements are stronger formalized and revised on a regular base (Töller, 2012). However, beyond the fact of stronger institutionalization, there is no uniform "German" type of voluntary agreement any more. There are rather sectoral patterns.
7. In 2012, I conducted seven qualitative interviews (oral or written): three with physicians (one working in a leading position in a hospital, two in residence), and one each with the secretary of the FSA, an activist of Transparency International, a representative of IQTG and an official in charge at the Federal Ministry of Health.
8. www.lexisnexis.de; https://www.wiso-net.de/; Search words were (single and in combination) "Pharmaindustrie," "Kodex"/"Codex," "Selbstkontrolle," "Korruption."
9. Most contributions on voluntary regulation deal with *transnational* voluntary regulation, which is often analyzed as something rather new. In this debate, the literature on voluntary regulation in the national context (which is long-established, in part) is not represented often. From my point of view, there is no fundamental difference between national and transnational voluntary regulation. The difference that does exist is that, in the transnational context, the institutions that could

elaborate a credible shadow of hierarchy are fewer and weaker. As a consequence, the role of NGOS and social pressure would be more important, and this is why this article—though it examines a case of national voluntary regulation—could also contribute to the debate on transnational voluntary regulation.

10. The Code adopted by EFPIA (European Federation of Pharmaceutical Industries and Associations) sets minimum standards which member associations have to comply with. *De facto* different rules are brought up by different national associations. To evaluate the precise impact of the EFPA Code on the FSA Codex would require a study of its own.
11. This is arguably the more European version of voluntary regulation while in the U.S. version it is the public authority that sets up programs and invites companies to participate, which in return expect some regulatory relief (see e.g., Maxwell & Lyon, 2004). Transnational variants include elements of both, plus a possible role for NGOs.
12. The subsequent empirical analysis of the FSA Codex will only deal with the first two aspects, i.e., the adoption and the regulatory substance of the FSA Codex.
13. The European Union is an exception, however.
14. This was the case with asbestos, PCP and CFC industries, as well as with chemical and nuclear operations in the 1980s (Gunningham & Rees, 1997, p. 379; Töller, 2013); with international wood production in the early 1990s (Bartley, 2003, p. 442; Gunningham & Rees, 1997, p. 379), apparel industry in the mid-1990s (Bartley, 2003, p. 442–45), and the market for diamonds in the early 2000s (Haufler, 2009).
15. For a similar—yet different institutionalist approach to explain the emergence of voluntary regulation see Bartley (2003, 2011).
16. See Töller, 2012. For contexts beyond the nation state, it is the shadow of anarchy that can motivate voluntary regulation when regulation is necessary, but there is no institutional structure that could intervene hierarchically, see Börzel (2008, p. 129); Mayntz and Scharpf (1995, p. 23).
17. Yet rational-choice institutionalism offers other causal mechanisms that can link institutions to voluntary regulation. One such mechanism is evasion. Various studies have shown that voluntary regulation is used because it allows state actors to evade legal restrictions or uncertainties stemming from the common market rules of EU-Treaties or WTO-law, for example (Bartley, 2003; Töller, 2017).
18. E.g., as a result of learning from new experiences or public discourse, or as a consequence of scandals (March & Olsen, 2009, p. 13, 18).
19. The fact that rational-choice institutionalism and normative institutionalism as such are based on very different concepts and assumptions is—in my view—no reason not to apply them in a complementary way. First, other authors (such as Gulbrandsen, Koop or Turcotte et al.) have applied both in a similar way, as mentioned above. Second, real life agency is rarely only driven by rational interest or social norms but mostly by a mixture of both.
20. Whether, and if so, to what extent such practices not only produce unnecessary costs for the health system but can also endanger patients and undermine the professional ethics of physicians is a much disputed issue. See, for example, a number of articles in Lieb, Klemperer and Ludwig (2011).
21. Most applies to both doctors working in a hospital and doctors in residence.
22. See for more details e.g., Badische Zeitung November 26, 2005; Nürnberger Nachrichten October 6, 2004; FAZ February 18, 2004. Deutsches Ärzteblatt January 26, 2007; Ärztezeitung Feburary 18, 2004; Brand Eins 3/2007; Deutsches Ärzteblatt November 14, 2011, der Spiegel January 18, 2011; Badische Zeitung November 26, 2005; Stern November 10, 2005.
23. There was a popular joke: One physician asks another: "Where are you going to spend your holidays this year?" Replies the other: "I have no idea so far, I haven't yet spoken to my pharma representative."
24. VfA was one of three associations of the German pharmaceutical industry at that time, organizing 39 companies that covered almost two thirds of the German market, FAZ (February 18, 2004).

25. These are the federal association of pharmaceutical manufacturers (*Bundesverband der Arzneimittelhersteller,* BAH) and the federal association of the pharmaceutical industry (*Bundesverband der Pharmazeutischen Industrie,* BPI).
26. The time lag between adoption and coming into force is due to the fact that the codex (and each revision) has to be approved by the German Federal Trust Agency since it is considered a cartel.
27. While in the EU product promotion to end-consumers is not allowed for prescription medicines, promotion here means promotion to physicians.
28. The background of this was that due to a number of legislative changes over time, doctors had become less important as decision makers concerning prescriptions, therefore pharmaceutical firms started to directly address patients by sponsoring patient's organizations (Brand eins 3/2007, p. 16–7).
29. Recently, media have started to amplify and discuss these pieces of information.
30. Representatives of physicians' associations argued however, that this was not a reaction to the proposed appointment of a commissioner for corruption, but that it had already been planned before.
31. "Big" Coalitions are Governments consisting of the two strongest parties in Parliament, (so far) the Christian Democrats (CDU/CSU) and Social Democrats (SPD). While in the past, such constellations were rare, Germany is currently witnessing the third Big Coalition in its history.
32. Accordingly, from 2013 onward, pharmaceutical firms have had to publish all payments and gifts to physicians amounting to more than 10 USD in a single case and to 100 USD in a year.
33. While the FSA Codex, regarding cooperation with patient's organizations, requires the publication of such data, initially the FSA did not provide data or a link to data. From 2012 on, FSA featured a list on their homepage that included links to the relevant information on the members' homepage. www.fs-arzneimittelindustrie.de/index.php?id=182, accessed March 3, 2017. However, the IQTG criticizes this, arguing that it allows the identification of firms which give money and to which patients' organizations, but that it is not as easy to trace which patients' organizations get money from which firms.
34. See details and changes here: www.bundesaerztekammer.de/downloads/Synopse_Stand_29.08.11.pdf, accessed March 3, 2017.
35. The paper, however, does not say how exactly the chambers would organize all the necessary seminars and who would pay for them.

References

BÄK AK (Bundesärztekammer, Arzneimittelkommssion). 2008a. *Stellungnahme der Arzneimittelkommission der deutschen Ärzteschaft zu dem Antrag des Vereins "Freiwillige Selbstkontrolle für die Arzneimittelindustrie e.V." auf Anerkennung der Wettbewerbsregeln. FSA-Kodex Fachkreise.* Berlin: Bundesärztekammer, Arzneimittelkommission.

BÄK AK (Bundesärztekammer, Arzneimittelkommssion). 2008b. *Stellungnahme der Arzneimittelkommission der deutschen Ärzteschaft zu dem Antrag des Vereins "Freiwillige Selbstkontrolle für die Arzneimittelindustrie e.V." auf Anerkennung der Wettbewerbsregeln. FSA-Kodex Patientenorganisationen.* Berlin: Bundesärztekammer, Arzneimittelkommission.

Bandelow, N., and A. Hartmann. 2015. "Gesundheitspolitik unter gelb-schwarzer Führung: begrenzte Erklärungskraft der Parteiendifferenz in einem vermachteten Politikfeld." In *Politik im Schatten der Krise,* ed. R. Zohlnhöfer, and T. Saalfeld. Wiesbaden: Springer, 427–49.

Baron, D. P. 2009. "Credence Standards and Social Pressure." In *Voluntary Programs: A Club Theory Perspective,* ed. M. Potoski, and A. Prakash. Cambridge MA: MIT Press, 41–66.

Bartley, T. 2003. "Certifying Forests and Factories: States, Social Movements, and the Rise of Private Regulation in the Apparel and Forest Products Fields." *Politics and Society* 31 (3): 433–64.

———. 2007. "Institutional Emergence in an Era of Globalization: The Rise of Transnational Private Regulation of Labor and Environmental Conditions." *American Journal of Sociology* 113 (2): 297–351.

———. 2011. "Certification as Mode of Social Regulation." In *Handbook on the Politics of Regulation*, ed. D. Levi-Faur. Cheltenham: Edward Elgar, 441–52.

Bell, St., and A. Hindmoor. 2011. "Governance without Government? The Case of the Forest Stewardship Council." *Public Administration* 90 (1): 144–59.

Berliner, D., and A. Prakash. 2014. ""Bluewashing" the Firm? Voluntary Regulations, Program Design, and Member Compliance with the United Nations Global Compact." *Policy Studies Journal* 43 (1): 115–38.

Black, J. 2001. "Decentring Regulation: Understanding the role of Regulation and Self-Regulation in a 'Post-Regulatory World'." *Current Legal Problems* 54 (1): 103–46.

BMG (Bundesministerium für Gesundheit). 2011. *Daten des Gesundheitswesens* [Online]. www.bundesgesundheitsministerium.de/fileadmin/Dateien/5_Publikationen/Gesundheit/Broschueren/Daten_des_Gesundheitswesens_2011.pdf. Accessed April 10, 2017.

Börzel, T. 2008. "Der "Schatten der Hierarchie"—Ein Governance-Paradox?" In *Governance in einer sich wandelenden Welt*, ed. G. F. Schuppert, and M. Zürn. Politische Vierteljahresschrift. Wiesbaden: VS Verlag, 118–31.

Bundesrat. 2016. *Gesetz zur Bekämpfung von Korruption im Gesundheitswesen*. Köln: Bundesanzeiger Verlag.

Büthe, T. 2010. "Private Regulation in the Global Economy. A (P) Review." *Business and Politics* 12(3): 1–38.

Cadbury, A. 2006. "The Rise of Corporate Governance." In *The Accountable Corporation, Corporate Governance*, Vol. 1, ed. M. J. Epstein, and K. O. Hanson. London: Praeger, 15–43.

Campbell, E. G., R. L. Gruen, J. Mountford, L. G. Miller, P. D. Cleary, and D. Blumenthal. 2007. "A National Survey of Physician-Industry Relationships." *The New England Journal of Medicine* 356 (17): 1742–50.

Croci, E. 2005. "The Economics of Environmental Voluntary Agreements." In *The Handbook of Environmental Voluntary Agreements*, ed. E. Croci. Dordrecht: Springer, 3–30.

Cummins, A. 2004. "The Marine Stewardship Council: A Multi-stakeholder Approach to Sustainable Fishing." *Corporate Social Responsibility and Environmental Management* 11 (2): 85–94.

DESTATIS. 2012. *Gesundheit. Ausgaben*. Fachserie 12 Reihe 7.1.2. 1995 bis 2010. Wiesbaden: Statistisches Bundesamt.

Dieners, P. 2007. *Zusammenarbeit der Pharmaindustrie mit Ärzten. Rechtliches Umfeld, Steuern und Compliance Governance*, 2nd ed. München: Verlag C. H. Beck.

Döhler, M. 2002. "Gesundheitspolitik in der Verhandlungsdemokratie." In *Paradigmenwechsel in der Gesundheitspolitik*. ed. W. Gellner, and M. Schön. Baden-Baden: Nomos, 25–39.

Eberlein, B., K. W. Abbott, J. Black, E. Meidinger, and St. Wood. 2014. "Transnational Business Governance Interactions: Conceptualization and Framework for Analysis." *Regulation & Governance* 8 (1): 1–21.

Edelman Trust Barometer. 2008. www.edelman.com/assets/uploads/2014/01/2008-Trust-Barometer-Global-Results.pdf. Accessed November 24, 2015.

Erices, R., A. Frewer, and A. Grumz. 2013. "Strafbare Bestechlichkeit von Vertragsärzten und Ethik. Überlegungen zu Grauzonen und Korruption im Gesundheitswesen." *Ethik in der Medizin* 25 (2): 103–13.

Francer, J., J. Z. Izquierdo, T. Music, K. Nasai, Ch. Nikidis, H. Simmonds, and P. Woods. 2014. "Ethical Pharmaceutical Promotion and Communications Worldwide: Codes and Regulations." *Philosophy, Ethics and Humanities in Medicine* 9 (7): 1–17.

FSA. 2004. *Kodex der Mitglieder des Vereins*. Berlin: Freiwillige Selbstkontrolle für die Arzneimittelindustrie e.V.

FSA. 2006. *Kodex der Mitglieder des Vereins*. Berlin: Freiwillige Selbstkontrolle für die Arzneimittelindustrie e.V.

FSA. 2008. *Kodex der Mitglieder des Vereins*. Berlin: Freiwillige Selbstkontrolle für die Arzneimittelindustrie e.V.

FSA. 2010. *Kodex der Mitglieder des Vereins*. Berlin: Freiwillige Selbstkontrolle für die Arzneimittelindustrie e.V.

FSA. 2011. *Kodex der Mitglieder des Vereins*. Berlin: Freiwillige Selbstkontrolle für die Arzneimittelindustrie e.V.

FSA. 2012. *Kodex der Mitglieder des Vereins*. Berlin: Freiwillige Selbstkontrolle für die Arzneimittelindustrie e.V.

FSA. 2013. *Kodex der Mitglieder des Vereins*. Berlin: Freiwillige Selbstkontrolle für die Arzneimittelindustrie e.V.

FSA. 2014. *Kodex der Mitglieder des Vereins*. Berlin: Freiwillige Selbstkontrolle für die Arzneimittelindustrie e.V.

Gerlinger, Th. 2009. "Der Wandel der Interessenvermittlung in der Gesundheitspolitik." In *Interessenvermittlung in Politikfeldern. Vergleichende Befunde der Policy- und Verbändeforschung*, ed. B. Rehder, von Winter Th., and U. Willems. Wiesbaden: Springer Verlag, 31–51.

Gøtsche, P. 2014. *Tödliche Medizin und organisierte Kriminalität: Wie die Pharmaindustrie unser Gesundheitswesen korrumpiert*. München: rivaVerlag.

Grande, D. 2009. "Limiting the Influence of Pharmaceutical Gifts on Physicians: Self-Regulation or Government Intervention?" *Journal of General Internal Medicine* 25 (1): 79–83.

Grill, M. 2007. *Kranke Geschäfte: wie die Pharmaindustrie uns manipuliert*. Reinbek: Rowohlt.

Grusa, M. 2011. "Freiwillige Selbstkontrolle für die Arzneimittelindustrie." In *Interessenkonflikte in der Medizin. Hintergründe und Lösungsmöglichkeiten*, ed. K. Lieb, D. Klemperer, and W. Dieter. Wiesbaden: Springer, 185–201.

Gulbrandsen, L. H. 2010. *Transnational Environmental Governance. The Emergence and Effects of the Certification of Forests and Fisheries*. Cheltenham: Edward Elgar.

Gunningham, N., and J. Rees. 1997. "Industry Self-Regulation: An Institutional Perspective." *Law & Policy* 19(4): 363–413.

Hartmann, A. 2010. "Die Gesundheitsreformen der Großen Koalition: Kleinster gemeinsamer Nenner oder offenes Hintertürchen?" In *Die zweite Große Koalition. Eine Bilanz der Regierung Merkel 2005-2009*, ed. Ch. Egle, and R. Zohlnhöfer. Wiesbaden: Springer, 327–49.

Haufler, V. 2009. "The Kimberley Process, Club Goods, and Public Enforcement of a Private Regime." In *Voluntary Programs. A Club Theory Perspective*, ed. M. Potoski, and A. Prakash. Cambridge: MIT Press, 89–106.

Hemphill, Th. A.. 2006. "Physicians and the Pharmaceutical Industry: A Reappraisal of Marketing Codes of Conduct." *Business and Society Review* 111 (3): 323–36.

Héritier, A., and S. Eckert. 2008. "New Modes of Governance in the Shadow of Hierarchy: Self-regulation by Industry in Europe." *Journal of Public Policy* 28 (1): 113–38.

Kahle, E. 2006. *Korruptionsbekämpfung und Transparenz in der Pharmaindustrie, Gesundheitswesen*. 6. Lüneburger Sicherheitsforum für die Wirtschaft 2005. Lüneburg: Universität Lüneburg.

Katz, D., A. L. Caplan, and J. F. Merz. 2010. "All Gifts Large and Small: Toward and Understanding of the Ethics of Pharmaceutical Industry Gift-Giving." *The American Journal of Bioethics* 10 (10): 11–7.

Koop, Ch. 2014. "Theorizing and Explaining Voluntary Accountability." *Public Administration* 92 (3): 565–81.

Kuhlen, L. 2010. "Strafrecht und freiwillige Selbstkontrolle der Wirtschaft: das Beispiel der Pharmaindustrie." In *Festschrift für Winfried Hassemer*, ed. F. Herzog, and U. Neumann. Heidelberg: C.F. Müller Verlag, 875–90.

Levi-Faur, D. 2010. "Regulation and Regulatory Governance." Jerusalem Papers on Regulation & Governance. Working Paper No. 1. Jerusalem: The Hebrew University.

Lieb, K., D. Klemperer, and W. D. Ludwig, ed. 2011. *Interessenkonflikte in der Medizin. Hintergründe und Lösungsmöglichkeiten*. Wiesbaden: Springer.

March, J. G., and J. P. Olsen. 1989. *Rediscovering Institutions: The Organizational Basis of Politics*. New York: Free Press.

———. 2009. "The logic of appropriateness." Arena Working Paper No. 04/09. University of Oslo, Centre of European Studies.

Marx, A. 2008. "Limits to Non-state Market Regulation: A Qualitative Comparative Analysis of the Internal Sport Footwear Industry and the Fair Labor Association." *Regulation and Governance* 2 (2): 253–73.

———. 2011. "Global Governance and the Certification Revolution: Types, Trends and Challenges." In *Handbook on the Politics of Regulation*, ed. D. Levi-Faur. Cheltenham: Edward Elgar, 590–603.

Marx, A., and D. Cuypers. 2010. "Forest Certification as a Global Environmental Governance Tool: What is the Macro-effectiveness of the Forest Stewardship Council?" *Regulation & Governance* 4 (4): 408–34.

Maxwell, J. W., and Th. P. Lyon. 2004. *Corporate Environmentalism and Public Policy*. Cambridge: Cambridge University Press.

Mayntz, R., and F. W. Scharpf. 1995. "Steuerung und Selbstorganisation in staatsnahen Sektoren." In *Gesellschaftliche Selbstregelung und politische Steuerung*, ed. R. Mayntz, and F. W. Scharpf. Frankfurt: Campus Verlag, 9–38.

Meyer, N. 2013. "Political Contestation of Self-regulation in the Shadow of Hierarchy." *Journal of European Public Policy* 20 (5): 760–76.

Newman, A., and D. Bach. 2004. "Self-Regulatory Trajectories in the Shadow of Public Power: Resolving Digital Dilemmas in Europe and the United States." *Governance* 17 (3): 387–413.

Offe, C. 1987. "Die Staatstheorie auf der Suche nach ihrem Gegenstand. Beobachtungen zur aktuellen Diskussion." In *Jahrbuch zur Staats- und Verwaltungswissenschaft*, ed. Th. Ellwein, J. J. Hesse, R. Mayntz, and F. W. Scharpf. Baden-Baden: Nomos, 309–20.

Paris, R., and W. Sofsky. 1998. "Drohungen. Über eine Methode der Interaktionsmacht." In *Stachel und Speer. Machtstudien*, ed. R. Paris. Frankfurt a.M.: Edition Suhrkamp, 13–57.

Peters, G. 2005. *Institutional Theory in Political Science*, 2nd ed. London: Bloomsbury Publishing.

Potoski, M., and A. Prakash. 2009a. "Voluntary Clubs. Introduction." In *Voluntary Programs: A Club Theory Perspective*, ed. M. Potoski, and A. Prakash. Cambridge, MA: The MIT Press, 1–14.

———. 2009b. "A Club Theory Approach to Voluntary Programs." In *Voluntary Programs: A Club Theory Perspective*, ed. M. Potoski, and A. Prakash. Cambridge, MA: The MIT Press, 17–39.

Potoski, M., and A. Prakash, ed. 2009c. *Voluntary Programs: A Club Theory Perspective*. Cambridge, MA: The MIT Press.

Rosenbrock, R., and Thomas Gerlinger. 2014. *Gesundheitspolitik. Eine systematische Einführung*, 3rd revised ed. Bern: Verlag Hans Huber.

Rübenstahl, M. 2011. "Korruptionsdelikte und Pharmamarketing—Sind Vertragsärzte Amtsträger oder Beauftragte der Krankenkassen?" *HRR Strafrecht* 8 (9): 333–8.

Schneider, H., and E. Strauß. 2011. "Die Zukunft der Anwendungsbeobachtung. Rechtssichere Grenzen zwischen Korruption und zulässiger Kooperation angesichts der aktuellen Vorlagebeschlüsse des 3. Und 5. Strafsenats des Bundesgerichtshofs." *HRR Strafrecht* 8 (9): 333–8.

Schorlau, W. 2011. *Die letzte Flucht, Denglers sechster Fall*. Köln: Kiwi-Verlag.

Schubert, K., and G. Glaeske. 2006. *Einfluss des pharmazeutisch-industriellen Komplexes auf die Selbsthilfe*. Universität Bremen, Zentrum für Sozialpolitik. www.vdek.com/vertragspartner/Selbsthilfe/selbsthilfe_werkstattbericht_01_2007.pdf. Accessed August 12, 2015.

TI (Transparency International). 2004. *Stellungnahme von Transparency International Deutschland zum "Kodex der Mitglieder des Vereins 'Freiwillige Selbstkontrolle für die Arzneimittelindustrie e.V.'"* Berlin: Transparency International Deutschland e.V.

TI (Transparency International). 2006. *Schwerpunkt: Korruption im Gesundheitswesen*. Berlin: Transparency International Deutschland e.V.

TI (Transparency International). 2008. *Transparenzmängel, Korruption und Betrug im deutschen Gesundheitswesen—Kontrolle und Prävention als Gesellschaftliche Aufgabe. Grundsatzpapier*, 5th ed. Berlin: Transparency International Deutschland e.V.

TI (Transparency International). 2009. *Stellungnahme der Arbeitsgruppe "Korruption im Gesundheitswesen" zum "Kodex für die Zusammenarbeit der pharmazeutischen Industrie mit Patientenorganisationen" der FS Arzneimittelindustrie"*. Berlin: Transparency International Deutschland e.V.

TI (Transparency International). 2010. *Transparency International Deutschland fordert gesetzliches Verbot der Anwendungsbeobachtungen*. Berlin: Transparency International Deutschland e.V.

TI (Transparency International). 2012. Umfrage im Gesundheitswesen: Trotz Verbot übertreten Ärzte die selbst gesetzten Standesregeln. Kaum Unrechtsbewusstsein bei der Gewährung und Annahme von Geldgeschenken in den Geschäftsbeziehungen. Press release, Berlin. https://www.transparency.de/2012-05-22-PM-Gesundheit.2090.0.html?&contUid=4472. Accessed March 3, 2017.

Töller, A. E. 2008. "Kooperation im Schatten der Hierarchie. Dilemmata des Verhandelns zwischen Staat und Wirtschaft." In *Governance in einer sich wandelnden Welt*, ed. G. F. Schuppert, and M. Zürn. Wiesbaden: VS Verlag, 288–312.

———. 2009. "Freiwillige Regulierung zwischen Staat und Markt: Der Deutsche Corporate Governance-Kodex (DCGK)." *Der moderne Staat (dms)* 9: 301–22.

———. 2011. "Voluntary Approaches to Regulation—Patterns, Causes and Effects." In *The Handbook of the Politics of Regulation*, ed. D. Levi-Faur. Cheltenham: Edward Elgar, 499–510.

———. 2012. *Warum kooperiert der Staat? Kooperative Umweltpolitik im Schatten der Hierarchie.* Schriftenreihe Staatslehre und politische Verwaltung. Baden-Baden: Nomos.

———. 2013. "The Rise and Fall of Voluntary Agreements in Germany Environmental Policy." *German Policy Studies* 9 (2): 49–92.

———. 2017. "Evasion as a Mechanism of Resistance (not only) to European Law." In *The Routledge Handbook of European Public Policy*, ed. N. Zahariadis, and L. Buonanno. London: Routledge, forthcoming.

Turcotte, M.-F., J. Reinecke, and F. den Hond. 2014. "Explaining Variation in the Multiplicity of Private Social and Environmental Regulation: A Multi-case Integration Across the Coffee, Forestry and Textile Sectors." *Business and Politics* 16 (1): 151–89.

Volz, M. 2008. "Der FSA Kodex—"Healthcare Compliance" in Deutschland." *Corporate Compliance Zeitschrift* 1: 22–6.

Wahl, A., and G. Q. Bull. 2014. "Mapping Research Topics and Theories in Private Regulation for Sustainability in Global Value Chains." *Journal of Business Ethics* 124: 585–608.

Walter, C., and A. Koblynski. 2010. *Patient im Visier. Die neue Strategie der Pharmakonzerne*. Hamburg: Hoffmann und Campe.

Weiß, H. 2008. *Korrupte Medizin. Ärzte als Komplizen der Konzerne*, 3rd ed. Köln: Kiwi-Verlag.

Wiesner, A., and K. Lieb. 2011. "Interessenkonflikte durch Arzt-Industrie-Kontakte in Praxis und Klinik und Vorschläge zu deren Reduzierung." In *Interessenkonflikte in der Medizin. Hintergründe und Lösungsmöglichkeiten*, ed. K. Lieb, D. Klemperer, and W.-D. Ludwig. Wiesbaden: Springer Verlag, 161–74.

The Utilization of Expert Knowledge in Times of Crisis: Budgetary and Migration Policies in the Netherlands

Frans K. M. van Nispen and Peter W. A. Scholten

Times of crisis, such as the financial and economic crisis and, more recently, the migration crisis, open windows of opportunity for agenda setting and policy change. However, the added value of policy analysis and utilization-focused evaluation is often more contested during crises: do crises provide opportunities for the utilization of expert knowledge and policy learning in order to punctuate policy deadlocks and to induce policy innovation or do crises rather inhibit opportunities for the utilization of expert knowledge and policy learning because of political contestation and establishment of a clear political primacy? Building on empirical data drawn from the Dutch comprehensive spending reviews (2010), advisory reports and policy studies, respectively, in the field of the Dutch migration and integration policy (2000–2015), we found that the utilization of expert knowledge is not much different in bad times than in good times. Rather, the type of expert knowledge as well as the way of utilization of expert knowledge is subject to change as boundary organizations are playing a key role as producers of expert knowledge in legitimating policy actors and structures and substantiating policy decisions. We conclude that expert knowledge may be a very important and powerful tool for policy coordination, precisely in the highly contested and politicized setting of a crisis.

KEY WORDS: boundary organizations, knowledge utilization, times of crisis, budgetary policy, migrant policy, The Netherlands

危急时刻利用专家知识:荷兰的预算政策和迁移政策

危急时刻, 例如金融和经济危机, 以及近期更常出现的迁移危机, 都为议程设置和政策变化打开了机会之窗。然而, 政策分析的附加价值和“以利用为重点”的评估却时常在危机中遭受质疑: 危机是否为“不断介入政策僵局”和“引入政策创新”提供了使用专家知识和政策学习的机会? 还是说, 因为政治竞争和建立明确的政治首要地位, 使得危机反而抑制了使用专家知识和政策学习机会? 基于2010年荷兰综合消费评论的实证数据、咨询报告和有关2000-2015年荷兰移民融合政策的研究, 本文发现: 危机背景的“好”与“坏”对利用专家知识而言并不会有太大差别。更准确地说, 专家知识的类型和利用方式都会发生变化, 因为边界组织在“将政策参与者和政策结构合法化”以及“将政策决定实体化”时扮演着专家知识生产者这一重要角色。本文结论认为: 专家知识可能是用于政策协调的一项非常重要和有力的工具, 严格地说, 是在危机背景存在高度争议和政治化的情况下使用的政策协调工具。

关键词: 边界组织, 知识利用, 危机时刻, 预算政策, 迁移政策, 荷兰

doi: 10.1002/epa2.1014

Introduction

The British prime-minister Winston Churchill is supposed to have said *"Never let a good crisis go to waste"* for the first time.[1] A crisis, such as the financial and economic crisis and the more recent migration crisis in Europe, promotes agenda setting and open "windows of opportunity" for policy change. Think about how the financial and economic crisis has not only put economic policy reform on the agenda but also promoted institutional dynamics in the European Union. However, what role policy analysis in particular and social science research more in general can play during crises is often more contested. Do crises also open opportunities for policy learning, by promoting knowledge utilization and reflection in order to punctuate policy deadlocks and promote innovation? Or do crises rather inhibit opportunities for policy learning and knowledge utilization because of political contestation and establishment of a clear political primacy?

As it is difficult, if not impossible, to make a distinction between academic and nonacademic research (Jasanoff, 1987), we have adopted the concept of "expert knowledge," which not only covers articles published in international peer reviewed journals but also to reports issued by advisory bodies and similar committees, which serve as boundary organizations at the nexus of policy and science.[2] As we will see, academics are often consulted as experts and even participate in the work of these boundary organizations (Guston, 2000). In addition, they are frequently hired by the government to do contract research.

The empirical data are taken from two policy areas that have been characterized by institutional crises over the last decade or so: economic (including fiscal) policies and migration policies. In the context of the financial and economic crisis in Europe, Dutch economic policies were reformed dramatically in order to manage spending within targets for the overall budget deficit. In the context of the broader European migration crises, Dutch migration policies (including policies at migrant integration) have also been under immense pressure to manage migration flows in a more restrictive way while promoting migrant integration to a much greater extent. Both cases do not apply to the Netherlands only but seem representative of broader crises driving policy change throughout Europe.

The theoretical ambition of this article is to learn more on what role expert knowledge plays in the context of crises. Following the work of Boswell (2009) and Jasanoff (2004), among others, we will examine what patterns of knowledge utilization can be identified and also what types of expert knowledge claims are involved. We believe that although patterns of "policy learning" may be difficult to identify empirically, patterns of knowledge utilization can be defined empirically and reveal much on the role that expert knowledge can play in policy processes. We will distinguish between instrumental and political or symbolic forms of knowledge utilization (Boswell, 2009). Furthermore, we will examine how and why actors select specific expert knowledge claims, while possibly ignoring others.

In the following sections we will first develop our key concepts and theoretical assumptions regarding the utilization of expert knowledge, and discuss the methodology of our research. Secondly, we develop our two case studies on knowledge utilization in two crises-prone policy areas in the Netherlands. Subsequently, we will analyze and compare patterns of knowledge utilization in both areas, and draw up some conclusions regarding the role of expert knowledge in contested policy areas.

Knowledge Utilization in Policy Processes

Within policy sciences a broad literature has emerged on the role of knowledge in policy processes. Studies have focused among others on how knowledge is used, by whom, in what stages of the policy process and to what effect in terms of policy change. A key reference in this literature is Carol Weiss's study on the enlightenment function of knowledge and her notion of the gradual "knowledge creep" (1979). Weiss was an early scholar to draw attention to what Heclo (1974) has described as the key role of "puzzling" besides the role of "powering" in policy processes. This has given birth to a long tradition in policy studies focusing on the instrumental use of knowledge in policy processes. A recent development in this tradition is the revival of attention for so-called "evidence-based policymaking" (see also Sanderson, 2002), which also exhibits a strong belief in the instrumental role of knowledge in all stages of the policy cycle.

This belief in the instrumental value of knowledge in policy processes is also manifest in the literature on "policy learning." Sabatier (1998) defines policy learning as "the adjustment of policy beliefs in response to knowledge, information, and experiences." The notion of knowledge learning thus creates a direct relation between knowledge utilization and policy change. However, as not only Sabatier (1998) but also Hall (1993) argue, the potential for learning may be limited for instance by the political and institutional setting in which learning takes place.

The prevailing view on knowledge utilization at the turn of the century is well articulated by Rob Hoppe claiming that the results of policy research are hardly used in a direct instrumental way, that is, for the solution of problem in society:

> The impact of professional policy analysis is limited, and adds only modest increments to the ordinary knowledge of politicians and public officials. Policy analysts are condemned to provide argumentative ammunition for the rhetorical struggles of politicians (policy analysis as argument or data, Weiss, 1979) only occasionally they discover a nugget of enlightenment (policy analysis as idea) (Hoppe, 1999, p. 206).

As has been argued by Christina Boswell, the basic assumption underling the "enlightenment function" of research is very much instrumental, that is, aimed at impact, although indirect and in the long run, on current policy (Boswell, 2009, p. 5).[3] She argues that we should look more at the political or symbolic modes of knowledge utilization, that is, for other purposes than the solution of problems in society. Following Christina Boswell, a distinction can be made between roughly three modes of knowledge utilization, which may be depicted as below (Figure 1).

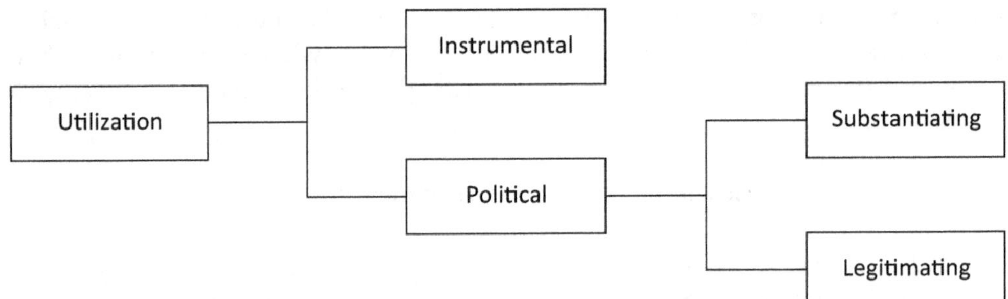

Figure 1. Three Modes of Knowledge Utilization.

Source: Boswell (2008).

The various modes of knowledge utilization may be characterized as follows:

1. Instrumental utilization, which covers both the problem-solving model (direct) and the enlightenment function (indirect) of knowledge utilization (Weiss, 1979, p. 427). It is closely related to the pursuit of evidence-based policy making (Scholten, Entzinger, Penninx & Verbeek, 2015, p. 6);
2. Political or symbolic utilization, which may be subdivided into two broad categories:
    a. Substantiating utilization, which may be either positive or negative. In the first case expert knowledge is used to justify a preferred, often predetermined policy choice. In the latter case, expert knowledge is used as ammunition to challenge or even undermine the position of an opponent in the political arena (Schrefler, 2010, p. 320);
    b. Legitimating utilization, which points to the effort of an organization to boost its authority, credibility, reputation, and/or power *vis-à-vis* other actors.

The various modes of knowledge utilization are not mutual exclusive. The generation of information may back a claim, which may add to the credibility of the policy maker and, ultimately, will solve a problem in society.[4] Consequently, we expect to find a combination of knowledge utilization.

The academic debate on knowledge utilization has got a boost recently by the attention to boundary organizations in the field of the policy sciences (Hoppe, 2010),[5] interalia, pointing at the role of advisory bodies and other institutions as in between (brokers, interpreters) at the interface of what Nathan Caplan once has called the two communities metaphor (Caplan, 1979).[6] As a result, both sides of the science-policy nexus have induced each other, leading to a "scientification of policy" and the "politicization of science" (Weingart, 1999). One may even argue that the policy space is now composed of three communities. The latter serves as a platform for dialogue and exchange of ideas (Lindquist, 1990; Radaelli, 1995, p. 175–6).

In this paper, we will look at the utilization of expert knowledge. It is usually associated with two characteristics, although they are not always met in reality. First, the qualification of the *producers* of information, which are typically located, although not exclusively, in an academic or a research institute.[7] Second, the qualification of the *outcome* of their work as measured by theoretical and methodological standards. However, the boundary between expert knowledge and laymen's knowledge is blurred, fluid, and frequently contested (Boswell, 2008; Bekkers 2015; Jasanoff, 1987). Furthermore, there is a trade-off between scientific (epistemological) and nonscientific (practical) standards, such as the implementability and connection with the existing strategy (van de Vall, 1980). It does not make much sense to come up with a proposal for which there is no support in politics or society (Leeuw, 1987, p. 164). Besides, the outcome of research that comes too late is perceived as mustard after dinner (Knott & Wildavsky, 1980, p. 548). What counts as expert knowledge is ultimately contingent on the beliefs and interests of the administrators who are making use of it (Boswell, 2009, 23–5).

The notion of boundary work draws attention to how research-policy relations also involve an element of selecting (and sometimes even producing) specific expert knowledge claims (Hoppe, 2005; Jasanoff, 1990). The relationship between research and policy is often not linear but mutual. This is also due to the plurality of knowledge claims that often characterizes specific policy subsystems. In any policy area there will mostly be multiple knowledge producers working with different methods, concepts, and theories, thus sustaining specific paradigms or research traditions. Some of these might find easier access to the policymaking process, leading to what Jasanoff (2004) has described as a *coproduction* of knowledge by researchers and policymakers. This resembles what in the broader policy science literature is described as epistemic communities or discourse coalitions of which both researchers and policymakers can be part.

A key type of actor on which we will focus in this article involves *boundary organizations* (Guston, 2000; Miller, 2001). This involves organizations that operate on the boundaries of research and policy and often play an intermediary or brokerage role in mutual relations. This can for instance involve advisory bodies that upon request of government institutions bring together the available knowledge and expertise on a specific topic (Stone, 1998). However, they can also involve think tanks, consultancy firms, government research , or so-called "universities without students." A characteristic for boundary organizations is that they often operate as "bridges" or "transmission belts" between the worlds of research and policy. It makes them well situated to play a key role not only in terms of the distribution of knowledge but also in terms of the (co)production of knowledge.

In this article, we examine what patterns of knowledge utilization emerge in times of crisis, based on qualitative analysis of policymaking in the two selected policy areas. The data are primarily taken from policy records (policy documents, policy memoranda, records/minutes of parliamentary hearings) issued from the start of the financial and economic crisis in 2008, respectively, in the context of Europe's debate on the migration crisis which emerged in the 2000s and recently intensified in the run-up to the current refugee crisis.

Methodological Note

The study follows a similar case study design of two policy areas that have in common that both have been prone to what is perceived as "crisis." However, in order to be able to draw more general inferences on the role of knowledge and knowledge utilization in policy areas in crisis, we selected two areas that have little in common apart from being in "crisis"; budgetary policies and migration/integration policies. The empirical data are taken from the Dutch budgetary policy and migration and integration policy, respectively. The question may be raised on how the crisis affects the production and utilization of expert knowledge. On the one hand, there may be demand for expert knowledge to deal with the crisis. On the other, time may be simply lacking to produce, if not to use expert knowledge. We zoom in on the role of boundary organizations in the production and, subsequently, utilization of expert knowledge.

For both policy areas a qualitative approach was adopted in the study of policy processes and the utilization of knowledge in those policy processes. The outcome of the Dutch spending review is analyzed with the help of a search engine, looking for literature references in the text of reports as well as endnotes and footnotes.[8] The *gross* number of literature references is controlled for overlap. that is, the figures below refer to the *net* number of literature references. Finally, the literature references are categorized in six broad categories of providers of expert knowledge. The advisory bodies stand for 36.4% of the sample (see Annex B), justifying a closer inspection of that category. As we will see, the Centaal Planbureau (Netherlands Institute for Economic Policy Analysis) happens to be the largest provider by far of expert knowledge with 23.4% of the advisory bodies (see Figure 3), which does not come as a surprise given the mission of the task forces.

For migration and integration policies also a qualitative analysis was made on the utilization of knowledge in policymaking. This involved a broad analysis of advisory reports and references to research reports in policy memoranda in the period 2000–2015. This analysis was part of a broader project into the relationship between research and policymaking in migration and integration policies in the Netherlands (see also Scholten et al., 2015).[9] This analysis revealed a key role of specific boundary organizations, in particular the Dutch Scientific Council for Government Policy and the Social and Cultural Planning Office. Consequently, the analysis in this paper focused in particular on the role of these two organizations.

The Dutch Comprehensive Spending Reviews (2010)

Introduction

The budgetary policy of the Dutch is the subject of coordination by the European Union, although the budgetary policy still belongs to the domain of the European member states.[10] More precisely, the European member states are obliged under the Stability and Growth Pact (SGP) to reduce their budget deficit below the reference value of 3 percent of GDP as well as their gross debt below the reference value of 60 percent of GDP.[11] In an effort to meet its requirements the Dutch government, building on a previous experience in the 1980s, launched a one-off comprehensive spending review (Brede Heroverwegingen [BHO]) in the run-up to the elections of 2010.

The comprehensive spending reviews may be considered as a mode of policy analysis or, more precisely, utilization-focused evaluation (Patton, 2008; van Nispen, 2015, p. 4) geared toward a more evidence-based budgetary, notably retrenchment policy. Consequently, one may expect that the outcome of the comprehensive spending reviews will be primarily used in an instrumental way. We distinguish basically two levels of knowledge utilization:

1. The utilization of both academic and nonacademic studies, which are often delivered for other purposes, in the context of the spending reviews;
2. The utilization of the findings of the comprehensive spending reviews for a reduction of public expenditures and, consequently, the budget deficit.

In sum, 20 special task forces have been assigned to generate cheaper alternatives for current policies of which of minus 20 percent of the baseline. Chaired by independent civil servants, they had 6 months to complete their mission.[12,13]

Boundary Organizations

In this section, we will look at the advisory bodies first and then zoom in on the role of the Netherlands Bureau for Economic Policy Analysis (Centraal Planbureau [CPB]) as the main supplier of expert knowledge in the context of the comprehensive spending reviews. At the same time we will expand the scope from literature references to the involvement of a researcher from the CPB as an expert in the work of the special task forces and the assessment of the impact of the potential savings (CPB 2010).

In sum, we found 330 references to the literature adjusted for duplication in the body text of the comprehensive spending reviews, which is 16.5 references per report. The front runner is the report on Public Safety and Terrorism (nr. 15) with not the less than 50 references. On the other side of the spectrum is the report on International Security (nr. 20) with one single reference to the literature. Clearly there is no academic culture in this field regarding the account for its sources of information. In addition, we may look at the reference list at the end of the report, showing that only 7 out of 20 task forces referred to the literature that they used to accomplish their mission.

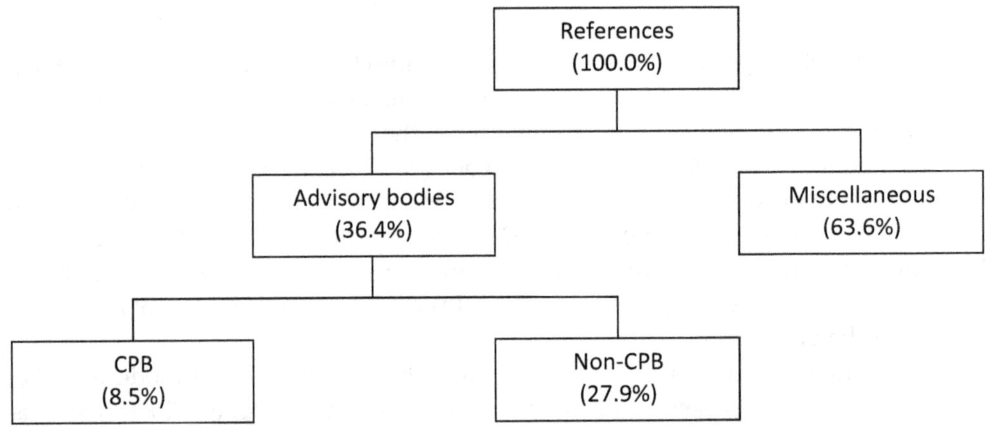

Figure 2. The Number of Literature References in the Comprehensive Spending Reviews.
Note: CPB stands for Centraal Planbureau (Netherlands Bureau for Economic Policy Analysis).

Source: BHO 2010 (Own Calculations).

A closer inspection of the comprehensive spending reviews reveals that more than a third of the references to the literature (36.4%) consists of publications of advisory bodies (see Figure 2), which justifies a closer inspection of this category. A breakdown of the advisory bodies is provided below (see Figure 3), showing that the CPB—not surprisingly—happens to be the main supplier of expert knowledge in the context of the comprehensive spending reviews (see Annex B).

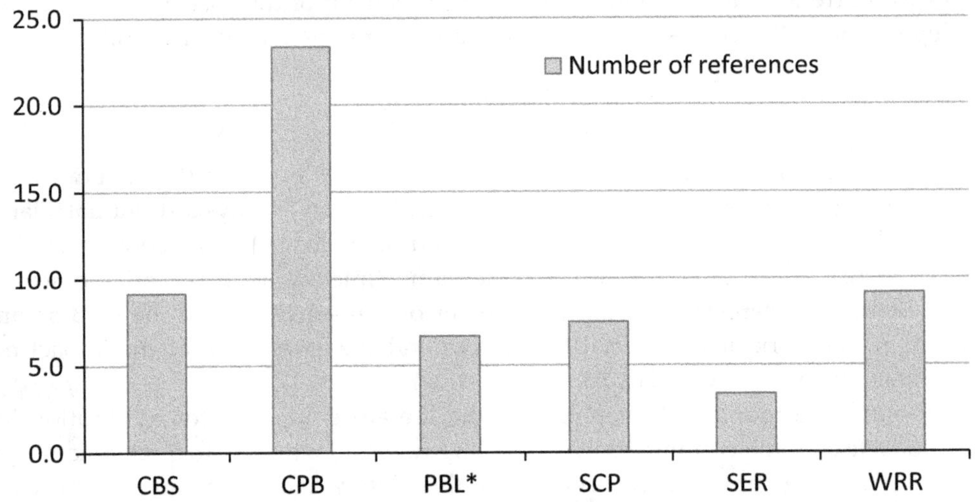

Figure 3. A Breakdown of the References to Advisory Reports in the Comprehensive Spending Reviews (n = 120).[14]
Note: PBL includes references to the RIVM and RPD that work in the same field.

Source: BHO 2010 (Own Calculations).

In total, 28 references to the CPB, adjusted for duplication, has been found, which stands for 8.5 percent of the sample.[15] However, the impact of the CPB should not be underestimated as 13 observers and researchers of the CPB were formally involved in the work of the special task forces, while many special task forces have consulted the CPB informally. Furthermore, 5 out 20 special task forces applied or followed the methodology used by the CPB and 10 out of 20 special task forces have invited the CPB to assess the potential savings critically with the help of a macroeconomic model (Centraal Planbureau [CPB], 2010), which points at the utilization of expert knowledge for legitimating and/or substantiating purposes.

Finally, a more in-depth analysis has been made of the references to the publications of the CPB, ranging from the enlightenment function by providing insight in the facts and figures to the substantiating function by drawing arguments or counterarguments regarding potential savings. However, this is mostly done in a methodological sound way, balancing information before adopting a specific course of action. As such, the comprehensive spending reviews happen to be more evidence-based than may be thought on the basis of the instrumental utilization of expert knowledge.

Knowledge Utilization

In sum, the special task forces identified € 42.5 billion of potential savings, amply exceeding the € 35 billion target. In fact, potential savings are even higher as saving options may be combined to even further reaching spending cuts.[16] In addition, the sum of the most far reaching options accounts for 25.0 percent of the review base and is, as such, topping the 20 percent mark.

However, it should be noted that most saving options were not completely new as they were already figured on the so-called Gerritse list, named after the then permanent secretary of the Dutch ministry of Finance, which may be characterized best as an educated guess of saving options. One may argue that the comprehensive spending reviews provided a reliable foundation to the Gerritse list and, as such, may be considered as substantiating utilization of expert knowledge.

The findings of the comprehensive spending reviews have served as input for the election manifestos of the political parties in the run-up to the elections due to the fall of the incumbent coalition and later became part of the negotiations about the new coalition agreement. The centerpiece of the agreement is an austerity package of € 18.0 billion in FY 2015, explicitly referring to the findings of the comprehensive spending reviews. In total, € 2.5 billion has been used, which equals about 16.9 percent of the austerity package. The instrumental utilization is even paler, that is, 5.4 percent, when it is related to the sum of the most far reaching options generated by the taskforces (Van Nispen and Klaassen, 2010).

Recently, the Court of Audit issued a report on the costs and benefits of six austerity packages, covering the period running from 2011 until 2016 (Algemene Rekenkamer 2016). As for the utilization of the outcome of the comprehensive spending reviews one may conclude that 7 out of 37 measures are not effectuated, reducing the added value of the comprehensive spending reviews by 0.7 billion euro's to 1.8 billion euro's. All but one has been replaced by other measures, so that the overall reduction in public expenditures is hardly touched by the cancelation of these measures. Furthermore, the CPB has calculated that a third (33.8%) of the Rutte I austerity package faded away due to a combination of (1) the multiplier effect of the spending cuts on the economy and (2) the elasticity of the budget to changes in the economy (Suyker, 2016; Algemene Rekenkamer 2016).[17] Applied to the measures that have been drawn from the comprehensive spending reviews, another 0.5 billion euros leaked away (see Annex A). As a result, almost 1.1 billion euros materialized (Figure 4), that is, 47.7 percent of the savings due to the comprehensive spending reviews. The outcome stands for 25.5 percent of the *realized* savings of the Rutte I austerity package.[18] Note that the exact amount is unclear as the impact of the savings on economic growth is calculated on the basis of the standard multiplier.[19]

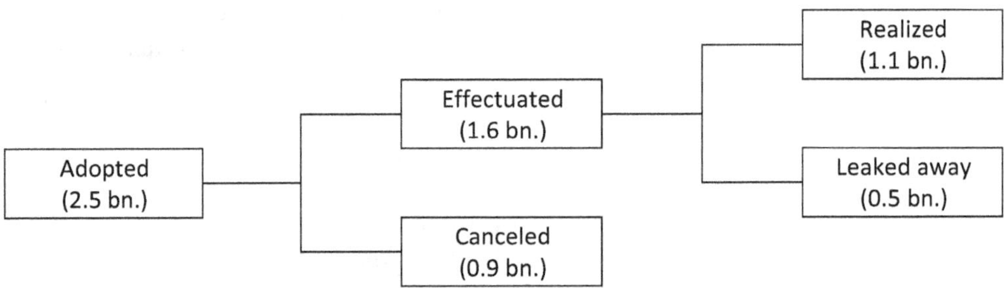

Figure 4. The Utilization of the Comprehensive Spending Reviews.

Source: Algemene Rekenkamer 2016; Suyker 2016 (Own Calculations).

At face value, the *instrumental* utilization of the comprehensive spending reviews may be somewhat disappointing, but it should be noted that it simply takes time to have effect. On one hand, the utilization of the comprehensive spending reviews may grow further over time, notably in case of ongoing austerity. Besides, comprehensive spending reviews are used as a lever during budget talks by preparing the ground for spending cuts that are not rooted in the comprehensive spending reviews. It goes too far to attribute these spending cuts to the comprehensive spending reviews, but it seems to be plausible that they would not be considered otherwise, let alone realized (van Nispen, 1993, p. 121; van Nispen, 2015, p. 12). On the other hand, a budget must be considered as a plan and saving options often do not materialize due to a wide variety of reasons. Finally, one may point at *noninstrumental*, that is, political utilization of the spending reviews as they backed the austerity package of the Rutte 1 coalition (substantiating). Although it is more common these days to refer to the source of information in public documents, we believe that the number of literature references in the reports of the task forces is not representative as it biased by a deliberate effort to substantiate the claims by expert knowledge provided by boundary organizations.

In addition it even further strengthened the position of the minister of Finance, which is already stronger during a downturn than during an upswing of the economy (Randma-Liiv & Savi, 2016, p. 239), by providing ammunition *vis-à-vis* the spending departments (legitimating) during the subsequent negotiations about next year's budget.

The Dutch Migration and Integration Policies (2000–2015)

Introduction

Just like in various other European countries, migration and integration have become issues of fierce public contestation over the last decade or so. This was due, on the hand, to the increase in migration flows into the Netherlands. Besides immigration from former Dutch colonies such as Surinam and the Antilles and from former guest-labor countries such as Turkey and Morocco, migration from especially other EU countries increased in the second half of the 2000s. Furthermore, since 2015, the number of refugee migrants increased steeply, as in many other European countries.

On the other hand, besides the impact of increasing immigration levels, the politicization of migration and integration within the national political arena also played a key role in policy contestation. Already in the early 2000s a strong influence emerged of populist parties such as first the Pim Fortuyn Party and later the more pronounced anti-immigrant Freedom Party. This created enormous political pressure for changes in Dutch policies to promote the sociocultural integration of newcomers and to impose restrictions for further immigration.

Although migration policies are to a large extent Europeanized, the Dutch policies on migrant integration did change significantly in the period under study in this article. The integration policy that had traditionally focused primarily on socioeconomic participation changed into an "Integration Policy New Style" (TK 2003–2004 29203, Nr. 1) with much more emphasis on sociocultural integration. For instance, basic knowledge of Dutch history, values and norms was included into civic integration tests that newcomers had to pass before getting a permanent residence permit. What is more, the responsibility for integration was individualized to the migrants themselves. This also includes financial responsibility. Migrants had to prepare and pay themselves for civic integration courses and the test itself.

Another side of this assimilationist turn in Dutch policies was a government retrenchment out of the field of migrant integration. The budget for migrant integration was brought down to almost zero. Moreover, the coordination structure was largely dismantled. Rather than having one integration policy with its own coordination structure, integration was now "mainstreamed" (Scholten et al., 2015) into generic policies. It became part of policies directed at the whole population, such as education, housing, and labor. As a consequence, much of the previous national integration policies were decentralized to the cities where most migrants lived.

Boundary Organizations

In the policy change that was defined above, several advisory bodies played a role. One advisory body that has traditionally played a key role in migrant integration policies was the Dutch Scientific Council for Government Policy (Wetenschappelijke Raad voor het Regeringsbeleid, WRR). The WRR is a semi-independent think thank that provides interdisciplinary reports on topics that are relevant to policy making in various departments and over a relatively long term. Reports from the WRR had already played a key role in major changes in migrant integration policies in the decades before (WRR 1979; WRR 1989) (Scholten, 2009). During the 2000s the WRR once again published two reports on migrant integration; one in 2001 (Netherlands as Immigration Society) and one in 2007 (Identification with the Netherlands).

These two reports echoed strongly with developments in the international migration literature that highlighted a growing mobility and diversification of societies in the context of the ongoing process of globalization. More people were able to migrate over greater distances, and as a consequence the diversity of society increased further. This also involved the formation of transnational communities with migrants keeping feet in more than one world, for instance leading to dual citizenship. As a consequence, identification with a society would no longer be exclusive in the context of an increasingly mobile world. Migrants can identify with societies in many different ways, in functional ways such as related to world, as well as in emotive ways (feeling at home) or cultural ways (feeling part of a broader community). One of the key conclusions of the 2007 report, as paraphrased by a Dutch princess at the time of the launch of the report, was that "the Dutchman does not exist."

Besides the WRR, another important boundary organization involved in this domain is the Social and Cultural Planning Office (SCP). Like the WRR, the SCP is a semi-independent knowledge producer, which formally resorts within the Department of Public Health and Welfare. Although the WRR produces mostly conceptual studies for policies on the longer term, the SCP produces statistics on the social and cultural position of Dutch society. This includes so-called "ethnic statistics," or data on the position of specific groups, such as migrant minorities. Together with the Central Planning Office (CPB), the SCP produces integration monitors that provide information on various aspects of the position of migrants, such as income, work, educational achievements, crime, and various social–cultural indicators such as mutual attitudes between migrants and natives.

An important foundation for the work of the SCP (and CPB) is a collection of "ethnic statistics" on migrants. Such statistics are based on a distinction between natives ("autochthonous") and immigrants ("allochthonous"). In the statistics, anyone who is born outside the Netherlands or of whom at least one of the parents is born outside the Netherlands is considered "allochthonous." This means that data allow for monitoring not just of first but also second-generation migrants, who actually are born in the Netherlands.

These data showed among others that although various "objective" indicators such as educational performance and language comprehension showed improvement, various "subjective" indicators such as mutual attitudes showed deterioration. It also showed that the labor market position of migrants was very vulnerable during the financial-economic crisis and that crime rates were particularly high among specific migrant groups (Moroccans and Antilleans).

Knowledge Utilization

The two boundary organizations identified above played very different roles in the policy changes that occurred in Dutch migrant integration policies in the last decade or so. Although earlier WRR reports (1979, 1989) had triggered major changes in migrant integration policies, the 2001 and 2007 reports remained largely ignored. There was a misfit between the reports' focus on internationalization and transnationalization and the policy focus on assimilation that emerged in the 2000s.

What is more, the scientific credibility and authority of the WRR was put on the line in public and political debate surrounding these reports (Scholten, 2011; Scholten & Timmermans, 2010). Especially, the 2007 report led to broad political indignation as it questioned the image of one clear Dutch identity. This indignation not only confronted the Dutch princess Maxima who held a speech at the launch of the report but also led to open questions by parliamentarians about the value of having a WRR in the first place. The report hardly had any concrete effect on policy, besides the discursive effect of functioning as an element from which assimilationists could distance themselves.

In contrast, the reports from the SCP became increasingly prominent markers for policy developments. For instance, various important policy documents (such as the latest "integration letter" of the Minister of Social Affairs in 2015) were positioned as government responses to SCP reports with updates of data on the position of "allochthonous." Also for the media, the launch of new data was often a key moment of agenda setting.

There are various aspects to how these SCP reports were used in the policy process. As the SCP delivers primarily data rather than policy advice, its instrumental use is very limited. On various occasions, government departments did announce concrete policy measures in response to the data from SCP, for instance when data showed that unemployment or crime had increased among specific groups.

However, both forms of symbolic knowledge utilization figured very prominently. Having data that distinguished between "autochthonous" and "allochthonous" and provided information on differences in their socialeconomic and sociocultural position, substantiated the idea of having an integration policy. It substantiated the belief that a policy is required to intervene in the position of migrants. Furthermore, especially in the context of government retrenchment, and budget cuts, the data from the SCP also legitimated the coordination of this integration policy. Apart from statistics, the coordinating minister actually had very few instruments let alone means to achieve policy goals. Due to the mainstreaming of migrant integration, the effectiveness of policy was dependent to a very large extent upon efforts made by other departments in other policy areas such as education, labor, and housing.

The case of the SCP reveals a clear element of coproduction as defined by Jasanoff (2004). The key symbolic importance of the ethnic statistics produced by SCP also legitimated the position of SCP as a leading knowledge producer on migrant integration. Consequently, this also legitimated the collection of ethnic statics on and the distinction between "allochthonous" and "autochthonous." At the same time, our case analysis showed how knowledge that was produced outside this intimate coproduction relationship between government and SCP, was largely ignored (Entzinger and Scholten 2015).

Conclusion

In this paper, we looked at the utilization of expert knowledge in times of crisis. Our analysis of two crisis-prone policy areas in the Netherlands shows only little proof of instrumental knowledge utilization. However, rather than knowledge being utilized less in contested crisis, our study shows rather that knowledge is utilized in different way. We found evidence of more political or symbolic forms of knowledge utilization. This not only involved substantiating existing policies but also legitimating policy actors and coordination structures. In fact, our study shows that in both cases knowledge could be considered a very important tool for policy coordination, precisely in a highly politicized setting of a crisis.

The findings of this study indicate that expert knowledge is used instrumentally, but modestly. As for the comprehensive spending reviews we expected to find more support for the instrumental mode of knowledge utilization as they are geared to a more evidence-based budgetary policy. In total, only 5.4 percent of the sum of the most far reaching options generated by the special task forces is used for the austerity package of the Rutte I cabinet. It makes up for 16.9 percent of the spending cuts of the austerity package.[20] So, we have to conclude that the budgetary policy is still not evidence-based, but rather opinion-based relying on "either the selective use of evidence ... or on the untested views of individuals or groups, often inspired by ideological stand points, prejudices or speculative conjecture" (Davies, 2004, p. 3).

In addition, one may argue that that the comprehensive spending reviews built up to the authority, if not the power of the ministry of Finance *vis-à-vis* the spending departments. It provides the civil servants of the ministry of Finance with ammunition during the annual negotiations about next year's budget. The outcome of the spending reviews often served as the opening bid during the negotiations to be replaced by another savings, which are not based on evidence, but on an educated guess. Although, it seems to be plausible that these savings would not be realized without the comprehensive spending reviews. Unfortunately, the lever function of expert knowledge is not easy to trace back as the negotiations take place behind closed doors and the proceedings are not accounted for in the budget. Contrary though to the past reference is made to the sources of information in the budget memorandum.

As for the role of expert knowledge in the comprehensive spending reviews, one may conclude that the outcome of research conducted for other purposes is mainly used selectively, that is, either as an argument or as a counter-argument, pointing at the substantiating function of utilization of expert knowledge. In addition, research is contracted out as many task forces have been commissioned the CPB to assess the potential savings critically with the help of a macroeconomic model. Besides, many experts of the CPB were involved in the work of the special task forces.

In the case of Dutch immigrant integration policies, our analysis shows that the context of crisis and the sharp politicization of Dutch integration policies did not mean that knowledge utilization became either more prominent or rare. Rather, the type of knowledge as well as the way it is used changed during the crisis. The focus of knowledge changed from the delivery of "conceptual" advice to the provision of data and descriptive statistics about the position of migrants. At the same time the instrumental type of knowledge utilization that had given the WRR reports from the past a key role in policy changes, made place for more symbolic forms of knowledge utilization due to the sharp politicization of migration.

It is important to note that the symbolic forms of knowledge utilization that we found in this case do not so much refer to political symbolism. Rather, within the politicized policy setting and in the context of growing fragmentation of integration policies ("mainstreaming"), knowledge played a key role in both substantiating and legitimating the remaining central integration policy and policy coordination structure. In fact, precisely within the politicized setting of this policy domain, knowledge was one of the few tools left for policy coordination. With the help of the facts and figures regarding the position of migrants, other departments could be made aware of the sense of urgency to implement integration policies. This shows that symbolic knowledge utilization can be a very powerful form of knowledge utilization.

To summarize, this analysis adds to our understanding of knowledge utilization at times of crisis. The policy studies literature has focused much on the instrumental use of knowledge in processes of policy learning, and has "found" that the potential role of learning in policy change often appears rather limited; especially when it comes to situations of "crises" where fundamental policy assumptions (deeper level policy beliefs) are at stake. However, our analysis shows that expert knowledge can be very important and powerful also in situations of contestation or crisis. Perhaps not contributing to learning *per se*, political or symbolic forms of knowledge utilization appear to play a key role in legitimating policy actors and structures as well as substantiating policy decisions.

Finally, the fact that these findings are based on an analysis of two policy areas that have little in common apart from being in crisis, speaks to the external validity of the argument made in this article. However, as a one-off effort to reduce the budget deficit, the Dutch comprehensive spending review is relatively unique and, as such, not representative for other policy fields. As mentioned before the political or symbolic utilization of expert knowledge provided by boundary organizations seems to be influenced positively by the pursuit of an evidence-based budgetary policy. One may question if that will also apply to other policy fields, notably those which are not subject to a crisis. The political or symbolic utilization of expert knowledge is of all times, but may be more prominent as well as more visible in times of crisis.

Frans van Nispen is currently Visiting Fellow at the Department of Political and Social Sciences of the European University Institute in San Domenico di Fiesole, Italy.
Peter Scholten is Associate Professor of Public Policy and Politics and director of IMISCOE at the Erasmus University of Rotterdam, The Netherlands.

Notes

1. He referred to the situation after the Second World War that allowed for the formation of the United Nations.
2. In the remaining sections of this paper we will use theory, knowledge, and research as being interchangeable, although they are not exactly the same.
3. In an earlier publication about the Dutch spending reviews in the 1980, I followed the line of direct vs. indirect knowledge utilization, the latter being composed of the conceptual function (enlightenment) and political function of research (van Nispen, 1993).
4. The essential difference between substantiating and legitimating is in the relation with the content of the policy solution (Rimkutė & Haverland, 2015, p. 438–39).
5. The issue of boundary work is usually attributed to the sociologist Thomas Gieryn in an effort to distinguish science from nonscience.
6. It is in the interest of both communities to keep the boundaries is tact. For scientists, it is crucial for sustaining their claim that they produce authoritative information; for policy makers, authoritative information may strengthen the credibility of the expertise (Boswell, 2009, p. 25).
7. Note that expert knowledge may be also produced by a special unit/"in house," but is generally not considered as part of the job description.
8. The literature references in the annexes are left out.
9. The DIAMINT project on "Research-Policy Dialogues on Migration and Integration in Europe." See: www.diamint.eu.
10. The European semester and the accompanying Six-Pack, Two-Pack, and Fiscal Compact still did not arrive at that time.
11. In fact, the constraints are more stringent as the country-specific Medium-Term Budgetary Objective (MTO), that is, the actual budget balance net of the cyclical component and one-off and other temporary measures, is set at −0.5 percent of GDP at market prices.
12. The task forces were established on September 25, 2009, following the submission of the budget memorandum for FY 2010. The reports were submitted to parliament on April 1, 2010 (BHO, 2009).
13. The reports have become subject of political debate due to the fall of the incumbent cabinet.
14. CBS = Centraal Bureau voor de Statistiek (Statistics Netherlands); CPB = Centraal Planbureau (Netherlands Bureau for Economic Policy Analysis); PBL = Planbureau voor de Leefomgeving (Netherlands Environmental Assessment Agency); SCP = Sociaal en Cultureel Planbureau

(Netherlands Institute for Social Research); SER = Sociaal-Economische Raad (Social and Economic Council); WRR = Wetenschappelijke Raad voor het Regeringsbeleid (Netherlands Scientific Council for Government Policy).

15. The reports of the CPB stand for 23.3 percent of the references to advisory bodies as the largest category of the references to the literature.
16. The amount is growing even further beyond FY 2015 to €55 billion.
17. The leakage of the six austerity packages reviewed by the AR/CPB is even higher: almost 50 percent of the savings faded away.
18. The austerity package of the Rutte I coalition was composed of 3.2 billion euros inherited from the Balkenende IV coalition and 14.8 billion euros of additional savings of which 5.0 billion euros faded away (33.8 percent).
19. As a rule of the thumb a multiplier of 0.5 may be used in the case of an average package of revenues and expenditures. However, there are signs that the multiplier is higher in times of recession (Suyker 2016, p. 8).
20. A substantial higher degree of instrumental utilization of expert knowledge is reported by Rimkutė & Haverland on the basis of a recent survey among 120 academics serving on expert groups under auspices of the Commission, as such adopting a supplier's perspective (Rimkutė & Haverland, 2015). In this study, we look at the utilization of expert knowledge from a user's perspective.

References

Algemene Rekenkamer. 2016. *Kosten en opbrengsten van saldoverbeterende maatregelen 2011–2016*. 's-Gravenhage: Algemene Rekenkamer.

Boswell, C. 2008. "The Political Functions of Expert Knowledge: Knowledge and Legitimation in European Union Immigration Policy." *Journal of European Public Policy* 15 (4): 471–488. doi: 10.1080/13501760801996634.

———. 2009. *The Political Uses of Expert Knowledge. Immigration Policy and Social Research*. Cambridge: Cambridge University Press.

Bekkers, V. J. J. M. 2015. Contested knowledge in theory-driven policy analysis: setting the Dutch stage. In Van Nispen & Scholten, Analysis and Evaluation in The Netherlands: Institutionalization and Performance, 231–246.

Brede Heroverwegingen (BHO). 2009. *Brief van de Minister-President aan de Voorzitter van de Tweede Kamer over de opzet van de brede heroverwegingen* d.d. 25 September 2009.

Brede Heroverwegingen (BHO). 2010. Aanbiedingsbrief van de Minister-President aan de Voorzitter van de Tweede Kamer van de rapporten van de brede heroverwegingen d.d. 1 April 2010.

Caplan, N. 1979. "The Two-Communities Theory and Knowledge Utilization." *American Behavioral Scientist* 22 (3): 459–470.

Centraal Planbureau (CPB). 2010. Nadere informatie t.b.v. doorrekening verkiezingsprogramma's.'s-Gravenhage 1 April 2010.

Davies, P. 2004. Is Evidence-Based Government Possible?, Jerry Lee Lecture 2004, delivered at the 4th Annual Campbell Collaboration Colloquium, Washington February 19, 2004.

Entzinger, H., and P. Scholten. 2015. "The Interplay of Knowledge Production and Policymaking: A Comparative Analysis of Research and Policymaking on Migrant Integration in Germany and the Netherlands." *Journal of Comparative Policy Analysis: Research and Practice* 17 (1): 60–74.

Guston, D. H. 2000. *Between Politics and Science. Assuring the Integrity and Productivity of Research*, New Jersey: Rutgers University.

Hall, P. A. 1993. "Policy Paradigms, Social Learning, and the State: The Case of Economic Policymaking in Britain." *Comparative Politics*, 25 (3): 275–296.

Heclo, H. 1974. *Social Policy in Britain and Sweden*. New Haven: Yale University Press.

Hoppe, R. 1999. "Policy Analysis, Science, and Politics: From 'Speaking Truth to Power' to 'Making Sense Together'." *Science and Public Policy*, 26 (3): 201–210.

———. 2005. "Rethinking the Science-Policy Nexus: From Knowledge Utilization and Science Technology Studies to Types of Boundary Arrangements." *Poiesis & Praxis* 3 (3): 199–215.

Hoppe, R. 2010. "From 'Knowledge Use' Towards 'Boundary Work': Sketch of an Emerging New Agenda for Inquiry into Science-Policy Interaction." In *Knowledge Democracy. Consequences for Science, Politics and Media*, ed. J. Roeland in't Veld. Berlin/Heidelberg: Springer-Verlag, 169–186.

Jasanoff, S. 1987. "Contested Boundaries in Policy-Relevant Science." *Social Studies of Science* 17 (2): 195–230.

———. 1990. *The Fifth Branch: Science Advisers as Policymakers*. London: Cambridge University Press.

———. 2004. *States of Knowledge; the Co-production of Science and Social Order*, New York: Routledge.

Knott, J., and A. Wildavsky. 1980. "If Dissemination Is the Solution, What Is the Problem?." *Knowledge: Creation, Diffusion, Utilization*, 1 (4): 537–578.

Leeuw, F. L. 1987. "De reconstructie en evaluatie van beleidstheorieën als methode van beleidsonderzoek: achtergronden, werkwijze, toepassing en relevantie." In *Sociaal beleidsonderzoek: differentiatie en ontwikkeling*, ed. Mark van de Vall, and Frans L. Leeuw. 's-Gravenhage: Vuga, 113–137.

Lindquist, E. A. 1990. "The Third Community, Policy Inquiry and Social Scientists." In *Social Scientists, Policy, and the State*, ed. S. Brooks, and A. G. Gagnon. New York/London: Praeger, 21–51.

Miller, C. A. 2001. "Hybrid Management: Boundary Organizations, Science Policy and Environmental Governance in the Climate Regime." *Science, Technology and Human Values* 26: 478–500.

Patton, M. Q. 2008. *Utilization-Focused Evaluation*, 4th ed. Los Angeles: Sage.

Radaelli, C. M. 1995. "The Role of Knowledge in the Policy Process." *Journal of European Public Policy* 2 (2): 159–183.

Randma-Liiv, T., and S. Riin. 2016. "Managing the public sector under fiscal stress." In *Public Administration Reforms in Europe. The View from the Top*, ed. G. Hammerschmid, S. Van de Walle, R. Andrews, and P. Bezes. Cheltenham/Northampton: Edward Elgar, 231–243.

Rimkutė, D., and M. Haverland. 2015. "How does the European Commission Use Scientific Expertise? Results from a Survey of Scientific Members of the Commission's Expert Committees." *Comparative European Politics* 13 (4): 430–449.

Sabatier, P. A. 1998. "The Advocacy Coalition Framework: Revisions and Relevance for Europe." *Journal of European Public Policy* 5 (1): 98–130.

Sanderson, I. 2002. "Evaluation, Policy Learning and Evidence-based Policy Making." *Public Administration*, 80 (1): 1–22.

Scholten, P. 2009. "The Coproduction of Immigrant Integration Policy and Research in the Netherlands: The Case of the Scientific Council for Government Policy." *Science and Public Policy* 36 (7): 561.

———. 2011. *Framing Immigrant Integration: Dutch Research-Policy Dialogues in Comparative Perspective*. Amsterdam: Amsterdam University Press.

Scholten, P., H. Entzinger, R. Penninx, and S. Verbeek, eds. 2015. *Integrating Immigrants in Europe Research-Policy Dialogues*. Dordrecht: Springer.

Scholten, P., and A. Timmermans. 2010. "Setting the Immigrant Policy Agenda: Expertise and Politics in the Netherlands, France and the United Kingdom." *Journal of Comparative Policy Analysis* 12 (5): 527–544.

Schrefler, L. 2010. "The Usage of Scientific Knowledge by Independent Regulatory Agencies." *Governance* 23 (2): 309–330. doi: 10.1111/j.1468-0491.2010.01481.x

Stone, D. 1998. *Capturing the Political Imagination: Think Tanks and the Policy Process*. London: Cass.

Suyker, W. 2016. *Opties voor begrotingsbeleid. Meer automatische stabilisatie gewenst*. 's-Gravenhage: CPB Policy Brief 2016/02.

van de Vall, M. 1980. *Sociaal beleidsonderzoek: Een professioneel paradigma.* Alphen aan den Rijn: Samsom.

van Nispen, F. K. M. 1993. *Het dossier Heroverweging [The Reconsideration Files].* Delft: Eburon.

———. 2015. "Policy Analysis in Times of Austerity: A Cross-National Comparison of Spending Reviews." *Journal of Comparative Policy Analysis: Research and Practice,* 479–501. doi: 10.1080/13876988.2015.1005929.

van Nispen, F. K. M., and H. L. Klaassen. 2010. "Heroverweging een beleidsanalytische manier van bezuinigen." *TPC, Tijdschrift Voor Public Governance, Audit & Control [Special Issue on Cut-Backs,* 8 (4): 4–10.

van Nispen, F. K. M., and Peter W. A. Scholten, ed. 2015. *Policy Analysis and Evaluation in The Netherlands: Institutionalization and Performance.* Bristol: The Policy Press.

Weingart, P. 1999. "Scientific Expertise and Political Accountability: Paradoxes of Science in Politics." *Science and Public Policy* 26 (3): 151–161.

Weiss, C. H. 1979. "The Many Meanings of Research Utilization." *Public Administration Review* 39 (5): 426–431.

Wetenschappelijke Raad voor het Regeringsbeleid, WRR. 1979. *Etnische Minderheden.* Den Haag: SDU.

Annex A
Overview of the Dutch Comprehensive Spending Reviews, FY 2010

Number	Name	Review Base	Maximum Option	Adopted	Effectuated	Canceled
1	Energy and Climate	1.85	0.47			
2	Environment and Nature	1.92	0.57	0.41	0.28	0.12
3	Mobility and Water	8.63	1.70	0.61	0.61	
4	Housing	12.73	5.60			
5	Schemes for Children	5.81	1.06	0.02		0.02
6	Productivity in Education	9.07	1.80	0.20		0.20
7	Higher Education	20.38	1.40	0.30		0.30
8	Innovation and Applied Research	1.87	0.38			
9	Programs for People with Few Skills	19.49	5.50			
10	Unemployment Benefits	6.69	3.10			
11	Curative Health Care	33.20	6.73	0.09	0.09	
12	Long-Term Health Care	20.81	4.40	0.21		0.21
13	International Cooperation	5.38	0.99	0.05	0.05	
14	Asylum, Immigration, and Integration	1.52	0.39	0.09	0.06	0.03
15	Public Safety and Terrorism	10.29	2.12	0.41	0.38	0.03
16	Tax Administration	2.00	0.18			
17	Supplementary Benefits	0.23	0.13			
18	Public Administration	N/A	1.80	0.12	0.12	
19	Public Management	N/A	2.00			
20	International Security	7.74	2.10			
Total		169.62	42.42	2.50	1.59	0.91

Source: Brede Heroverwegingen (BHO), 2010 (own calculations).

Annex B
Literature References to Advisory Bodies in the Comprehensive Spending Reviews, FY 2010

Number	Name	Body Text			Reference List
		Total	Advisory Body	CBP	
1	Energy and Climate	20	5	1	16
2	Environment and Nature	15	5	0	
3	Mobility and Water	6	4	3	38
4	Housing	5	2	2	
5	Schemes for Children	34	6	2	
6	Productivity in Education	32	10	5	29
7	Higher Education	26	8	2	
8	Innovation and Applied Research	10	3	1	
9	Programs for People with Few Skills	9	4	1	
10	Unemployment Benefits	25	13	4	27
11	Curative Health Care	13	5	1	
12	Long-Term Health Care	20	7	2	
13	International Cooperation	6	4	1	49
14	Asylum, Immigration, and Integration	14	2	0	
15	Public Safety and Terrorism	50	23	1	47
16	Tax Administration	2	1	1	
17	Supplementary Benefits	3	1	0	
18	Public Administration	35	16	1	36
19	Public Management	4	1	0	
20	International Security	1	0	0	
Total		330	120	28	242
Average/Total		100.0	36.4	8.5	

European Policy Analysis, Vol. 3, No. 1, 2017

Legislative Dynamics of Mitigation and Adaptation Framework Policies in the EU

Andreas Fleig, Nicole M. Schmidt and Jale Tosun

In this study we examine the adoption of climate framework laws in 20 member states of the European Union (EU) from 1990 until 2015. Our analysis is guided by the following research questions: First, which EU member states have adopted climate change legislation that addresses mitigation, adaptation, or both? Second, do EU countries act coherently or do we observe differences across countries regarding the response strategy or point in time of policies directed towards climate change? Third, comparing mitigation and adaptation frameworks, which approach came first and did it affect the adoption of the respective other? Our findings show that all countries save one (i.e., Hungary) covered in the analysis have adopted framework laws tackling mitigation and/or adaptation to climate change. While we did not observe a coherent pattern with respect to timing or sequence of adaptation and mitigation frameworks, we found that the best predictor of a national government's behavior is the behavior of the governments of other countries. However, the response of EU member states to climate change is less homogenous than one would have expected based on previous literature. In addition, by highlighting that mitigation and adaptation measures are equally prominent, at least within our sample of EU countries, we complement current climate change literature that often places mitigation efforts at the forefront in terms of legislation activity. Future research should examine this issue more closely, as this dynamic is likely to continue since the Paris Agreement gave prominence to adaptation.

KEY WORDS: adaption, climate change, European Union, legislation, mitigation

欧盟气候减缓和适应框架政策的立法动态

本文检验了*1990-2015*年间欧盟*20*个成员国采用的气候框架法律。研究了下列几个问题: 第一, 哪些欧盟成员国采用了减缓气候变化的立法? 哪些采用了适应气候变化的立法? 哪些两者都采用了? 第二, 关于气候变化的应对措施和政策时间点, 欧盟各国的回应是否一致? 第三, 对比减缓框架和适应框架, 哪种措施最先诞生? 它是否影响了对方的采用? 结果表明: 除匈牙利外, 其他欧盟成员国都采用了处理减缓和(或)适应气候变化的框架法律。然而, 本文并未发现减缓和适应框架出现的时间点或顺序存在连贯模式; 本文发现, 预测一个国家的政府行为, 最好的方式是通过观察其他国家的政府行为。然而, 基于以往的文献, 各成员国对气候变化的回应并不如预期那样相同。另外, 通过强调减缓和适应措施的同等重要性, 本文以欧盟国家样本, 对当前把减缓气候变化的立法措施 作 为主要研究的文献进行了补充。未来研究应更加密切检验适应问题, 因为巴黎协议突出强调了适应的重要性, 该动态很可能持续下去。

关键词: 适应, 气候变化, 欧盟, 立法, 减缓

doi: 10.1002/epa2.1002

Introduction

After a series of unsatisfactory outcomes of the past conferences held by the United Nations Framework Convention on Climate Change (UNFCCC) (Falkner, Stephan & Vogler, 2010), the Paris Agreement was settled amongst all member states in December 2015 and is widely regarded as a negotiation success (Rajamani, 2016). The five-year evaluation cycle in which every country needs to submit its efforts regarding climate change through their Nationally Determined Contributions (NDCs) is a particularly important and noteworthy commitment by UNFCCC member states. It represents the first distinctive characteristic of the Paris Agreement and brings national climate actions into the limelight of the coordinated efforts to respond to climate change at the global level (Fankhauser, Gennaioli & Collins, 2015; Jordan & Huitema, 2014a; Jordan et al., 2015; Lachapelle & Paterson, 2013; Massey, Biesbroek, Huitema & Jordan, 2014; Townshend et al., 2011, 2013a).

The second remarkable feature of the Paris Agreement is that it explicitly recognizes the need to adapt to climate change (Obergassel et al., 2017). Of the two major responses to climate change—in other words, mitigation and adaptation—both scholarly and political attention has predominantly concentrated on mitigation measures (Biesbroek, Swart & van der Knaap, 2009; Dubash, Hagemann, Höhne & Upadhyaya, 2013; Javeline, 2014; Lachapelle & Paterson, 2013; Widmer, 2014). Over time, however, more and more scholars have acknowledged that a dichotomy between mitigation and adaptation research limits the production of cumulative knowledge and that "mitigation and adaptation were erroneously regarded as two fundamentally different approaches to the same problem" (Biesbroek et al., 2009, p. 230; see also Schipper, 2006; Huitema et al., 2009). The dominant view is now that no matter how successful mitigation measures may be, some degree of climate change is inevitable, and this is why countries have started to focus on adaptation alongside mitigation (Keskitalo, 2010a,b). The Paris Agreement embraced exactly this perspective.

A small but growing literature exists that investigates the interrelation of the two approaches (Daniell et al., 2011; Jones, Dettmann, Park, Rogers & White, 2007; Touza & López-Gunn, 2011). Most of the studies argue that synergies between mitigation and adaptation exist and are prevalent in almost every sector (Moser, 2012), while simultaneously also pointing to potential challenges and undermining dynamics (Klein et al., 2007; Martens, McEvoy & Chang, 2009; Moser, 2012). Admittedly, most of these contributions focus on the actual implementation of climate change measures. We supplement the ongoing discussion by looking at the legislative domain in which proposals for mitigation and adaption might very well either compete against or encourage one another in aiming to reach the decision-makers' agenda.

More specifically, the Paris Agreement's recognition of both mitigation and adaptation measures motivates us to investigate the legislative dynamics between the two approaches. The literature suggests that the drivers underlying the adoption of these two response strategies towards climate change are different (Pielke,

Prins, Rayner & Sarewitz, 2007), that they are applied by different groups (Adger, Huq, Brown, Conway & Hulme, 2003; Bauer, Feichtinger & Steurer, 2012), and that they are used at different points in time (Keskitalo, 2010a,b; Tol, 2005).

We are, therefore, interested in the following research questions: First, which EU member states have adopted climate change legislation that addresses mitigation, adaptation, or both? Second, do EU countries act coherently or do we observe differences across countries regarding the strategy or point in time of policies directed towards climate change? Third, comparing mitigation and adaptation frameworks, which approach came first and did it affect the adoption of the respective other? To answer these questions, we empirically draw on the Global Climate Legislation Study (GLOBE), which provides data on both mitigation and adaptation-related legislation (Nachmany et al., 2015; Townshend et al., 2011, 2013b). Our focus is on framework policies towards climate change in 20 member states of the European Union (EU) from 1990 until 2015.

The remainder of this study is structured as follows. The section Policies for Mitigating and Adapting to Climate Change details the characteristics of those approaches that lie at the heart of our analysis. Here, we also explain our rationale to focus on framework legislation as well as on the national level of climate change governance. Subsequently, the Mitigation and Adaptation Policies at the European and Local Level section provides a common background for further analysis. The next section then investigates our sample to answer the raised research questions. In addition, we relate our findings to earlier studies on the underlying national as well as international drivers for both mitigation and adaptation policies. Finally, we summarize our main findings and discuss avenues for further research.

Policies for Mitigating and Adapting to Climate Change

Describing the complex dichotomy between climate change mitigation and adaptation is not an easy matter, and various scholarly works dealing with the two approaches differ substantially from one another. In a nutshell, adaptation-related research oftentimes adopts a planning focus (Eisenack et al., 2014; Juhola, Peltonen & Niemi, 2012; Webler, Tuler, Dow, Whitehead & Kettle, 2016), whereas studies on climate mitigation tend to concentrate on political costs and benefits (Bernauer, 2013; Gillard & Lock, 2016; Maor, Tosun & Jordan, 2017). In addition, for a long time, climate change adaptation was mostly associated with developing countries (Adger et al., 2003) and mitigation with developed countries. The next paragraphs investigate the characteristics and discuss a (non-exhaustive) list of the implementation of both policies in more detail. Thereby, we highlight the versatile character (Schaffrin, Sewerin & Seubert, 2014, 2015) of mitigating and adapting to climate change as well as the importance of national-level legislation.

The different goals and logics of mitigation and adaptation policies become evident when looking at what these two approaches actually comprise. As the IPCC (2014) states, climate mitigation policies include measures that aim at reducing or eliminating the drivers of climate change, while adaptation measures aim to manage or limit the degree of actual or expected climate change impacts. Ultimately, adaptation was pejoratively regarded as an inappropriate strategy to combat climate change and hence long considered "taboo" (Pielke et al., 2007; Tol, 2005). This is largely due to the fact that policymakers were initially convinced that reducing greenhouse gas (GHG) emissions would suffice and that technical improvements, as well as innovations, would help to combat climate change repercussions (Juhola et al., 2012; King, 2004).

Mitigation policies predominantly include measures aiming to lower emissions of GHG like carbon dioxide (CO_2), as those, among others, lead to an increase in temperature (Matthews et al., 2014). For example, some measures of climate mitigation action concentrate on protecting natural CO_2 sinks like forests and oceans, or creating new sinks through afforestation or reforestation and the greening of agriculture. Since forests play as important a role as CO_2 emissions sinks, the Reducing Emissions from Deforestation and Degradation (REDD+) mechanism was developed by the UNFCCC, aiming to provide an incentive for developing countries to protect their forest resources (Hickmann, 2013; Lederer, 2011; Wibowo & Giessen, 2015). However, most principal mitigation actions include measures that aim to cut emissions and are predominantly achieved by replacing fossil fuels by renewable energy (i.e., by fostering new technologies; see Cheon & Urpelainen, 2012; Negro, Alkemade & Hekkert, 2012; Pacala & Socolow, 2004) and energy savings (i.e., by promoting more energy efficient equipment; see Lechtenböhmer & Luhmann, 2013; Lipscy & Schipper, 2013).

Addressing climate mitigation measures in developing countries can further include improving the design of cook stoves (Jeuland & Pattanayak, 2012). Companies as well as individuals can be the targets of climate mitigation actions to reduce their CO_2 emissions by changing their consumption behaviors. In terms of relevant policy sectors, climate mitigation measures usually focus on agriculture, buildings, energy, manufacturing, and transport, which again shows that mitigation measures are versatile yet directed mainly at reducing GHG emissions (Hildén, 2011; Smith et al., 2008).

Turning to *adaption policies*, we broadly observe that these concentrate on preparing for the effects of climate change in such a way that the expected damage will be prevented or at least minimized. Following Dupuis and Biesbroek (2013, p. 1480), this includes any action that "deals intentionally with climate change impacts, and whose outcomes attempt to substantially impact actor groups, sectors, or geographical areas that are vulnerable to climate change." Most adaptation measures concentrate on developing strategies for using scarce water resources efficiently and managing drought periods as well as adapting buildings to global temperature increases, extreme weather conditions, and flood management. Policies can either be designed in anticipation of change (anticipatory adaptation) or in response to change (reactive adaptation), as both aim at building up resilience (Adger, Arnell & Tompkins, 2005). Furthermore, adaptation primarily focuses on local domains, such as coastal zone management, agriculture, health services, and spatial and urban planning (Brouwer, Rayner & Huitema, 2013; Nalau, Preston & Maloney, 2015).

All adaptation measures share the commonality that they are strongly concerned with questions regarding the costs incurred from climate change. Certainly, mitigation policies likewise fuel debates about costs. However, adaptation-related costs have always had a strong development-related component (Fankhauser, 2010), a fact that would explain why financial estimates usually vary enormously. At both COP 21 and COP 22, renewed commitment by developed countries and efforts to raise capital for the Green Climate Fund and the Adaptation Fund further address the circumstance that countries least responsible for increases in temperature will disproportionally be affected by climate change impacts (UNFCCC, 2016). Many other initiatives such as the Climate Technology Centre and Network also support technology development and transfer in developing nations to facilitate their commitments under the Paris Agreement (UN Climate Change Newsroom, 2016).

This described "multifaceted" character of both mitigation and adaptation is challenging in many ways (Van Buuren et al., 2013; for an overview of the "wicked-problem" character of climate change, see Levin, Cashore, Bernstein & Auld, 2012; Termeer, Dewulf & Breeman, 2013). For scholars, data collection and subsequent analysis are often tremendously difficult as initiatives are scattered and not all climate change policies are self-evident. For policymakers, the fact that both avenues for combating climate change suffuse so many sectors at the same time poses particular problems for the stage of policy design (Howlett & Rayner, 2006). Steurer and Clar (2015) highlight the importance of horizontal coordination and integration between sectors while Rayner and Howlett (2009) add that such coordination is also vital for designing coherent and consistent policy. These "smart" governance arrangements can avoid costly "layered" regimes (Feindt & Flynn, 2009) of very similar policies (Rayner & Howlett, 2009). In general terms, benefits from adaptation measures are mostly felt at the local level and are hence usually more decentralized than mitigation measures.

There is a growing appreciation in social science literature that the governance of climate change has become much more multi-leveled and dynamic and that international climate negotiations represent only one of many approaches that aim to address the challenges of climate change (Bernauer, 2013; Nilsson & Persson, 2012). For example, Dupuis and Biesbroek (2013) point towards public and private actors at different administrative levels as potential actors. Yet, across the "new" forms of climate governance (Jordan & Huitema, 2014b), the national level in particular seems to have taken over the leadership role—not only for climate change mitigation but also for adaption (Lesnikowski, Ford, Biesbroek, Berrang-Ford & Heymann, 2016). A number of recent studies such as Dubash et al. (2013), Lachapelle and Paterson (2013), Townshend et al. (2013a,b), Somanathan et al. (2014), and Boasson (2014) have revealed that climate change-related national legislation has been adopted in many countries across the globe in the last decade. Yet, research on comparative national climate policy is still in its early stages and is only beginning to emerge (Bernauer & Böhmelt, 2013; Lachapelle & Paterson, 2013; Ward & Cao, 2012).

With this paper we contribute to the existing literature by taking the increasing importance of the national level of climate change legislation into account. Therefore, we focus on *framework laws* that combine various efforts within mitigation, adaptation, or both. Such "framework legislation [. . .is] a law or regulation with equivalent status, which serves as a comprehensive, unifying basis for climate change policy, which addresses multiple aspects or areas of climate change mitigation or adaptation (or both) in a holistic, overarching manner" (Nachmany et al., 2015, p. 15). Hence, frameworks, by definition, cover more than one sector and are therefore particularly well equipped as an indicator of a country's overall policy performance—especially so as research has shown that such "flagship legislation" is a powerful driver of further climate policies (Fankhauser et al., 2015).

In comparison to policies that only address a singular issue, they are dispersed over multiple domains and aim to coordinate cross-sectoral climate change activities in a "holistic" (Jordan & Huitema, 2014b, p. 715) manner. By using this perspective, our study shares some features with ongoing discussions in both the Environmental Policy Integration (EPI) and Climate Policy Integration (CPI) literature (Adelle & Russel, 2013; Dupont, 2016; Tosun & Solorio, 2011). Yet, we clearly delineate framework policy analysis from these fields, as our analysis is just one of the many possible ways to look at climate policies. Furthermore, our study cannot contribute to the topic of vertical integration—which CPI scholars recognize as at least equally important (Gupta, 2007; Rayner & Howlett, 2009).

Mitigation and Adaptation Policies at the European and Local Level

Despite its complex institutional design, the EU has played and continues to play a significant role in designing European climate change legislation (Damro, Hardie & MacKenzie, 2008; Marcinkiewicz & Tosun, 2015; Rayner & Jordan, 2013). Yet some scholars have argued that the EU could do more and has, thus far, not fully utilized its leadership potential (Gupta & Ringius, 2001). Partially, this analysis holds truth if we look at individual member states' commitments, which have been largely underwhelming and in the past evidently failed to meet their Kyoto targets (Parker & Karlsson, 2010). Without a doubt, however, climate change as such has been, in comparison with other environmental fields, particularly high on the EU agenda. Table 1 provides an overview of EU legislation on climate change as listed in GLOBE. From the early 1990s onwards, the EU has repeatedly proclaimed to be aspiring a leading role within the international community in combating climate change (Dupont, 2016; Huitema et al., 2011; Oberthür & Roche Kelly, 2008; Selin & VanDeveer, 2015).

Empirically, we find that several mitigation measures were adopted at the EU level. This includes an increased use of renewable energy and combined heat and power installations; improved energy efficiency in buildings, industry, and household appliances; the reduction of CO_2 emissions from new passenger cars; abatement measures in the manufacturing industry; and measures to reduce emissions from landfills (European Environmental Agency (EEA), 2016). The EU's "own" (Bäckstrand & Elgström, 2013, p. 1373) landmark legislation is the Climate and

Table 1. EU Legislation on Climate Change

Directive/Regulation	Name/Short Description	Year	Related Sectors
	2020 Climate and Energy Package	2014	Mitigation framework; Carbon Pricing, Energy Supply, Energy Demand, Institutions/ Administrative arrangements
	2030 framework for climate and energy policies	2014	Mitigation framework; Carbon Pricing, Energy Supply, Energy Demand, Institutions/ Administrative arrangements
	European Energy Security Strategy	2014	Energy Supply, Energy Demand, Institutions/Administrative arrangements
517/2014	Fluorinated greenhouse gases	2014	Institutions/Administrative arrangements
	Common Agricultural Policy 2014–2020	2013	REDD+ and LULUCF, Institutions/Administrative arrangements
529/2013/EU	Land Use, Land Use Change and Forestry (LULUCF)	2013	REDD+ and LULUCF, Institutions/Administrative arrangements
2012/27/EU	Energy Efficiency	2012	Energy Supply, Energy Demand, Institutions/Administrative arrangements
510/2011	Emission performance standards for new light commercial vehicles	2011	Transportation
2010/30/EU	Energy labeling	2010	Energy Demand, Institutions/ Administrative arrangements
2009/33/EC	Clean and energy-efficient road transport vehicles	2009	Transportation
2009/125/EC	Eco-design	2009	Energy Demand
2009/72/EC	Third Energy Package	2009	Energy Supply, Institutions/ Administrative arrangements
406/2009/EC	Effort Sharing Decision	2009	Energy Demand, REDD+ and LULUCF, Transportation
443/2009	Emission performance standards for new passenger cars	2009	Carbon Pricing, Transportation
2009/30/EC	Fuel Quality	2009	Energy Supply, Energy Demand, Transportation
2009/31/EC	Geological storage of carbon dioxide	2009	Carbon Pricing, Energy Supply, Research and Development
2009/29/EC	Revision of the EU Emission Trading System (EU ETS)	2009	Carbon Pricing, Energy Supply, REDD+ and LULUCF, Transportation, Institutions/ Administrative arrangements
71/2007	Clean Sky	2008	Transportation, Research and Development
2004/8/EC	Cogeneration	2004	Energy Supply
2003/96/EC	Energy taxation	2004	Carbon Pricing, Energy Demand

Table 1. Continued

Directive/Regulation	Name/Short Description	Year	Related Sectors
280/2004/EC	Monitoring greenhouse gas emissions	2004	Institutions/Administrative arrangements
2003/87/EC	EU Emission Trading Scheme (EU ETS)	2003	Carbon Pricing, Energy Supply, Transportation, Institutions/ Administrative arrangements
2002/91/EC	Energy performance of buildings	2002	Energy Demand
1999/94/EC	Information on the fuel consumption and CO_2 emissions of new cars	2000	Energy Demand, Transportation

(*Source*: Nachmany et al., 2015)

Energy Package adopted in 2009, which pursues a triple goal: a 20 percent reduction of GHG emissions compared to 1990; a 20 percent share of renewables in EU energy consumption; and energy improvement by 20 percent (European Commission 2016a).

To attain these goals, the EU adopted the Emissions Trading Scheme (ETS) and an Effort Sharing Decision for non-ETS target sectors, which covers CO_2 emissions in buildings, transport and non-ETS industry, and non-CO_2 GHG emissions (Harmsen, Eichhammer & Wesselink, 2011). The EU ETS mostly covers GHG emissions from large-scale facilities in the power and industry sectors, as well as the aviation sector (Dessler & Parson, 2010). Overall, the EU ETS covers around 45 percent of the EU's GHG emissions (European Commission, 2016a). In addition, EU member states adopted binding annual targets until 2020 for cutting emissions in these sectors (compared to 2005) and a legal framework to promote the development and use of carbon capture and storage. The EU's mitigation efforts are supported by the energy efficiency action plan, which will help to achieve a 20 percent energy saving by 2020 (da Graça Carvalho, 2012). Overall, the EU's climate policy regarding mitigation is characterized by a multifaceted character, with the ETS as its centerpiece (Boasson, 2014).

By contrast, only in April 2013 did the European Commission adopt an EU strategy on adaptation to climate change. This strategy is markedly different from the mitigation measures promoted by the EU, as it mostly encourages the member states to adopt comprehensive adaptation strategies by means of knowledge production and sharing, as well as by providing financial assistance. Furthermore, the EU Commission supports the cities' role in adapting to climate change through the Mayor's Adapt Initiative, a voluntary commitment within the framework of the Covenant of Mayors (European Commission, 2016b). Altogether, the EU's role in climate adaptation policies is reduced and does not reflect its involvement in mitigation activities. This is due to the EU's lack of formal competence and authority in a variety of areas, such as in energy policy for buildings (Boasson, 2014).

Overall, much EU legislation is implemented at the local level (Marshall, 2005) and even more so if the regulation relates to environmental, energy, or communal policy aspects (Rezessy, Dimitrov, Urge-Vorsatz & Baruch, 2006). The literature refers to these municipal measures as "climate experiments" (Broto & Bulkeley, 2013, p. 92) as they provide strongly needed opportunities for testing new ideas and methods in the context of the enormous uncertainties that relate to climate change. This is why climate change is often described as being simultaneously global and local (Gupta, Van der Leeuw & de Moel, 2007). Following this line of reasoning, a broad strand of literature argues that local actors are better equipped to cope with transnational problems such as climate change (Barber, 2013).

A prominent development that we observed over the past few years is that cities are becoming more and more active in reducing CO_2 emissions, since they are responsible for emitting the majority of the world's GHG (Bulkeley, 2010; Bulkeley, Broto & Edwards, 2012). Here, systems such as Transnational Municipal Networks (TMNs) are important driving forces in tackling climate change (Betsill & Bulkeley, 2007; Broto & Bulkeley, 2013; Bulkeley et al., 2014; Hakelberg, 2014; Kern & Bulkeley, 2009). While energy policy and issues of power supply are most significant for many cities, other aspects of climate change such as health policy (Shipan & Volden, 2012) are discussed within the networks, too, highlighting the importance of the local level (Urpelainen, 2009).

This brief overview of climate policies within the EU shows that the legislative approach towards climate change is a dynamic but also diverse field. While the EU's aspiration for international leadership in combating climate change is clear (Oberthür & Roche Kelly, 2008), scholars have also noted that many European countries have adopted climate policies of varying ambition. While some nations such as Germany have been investing and actively pushing forward in the climate policy field, other countries such as Austria have lagged behind (Burck, Bals, Wittger & Beck, 2007; Burck, Marten & Bals, 2014). Thus, only by considering all levels of governance can a comprehensive overview of climate change legislation be achieved. While the current section focused on the European and local level, the following section investigates the national level and its corresponding dynamics of legislation on mitigation and adaptation policies. It is important to keep in mind that all national laws are adopted within the context of international negotiations and local circumstances.

Mitigation and Adaptation Policies at the National Level

We now focus on national-level legislation towards climate change in order to address our research questions. Throughout the analysis, we delineate in detail the used data sources, country sample, and operationalization of our dependent variable. The following empirical assessment uses two steps. Firstly, we provide an overview of the spread of mitigation as well as adaptation policies across the countries under scrutiny. Secondly, we relate our observations to earlier studies on the underlying drivers for climate change framework laws.

Data on National Climate Change Mitigation and Adaptation Frameworks

The respective dependent variables are extracted from the 2015 release of the GLOBE (Nachmany et al., 2015), which covers climate change legislation in 99 countries (treating the EU as a whole and single additional entity) from 1968 to 2015. More specifically, our unit of analysis is country-level data per year on climate change legislation during the sample period from 1990 to 2015. We focus on those 20 EU member states that are included in this dataset, which forces us to exclude Croatia, Cyprus, Estonia, Latvia, Lithuania, Luxembourg, Malta, and Slovenia from our analysis.

Thus far, the GLOBE is the most reliable, comprehensive and still growing dataset on national climate policy activities. One of the most noteworthy features is that it also includes legislation on adaptation. However, we are well aware of potential drawbacks of this data source (Fankhauser et al., 2015). With respect to our research, two limitations are most relevant. First, adaptation measures are rarely "stand-alone initiatives" (Dupuis & Biesbroek, 2013, p. 1487) as they are often embedded in various overarching legislative packages (see, section Policies for Mitigating and Adapting to Climate Change). Since the GLOBE only captures policies which explicitly refer to climate change (Nachmany et al., 2015), the available information just represents the lower bound of enacted adaptation policies. Second, the information available enables neither an analysis of the scope of climate policies nor allows one to make any informed statements on the effectiveness of these legislative efforts. Thus, our approach is purely enumerative, as any qualitative or outcome measures are not considered. Yet we do not simply count the amount of national legislation, but focus on the incidence of legislative adoption.

We argue that the domestic prominence of climate policies can be assessed by focusing on national framework legislation (Nachmany et al., 2015). It is in particular because of their comprehensive nature that framework legislation allows us to draw inferences on the influence of different aspects on a country's climate policy (see, section Policies for Mitigating and Adapting to Climate Change).

The Spread of National Climate Change Mitigation and Adaptation Frameworks within the EU

As a first step, Table 2 presents the amount of climate legislation that has been passed by the 20 EU members in our sample. With respect to our first research question we can observe that, with the exception of Hungary, all countries acted on climate change by passing frameworks laws on mitigation, adaptation, or a combination of the two.[1] Overall, 14 of the 20 countries targeted both approaches with framework legislation. Only Bulgaria, the Czech Republic, Greece, Poland, and Slovakia adopted a framework for either mitigation or adaptation.

Altogether, the information presented in Table 2 offers two more observations worth noting. Firstly, we do not observe any kind of coordinated behavior of mitigation and adaptation frameworks across countries. Thus, related to our second research question, we cannot identify a robust pattern with respect to the timing

Table 2. Overview of Climate Change Framework Legislation in Europe from 1990 to 2015

	Adoption date of Framework Law		
Country	Mitigation	Adaptation	Combined
Austria	2011	2012	
Belgium	2002	2010	
Bulgaria	2014		
Czech Republic	2004		
Denmark	2014	2008	
Finland	2015	2005	
France	2015	2011	
Germany	2014	2008	
Greece	2003		
Hungary			
Ireland		2012	2015
Italy	2007	2015	
Netherlands			2013
Poland		2013	
Portugal	2006	2010	
Romania			2013
Slovakia		2014	
Spain	2007	2006	
Sweden			2009
United Kingdom	2008	2013	
EU level	2009, 2014		

(*Source*: Nachmany et al., 2015)

or response strategies of EU member states towards climate change. To be sure, the literature has repeatedly argued that adaptation is only considered an option when mitigation efforts have failed or are expected to fail. In our data, however, we find five instances in which an adaptation framework law was passed before one for mitigation. And four countries adopted framework laws that commonly address mitigation and adaptation, in other words, both approaches were enacted at the same time. This therefore answers research question three, namely that the EU member states' approach towards climate change legislation is less uniform than expected.

Drivers for National Climate Change Mitigation and Adaptation Frameworks within the EU

In order to investigate these findings further, we relate our observations to earlier comprehensive assessments on the underlying national as well as international drivers for both mitigation and adaptation policies. Foremost, this refers to the contributions of Fankhauser, Gennaioli and Collins (2014, 2015, 2016), who used a previous version of the GLOBE (Nachmany et al., 2014) to investigate 66 countries across various geographical regions. Overall, scholarly literature so far has primarily used the GLOBE to support and refer to the rapid increase in national-level legislation on climate change (Benson & Lorenzoni, 2014; Jordan et al., 2015; Watts et al., 2015). We supplement these studies by relying on the most recent data and by shifting the focus towards EU member states as well as on the dynamics between mitigation and adaptation policies.

The focal explanatory variables are selected in accordance with earlier studies and comprise, in short, the previous diffusion of framework laws (Jordan & Huitema, 2014a,b; Massey et al., 2014), and the political ideology of the acting government. While Fankhauser et al. (2015) found that within their sample set of countries climate change was very much a two-party concern, the literature suggests that left governments are more inclined to pass environmental legislation (Aklin & Urpelainen, 2013; Jensen & Spoon, 2011). In fact, left-wing governments seem to be more in favor of a comprehensive legislative approach and more prone to adopt framework laws (Fankhauser et al., 2015). Our analysis examines if one can reach the same verdict when confined to looking at EU members by relying on data on the relative power position of left parties in government (Government, left party) as provided by Armingeon, Isler, Knöpfel, Weisstanner and Engler (2016).

Fankhauser et al. (2016) further argue that the propensity to adopt climate laws is influenced by the passage of similar laws elsewhere (Busch & Jörgens, 2005). In the European context, peer behavior should be particularly influential given the ongoing exchange of views, opinions, and ideas as well as the overall commitment of the EU member states to strive for international leadership in combating climate change (see section Mitigation and Adaptation Policies at the European and Local Level and Oberthür & Roche Kelly, 2008). Yet, keeping our previous findings in mind, this spread seems to require quite some time, which hints towards an alignment gap across EU members. We investigate this by means of horizontal diffusion variables (for a conceptual overview see Jahn & Stephan, 2015) that we generated ourselves based on the data provided by the GLOBE. These cover the number of mitigation and adaptation frameworks ("Diffusion, mitigation"/"Diffusion, adaptation") in other countries within the sample. For this specific operationalization, we follow Fankhauser et al. (2016) by considering all EU members and not just neighboring countries as the relevant peer group (for an overview on spatiotemporal-autoregressive processes see Franzese, Hays & Cook, 2016).

Selected control variables are also based on these earlier investigations (Fankhauser et al., 2014, 2015, 2016). They cover information on political, sociodemographic, economic, and environmental country characteristics. The summary statistics of the variables together with their definition and the sources from which the data were extracted are presented in alphabetical order in Table 3.

While our focus on the adoption of legislation would suggest relying on an event-history model, the data structure does not allow for the use of this estimation technique. This results from the insufficient variance of the obligatory explanatory and necessary control variables within the sample of EU countries. We deal with this predicament in two ways. As discussed, we rely on the findings of previous studies that investigated a larger sample (Fankhauser et al., 2015, 2016). Thus, our investigations constitute a specific extension of these contributions with respect to our specific research interest. In addition, we use logistic regression models that enable us to address potential time dependence through cubic splines and polynomial approximation (Carter & Signorino, 2010).[2]

Table 3. Summary Statistics of the Explanatory Variables

Variable	Obs	Mean	Std. Dev.	Min	Max	Short Description	Source
CO_2 per capita	520	8.03	2.19	3.92	13.71	CO_2 emissions in metric tons per capita	WDI
Diffusion, adaptation	520	3.73	4.65	0	17	Cumulative amount of adaptation frameworks in other countries within the sample	Own calculations based on Nachmany et al. (2015)
Diffusion, mitigation	520	3.11	4.92	0	17	Cumulative amount of mitigation frameworks in other countries within the sample	Own calculations based on Nachmany et al. (2015)
Executive initiative	520	0.09	0.29	0	1	Indicates whether the respective framework was passed by the executive branch of government and not superseded by a legislative act	Nachmany et al. (2015)
Energy, nuclear	520	22.77	22.93	0	19.67	Electricity production from nuclear sources (% of total)	WDI
Energy, renewable	520	18.75	18.08	0.58	78.00	Electricity production from renewable sources (% of total)	WDI
EU mitigation framework	520	0.27	0.44	0	1	Indicates whether a climate change mitigation framework was previously passed at the European level	Nachmany et al. (2015)
Federalism index	511	0.34	0.72	0	2	Indicates whether the respective country is categorized with "no" (0), "weak" (1) or "strong" (2) federalism	CPDS
GDP	520	26.32	1.37	23.00	28.98	GDP (log) in 2015 U.S. $	WDI
Government, left party	499	41.07	38.33	0	100	Relative power position of left parties in government	CPDS
Laws count	520	3.46	4.33	0	21	Cumulative amount of climate change legislation in this country	Own calculations based on Nachmany et al. (2015)
Population density	520	1.44	1.08	0.16	5.00	1,000 people per km² of land area	WDI
Resource rent	520	0.86	1.25	0	9.36	Total natural resources rents as % of GDP	WDI
Veto player	520	4.66	6.27	0	30.85	Veto player score over time	Jahn (2016)

Note: The control variables are all selected in accordance with earlier studies on the political economy of climate change legislation (see, section Mitigation and Adaptation Policies at the National Level) and most of them could directly be obtained from the respective data source. The only measures based on own calculations (besides diffusion) are "Laws, count" which depicts the amount of "ordinary" climate change laws passed within the respective country and "EU mitigation framework" which indicates if a respective framework was passed at the European level. Further robustness checks (including supplementary control variables) are available for interested readers upon request to the authors.

Abbreviations: CPDS = Comparative Political Data Set (Armingeon et al., 2016); WDI = World Development Indicators of the World Bank.

Our variable of interest is the incidence of adopting a mitigation or adaptation framework. For our following estimation, we do not distinguish whether or not the framework was passed along with the respective other or alone. Townshend et al. (2013a) argue that every country's approach to climate change is distinct and first and foremost mirrors a country's respective institutional context and capacities, among others. This is why we are interested if countries pass comprehensive climate legislation, and not if this happens simultaneously. Accordingly, we split combined frameworks on mitigation and adaptation into one adaptation and one mitigation framework. From this, it follows that we analyze two dependent variables. The findings for the causes driving the adoption of a mitigation framework law are presented in Table 4 and the findings for the adaptation framework laws are depicted in Table 5. In both cases, we specifically address time dependence by including models with cubic polynomial approximation (Model 1) and cubic splines (Model 2). However, we do not use these terms when expanding the model specification to the measures of legislative diffusion, as

Table 4. Estimates for Mitigation Frameworks

DV: Mitigation Framework	(1)	(2)	(3)	(4)	(5)
CO_2 per capita	0.08	0.09	0.11	0.11	0.08
	(0.18)	(0.18)	(0.22)	(0.22)	(0.21)
Energy, nuclear	−0.02	−0.02	−0.02	−0.02	−0.02
	(0.01)	(0.01)	(0.01)	(0.01)	(0.01)
Energy, renewable	0.01	0.01	0.01	0.00	0.01
	(0.02)	(0.02)	(0.01)	(0.01)	(0.01)
Executive initiative	0.81	0.75	0.98	0.97	1.02
	(0.72)	(0.72)	(0.82)	(0.83)	(0.82)
Federalism index	0.11	0.08	0.18	0.20	0.22
	(0.29)	(0.31)	(0.24)	(0.28)	(0.28)
GDP	−0.20	−0.17	−0.04	−0.07	−0.13
	(0.21)	(0.21)	(0.22)	(0.27)	(0.29)
Government, left party	0.03***	0.03***	0.03***	0.03***	0.03***
	(0.01)	(0.01)	(0.01)	(0.01)	(0.01)
Population density	0.34*	0.34*	0.24	0.24	0.29
	(0.20)	(0.20)	(0.19)	(0.19)	(0.19)
Resource rent	−0.66	−0.69	−0.48	−0.48	−0.57
	(0.52)	(0.53)	(0.47)	(0.46)	(0.49)
Veto player	−0.01	−0.01	−0.02	−0.02	−0.02
	(0.08)	(0.08)	(0.07)	(0.07)	(0.07)
Diffusion, mitigation			0.19**	0.17**	0.27**
			(0.07)	(0.08)	(0.12)
Laws count				0.02	0.03
				(0.07)	(0.07)
EU mitigation framework					−1.32
					(1.15)
Polynomials	Yes	No	No	No	No
Splines	No	Yes	No	No	No
N	491	491	491	491	491
Pseudo R^2	0.292	0.286	0.213	0.214	0.223
AIC	118.08	118.79	124.09	126.04	126.83
BIC	176.83	177.54	174.45	180.59	185.58

Note: All models are estimated with robust standard errors clustered at the country level. The table depicts every explanatory variable's regression coefficient, significance, and standard error (in brackets).

$^*p < 0.1$; $^{**}p < 0.05$; $^{***}p < 0.01$.

Table 5. Estimates for Adaptation Frameworks

DV: Adaptation Framework	(1)	(2)	(3)	(4)
CO_2 per capita	0.05	0.05	−0.05	−0.04
	(0.17)	(0.18)	(0.19)	(0.19)
Energy, nuclear	−0.01	−0.01	−0.00	−0.00
	(0.01)	(0.01)	(0.01)	(0.01)
Energy, renewable	−0.01	−0.01	0.00	0.00
	(0.01)	(0.01)	(0.01)	(0.01)
Executive initiative	2.30***	2.32***	2.52***	2.51***
	(0.75)	(0.75)	(0.72)	(0.71)
Federalism index	−0.02	−0.00	0.18	0.18
	(0.27)	(0.26)	(0.23)	(0.24)
GDP	−0.03	−0.04	0.11	0.06
	(0.21)	(0.21)	(0.19)	(0.17)
Government, left party	0.01	0.00	0.00	0.00
	(0.01)	(0.01)	(0.01)	(0.01)
Population density	−0.16	−0.13	−0.04	−0.04
	(0.16)	(0.16)	(0.12)	(0.13)
Resource rent	−0.54	−0.53	−0.07	−0.09
	(0.44)	(0.42)	(0.36)	(0.40)
Veto player	0.15***	0.15***	0.11***	0.12***
	(0.04)	(0.04)	(0.04)	(0.04)
Diffusion, adaptation			0.15***	0.13*
			(0.04)	(0.07)
Laws count				0.04
				(0.08)
Polynomials	Yes	No	No	No
Splines	No	Yes	No	No
N	491	491	491	491
Pseudo R^2	0.373	0.378	0.280	0.281
AIC	112.13	111.48	120.62	122.44
BIC	170.88	170.23	170.98	176.99

Note: All models are estimated with robust standard errors clustered at the country level. The table depicts every explanatory variable's regression coefficient, significance, and standard error (in brackets).
$^*p < 0.1$; $^{**}p < 0.05$; $^{***}p < 0.01$.

those variables are strongly correlated and do not allow the optimization algorithm to converge.

Focusing on our vocal explanatory variables, we find a stable and significant positive effect of left government parties on mitigation frameworks (Table 4, Models 1–5) as well as strong evidence that countries adopt climate change frameworks when other EU members have previously done so for both mitigation (Table 4, Models 3, 4, and 5) and adaptation (Table 5, Models 3 and 4). In sum, our results are comparable to other studies that argue that whether or not a country is actively engaged in the field of climate legislation is influenced by how other countries previously acted (Fankhauser et al., 2016). We supplement these past findings by using only EU countries and focusing on framework laws. Yet, we can still confirm the positive effect of peer behavior in this specific context.

Framework legislation has been judged to possess a "signaling character" because such legislation provides the basis for further negotiations (Fankhauser et al., 2015, p. 58) and serves as a good indicator for more and supplementary laws on climate change. This relationship does not hold for both directions, as a larger amount of climate change laws within a country does not significantly affect the passing of framework legislation (Tables 4, Model 4 and 5; Table 5, Model 4).

Looking at the controls, we observe that a higher population density is associated with mitigation frameworks (Table 4, Models 1 and 2), but the effect becomes insignificant when controlling for diffusion. More importantly, positive and significant effects of veto players and executive initiatives for adaptation frameworks are noticeable (Table 5, Models 1–4). That climate change adaptation in the EU is mainly based upon executive instruments represents an interesting avenue for further research, in particular when investigating qualitative information.

With respect to veto players, the initial approach would suggest that more veto points make the adoption of a comprehensive climate framework more challenging (Tsebelis, 2002). Yet, our finding is well in line with recent contributions on institutions and their corresponding environmental performance (Jahn, 2016; Knill, Schulze & Tosun, 2012). Here, less (complex) institutional procedures might undermine efforts to improve the environmental record (Wälti, 2004). Taking a deeper look at the data, it becomes evident that we observe a somewhat "Nordic"-country effect. Finland (2005), Denmark (2008), and Sweden (2009) adopted framework legislation on adaptation relatively *early* in comparison with other EU countries, alongside with Spain (2006) and Germany (2008). These countries are characterized by a particularly high veto player score, which is driving the respective estimation results.[3] Overall, this finding is in line with studies that examine the efforts of Nordic countries with regard to climate change (Juhola et al., 2012) and potential institutional safeguards for the environment (Jahn, 2016).

Summing up, the findings show that the odds of adopting a mitigation framework law increase with having a left government in place. Most importantly, the adoption of a framework is affected by the passing of such laws in other countries. We agree with Fankhauser et al. (2016, p. 7) that peer behavior might serve as a "powerful predictor" of how countries behave regarding the adoption of climate framework legislation and supplement that this holds true for both approaches. Here we want to note that, clearly, diffusion takes place. However, considering the observed time gaps across countries in terms of adopting mitigation and adaptation frameworks, we still need to point out existing delays across EU members. In addition, for adaptation, we find that within the EU members under scrutiny the number of veto players and a well-disposed executive branch of government have a positive impact on the chances of adoption.

Conclusion

In this paper we investigated the legislative dynamics of mitigation and adaptation policies in the EU. We showed that by the end of 2015, with the exception of Hungary, all of the 20 EU countries under scrutiny adopted a framework law that addresses mitigation, adaptation, or both. By considering these national as well as European level legislation we can, overall, substantiate the EU's aspiration for international leadership in combating climate change (Bäckstrand & Elgström, 2013; Oberthür & Roche Kelly, 2008). In a similar way, our analysis affirmed previous studies (Fankhauser et al., 2015, 2016) in that peer behavior indeed has a positive impact on the likelihood of adopting a framework law (regardless of whether it is adaptation or mitigation).

Taking a closer look at our findings, we contribute to the state of research in three ways. First, the approach of the EU states in responding to climate change is less homogenous than one would have expected based on the EU's climate change leadership aspiration. While most countries act on climate change and use mitigation as well as adaptation measures, both approaches do not exist in all countries and the timing as well as the sequence of the policies differ greatly. Thus, legislative activity concerning climate change within Europe does not convey a consistent image to the outside world. One broader implication of this finding is that the EU might fail to act as an international leader in the field, as it does not represent a coherent position on (effectively) implementing climate policy (Gupta & Ringius, 2001; Marcinkiewicz & Tosun, 2015; Parker & Karlsson, 2010).

Second, we found the patterns regarding the temporal order of the passage of mitigation and adaptation framework laws to be noteworthy. In our data we could not see whether or not governments embrace adaptation measures only as soon as they perceive mitigation measures to be insufficient. Rather, governments seem to pursue a dual strategy. In the future, it is likely that adaptation will gain even greater prominence.

Our third and last observation is that mitigation and adaptation measures are equally prominent. Yet again, one can imagine that this dynamic is likely to continue as the Paris Agreement gave greater prominence to adaptation. Now, countries are formally asked to submit their NDCs, in which they report their efforts not only for mitigation but also for adaptation on a regular five-year basis. This is particularly noteworthy as it presents an empirical finding that is not prominently depicted within the current climate change literature, which instead reports that mitigation efforts remain at the forefront in terms of legislation activity. Supporting this line of assessment further is that at COP 22 in Marrakech, negotiations also prominently focused on establishing NDC Partnerships programs to support the formulation and implementation of NDCs in developing countries. Again, both mitigation and adaptation under the NDCs were c issues in the debate.

While we believe that these are important findings, we also acknowledge several limitations of this study. Empirically, the most evident limitation is that we had to rely on policy density and could not seize the empirical insights yielded by using an indicator that draws on policy intensity (Knill et al., 2012; Schaffrin et al., 2014, 2015). In other words, our dataset is suitable for assessing the presence or absence of policies (policy density), but not their quality (intensity). A second limitation is that our dataset does not cover all 28 EU member states and is restricted to climate action at the national level. In addition, while we addressed both mitigation and adaptation measures, we did not aim to formulate a theoretical and systematic connection between them (Kane & Shogren, 2000; Klein et al.,

2007). In our view, these limitations provide an opportunity for future studies to advance the state of research on the basis of our findings. Another such opportunity might be to thoroughly investigate the "mixture" of framework legislation. As we are well aware of the importance of multi-sectoral policy approaches to climate change, we deem looking at the various sectors of framework laws an important future avenue for research. Finally, obtaining qualitative information on the various country cases as well as particular policies and frameworks would enable us to infer assessments regarding the effectiveness of these legislative activities.

Andreas Fleig is a postdoctoral researcher at the Institute of Political Science at Heidelberg University. His research addresses energy policy and the regulation of environmental risks.

Nicole M. Schmidt is a PhD candidate at the Institute of Political Science at Heidelberg University. Her research addresses comparative EU and global climate change policy, with a focus on adaptation.

Jale Tosun is a Professor of Political Science at the Institute of Political Science, Heidelberg University. She works on a range of topics in the fields of public policy, international political economy, European integration, and public administration.

Notes

This work was supported by the COST Action IS1309 "Innovations in Climate Governance: Sources, Patterns and Effects" (INOGOV) and the Fritz Thyssen Foundation under Grant Number: 10.13.2.141.

1. Please note that, as our analysis focuses on framework laws, we do not discuss "ordinary" legislation on single issues. Thus, we do not argue that Hungary did not pass any climate change law; they just did not adopt an overarching legislative framework in this policy field. Why Hungary behaved that way is subsequently an interesting avenue for future research, but addressing these questions lies beyond the scope of this analysis.
2. An alternative measurement of the dependent variables would have resulted in count variables. However, considering that our count variable would only vary between 0 and 1 (as no country passed more than one framework on mitigation or adaptation), this approach would not be appropriate for the present investigation.
3. Based on a Mann-Whitney U-test we see that the veto player scores of Denmark, Finland, Germany, Spain, and Sweden (observations 130; mean 11.13; standard deviation 7.96) are significantly different from the other 15 countries in our sample (observations 390; mean 2.50; standard deviation 3.57) and all other 93 countries in the GLOBE data set (observations 2418; mean 0.94; standard deviation 3.68).

References

Adelle, C., and D. Russel. 2013. "Climate Policy Integration: A Case of déjà vu?" *Environmental Policy and Governance* 23 (1): 1–12.

Adger, W., N. Arnell, and E. Tompkins. 2005. "Successful Adaptation to Climate Change Across Scales." *Global Environmental Change* 15 (2): 77–86.

Adger, W., S. Huq, K. Brown, D. Conway, and M. Hulme. 2003. "Adaptation to Climate Change in the Developing World." *Progress in Development Studies* 3 (3): 179–95.

Aklin, M., and J. Urpelainen. 2013. "Political Competition, Path Dependence, and the Strategy of Sustainable Energy Transitions." *American Journal of Political Science* 57: 643–65.

Armingeon, K., C. Isler, L. Knöpfel, D. Weisstanner, and S. Engler. 2016. *Comparative Political Data Set 1960–2014*. Bern: Institute of Political Science, University of Berne.

Bäckstrand, K., and O. Elgström. 2013. "The EU's Role in Climate Change Negotiations: From Leader to 'Leadiator'." *Journal of European Public Policy* 20 (10): 1369–86.

Barber, B. 2013. *If Mayors Ruled the World: Dysfunctional Nations, Rising Cities*. New Haven, CT: Yale University Press.

Bauer, A., J. Feichtinger, and R. Steurer. 2012. "The Governance of Climate Change Adaptation in 10 OECD Countries: Challenges and Approaches." *Journal of Environmental Policy & Planning* 14 (3): 279–304.

Benson, D., and I. Lorenzoni. 2014. "Examining the Scope for National Lesson-drawing on Climate Governance." *The Political Quarterly* 85 (2): 202–11.

Bernauer, T. 2013. "Climate Change Politics." *Annual Review of Political Science* 16: 421–48.

Bernauer, T, and T. Böhmelt. 2013. "National Climate Policies in International Comparison." *Environmental Science and Policy* 25: 196–206.

Betsill, M., and H. Bulkeley. 2007. "Looking Back and Thinking Ahead: A Decade of Cities and Climate Change Research." *Local Environment: The International Journal of Justice and Sustainability* 12: 447–56.

Biesbroek, R., R. Swart, and W. van der Knaap. 2009. "The Mitigation–Adaptation Dichotomy and the Role of Spatial Planning." *Habitat International* 33 (3): 230–7.

Boasson, E. 2014. *National Climate Policy: A Multi-field Approach*. New York, NY: Routledge.

Broto, V., and H. Bulkeley. 2013. "A Survey of Urban Climate Change Experiments in 100 Cities." *Global Environmental Change* 23 (1): 92–102.

Brouwer, S., T. Rayner, and D. Huitema. 2013. "Mainstreaming Climate Policy: The Case of Climate Adaptation and the Implementation of EU Water Policy." *Environment and Planning C: Government and Policy* 31 (1): 134–53.

Bulkeley, H. 2010. "Cities and the Governing of Climate Change." *Annual Review of Environment and Resources* 35: 229–53.

Bulkeley, H., L. Andonova, M. Betsill, D. Compagnon, T. Hale, M. Hoffmann, P. Newell, M. Paterson, C. Roger, and S. VanDeveer. 2014. *Transnational Climate Change Governance*. Cambridge: Cambridge University Press.

Bulkeley, H., V. Broto, and G. Edwards. 2012. "Bringing Climate Change to the City: Towards Low Carbon Urbanism?" *Local Environment* 17 (5): 545–51.

Burck, J., C. Bals, B. Wittger, and M. Beck. 2007. *The Climate Change Performance Index 2007* [Online]. http://germanwatch.org/klima/ccpi07.pdf. Accessed October 23, 2016.

Burck, J., F. Marten, and C. Bals. 2014. *The Climate Change Performance Index 2014* [Online]. https://germanwatch.org/de/download/8599.pdf. Accessed November 23, 2016.

Busch, P., and H. Jörgens. 2005. "The International Sources of Policy Convergence: Explaining the Spread of Environmental Policy Innovations." *Journal of European Public Policy* 12 (5): 860–84.

Carter, D., and C. Signorino. 2010. "Back to the Future: Modeling Time Dependence in Binary Data." *Political Analysis* 18 (3): 271–92.

Cheon, A., and J. Urpelainen. 2012. "Oil Prices and Energy Technology Innovation: An Empirical Analysis." *Global Environmental Change* 22 (2): 407–17.

Damro, C., I. Hardie, and D. MacKenzie. 2008. "The EU and Climate Change Policy: Law, Politics and Prominence at Different Levels." *Journal of Contemporary European Research* 4 (3): 179–92.

Daniell, K., M. Costa, N. Ferrand, A. Kingsborough, P. Coad, and I. Ribarova. 2011. "Aiding Multi-level Decision-making Processes for Climate Change Mitigation and Adaptation." *Regional Environmental Change* 11 (2): 243–58.

Dessler, A., and E. Parson. 2010. *The Science and Politics of Global Climate Change: A Guide to the Debate*. Cambridge: Cambridge University Press.

Dubash, N., M. Hagemann, N. Höhne, and P. Upadhyaya. 2013. "Developments in National Climate Change Mitigation Legislation and Strategy." *Climate Policy* 13: 649–64.

Dupont, C. 2016. *Climate Policy Integration into EU Energy Policy: Progress and Prospects*. London: Routledge.

Dupuis, J., and R. Biesbroek. 2013. "Comparing Apples and Oranges: The Dependent Variable Problem in Comparing and Evaluating Climate Change Adaptation Policies." *Global Environmental Change* 23 (6): 1476–87.

Eisenack, K., S. Moser, E. Hoffmann, R. Klein, C. Oberlack, A. Pechan, M. Rotter, and C. Termeer. 2014. "Explaining and Overcoming Barriers to Climate Change Adaptation." *Nature Climate Change* 4 (10): 867–72.

European Commission. 2016a. *2020 Climate & Energy Package* [Online]. http://ec.europa.eu/clima/policies/strategies/2020/index_en.htm. Accessed June 23, 2016.

European Commission. 2016b. *Covenant of Mayors* [Online]. http://edgar.jrc.ec.europa.eu/covenant_of_mayors.php. Accessed November 23, 2016.

European Environmental Agency (EEA). 2016. *Climate Change Policies* [Online]. http://www.eea.europa.eu/themes/climate/policy-context. Accessed July 13, 2016.

Falkner, R., H. Stephan, and J. Vogler. 2010. "International Climate Policy After Copenhagen: Towards a 'Building Blocks' Approach." *Global Policy* 1: 252–62.

Fankhauser, S. 2010. "The Costs of Adaptation." *Wiley Interdisciplinary Reviews: Climate Change* 1 (1): 23–30.

Fankhauser, S., C. Gennaioli, and M. Collins. 2014. "Domestic Dynamics and International Influence. What Explains the Passage of Climate Change Legislation." Working Paper 156, Grantham Research Institute, London School of Economics.

———. 2015. "The Political Economy of Passing Climate Change Legislation: Evidence from a Survey." *Global Environmental Change* 35: 52–61.

———. 2016. "Do international Factors Influence the Passage of Climate Change Legislation?" *Climate Policy* 16 (3): 318–31.

Feindt, P., and A. Flynn. 2009. "Policy Stretching and Institutional Layering: British Food Policy Between Security, Safety, Quality, Health and Climate Change." *British Politics* 4 (3): 386–414.

Franzese, R., J. Hays, and S. Cook. 2016. "Spatial- and Spatiotemporal-Autoregressive Probit Models of Interdependent Binary Outcomes." *Political Science Research and Methods* 4 (1): 151–73.

Gillard, R., and K. Lock. 2016. "Blowing Policy Bubbles: Rethinking Emissions Targets and Low-carbon Energy Policies in the UK." *Journal of Environmental Policy and Planning* 1–16. doi: 10.1080/1523908X.2016.1266931.

da Graça Carvalho, M. 2012. "EU Energy and Climate Change Strategy." *Energy* 40 (1): 19–22.

Gupta, J., and L. Ringius. 2001. "The EU's Climate Leadership: Reconciling Ambition and Reality." *International Environmental Agreements: Politics, Law and Economics* 1 (2): 281–99.

Gupta, J. 2007. "The multi-level governance challenge of climate change." *Environmental Sciences* 4 (3): 131–7.

Gupta, J., K. Van der Leeuw, and H. de Moel. 2007. "Climate Change: A "Glocal" Problem Requiring "Glocal" Action." *Environmental Sciences* 4 (3): 139–44.

Hakelberg, L. 2014. "Governance by Diffusion: Transnational Municipal Networks and the Spread of Local Climate Strategies in Europe." *Global Environmental Politics* 14 (1): 107–29.

Harmsen, R., W. Eichhammer, and B. Wesselink. 2011. "Imbalance in Europe's Effort Sharing Decision: Scope for Strengthening Incentives for Energy Savings in the Non-ETS Sectors." *Energy Policy* 39 (10): 6636–49.

Hickmann, T. 2013. "Private Authority in Global Climate Governance: The Case of the Clean Development Mechanism." *Climate and Development* 5 (1): 46–54.

Hildén, M. 2011. "The Evolution of Climate Policies—The Role of Learning and Evaluations." *Journal of Cleaner Production* 19 (16): 1798–811.

Howlett, M., and J. Rayner. 2006. "Convergence and Divergence in 'New Governance' Arrangements: Evidence from European Integrated Natural Resource Strategies." *Journal of Public Policy* 26 (02): 167–89.

Huitema, D., A. Jordan, E. Massey, T. Rayner, H. van Asselt, C. Haug, R. Hildingsson, S. Monni, and J. Stripple. 2011. "The Evaluation of Climate Policy: Theory and Emerging Practice in Europe." *Policy Science* 44 (2): 179–98.

Huitema, D., E. Mostert, W. Egas, S. Moellenkamp, C. Pahl-Wostl, and R. Yalcin. 2009. "Adaptive Water Governance. Assessing Adaptive Management from a Governance Perspective." *Ecology and Society* 4 (1): 26.

IPCC. 2014. Impacts, Adaptation, and Vulnerability. Part A: Global and Sectoral Aspects. Contribution of Working Group II to the Fifth Assessment Report of the Intergovernmental Panel on Climate Change. Cambridge University Press.

Jahn, D. 2016. "*The Politics of Environmental Performance. Institutions and Preferences in Industrialized Democracies.*" Cambridge: Cambridge University Press.

Jahn, D., and S. Stephan. 2015. "The Problem of Interdependence." In *Comparative Politics—Theoretical and Methodological Challenges*, ed. D. Braun, and M. Maggetti. Cheltenham: Edward Elgar Publishing, 14–54.

Javeline, D. 2014. "The Most Important Topic Political Scientists Are Not Studying: Adapting to Climate Change." *Perspectives on Politics* 12 (2): 420–34.

Jensen, B., and J.-J. Spoon. 2011. "Testing the 'Party Matters' Thesis: Explaining Progress towards Kyoto Protocol." *Political Studies* 59: 99–115.

Jeuland, M., and S. Pattanayak. 2012. "Benefits and Costs of Improved Cookstoves: Assessing the Implications of Variability in Health, Forest and Climate Impacts." *PLoS ONE* 7 (2): 30338.

Jones, R., P. Dettmann, G. Park, M. Rogers, and T. White. 2007. "The Relationship Between Adaptation and Mitigation in Managing Climate Change Risks: A Regional Response from North Central Victoria, Australia." *Mitigation and Adaptation Strategies for Global Change* 12 (5): 685–712.

Jordan, A., and D. Huitema. 2014a. "Policy Innovation in a Changing Climate: Sources, Patterns and Effects." *Global Environmental Change* 29: 387–94.

———. 2014b. "Innovations in Climate Policy: The Politics of Invention, Diffusion, and Evaluation." *Environmental Politics* 23 (5): 715–34.

Jordan, A., D. Huitema, M. Hildén, H. van Asselt, T. Rayner, J. Schoenefeld, J. Tosun, J. Foster, and E. Boasson. 2015. "Emergence of Polycentric Climate Governance and its Future Prospects." *Nature Climate Change* 5 (11): 977–82.

Juhola, S., L. Peltonen, and P. Niemi. 2012. "The Ability of Nordic Countries to Adapt to Climate Change: Characterising Adaptive Capacity at the Regional Level." *Local Environment* 17 (6–7): 717–34.

Kane, S., and J. Shogren. 2000. "Linking Adaptation and Mitigation in Climate Change Policy." *Climatic Change* 45 (1): 75–102.

Kern, K., and H. Bulkeley. 2009. "Cities, Europeanization and Multi-level Governance: Governing Climate Change Through Transnational Municipal Networks." *Journal of Common Market Studies* 47 (2): 309–32.

Keskitalo, E. 2010a. "Introduction—Adaptation to Climate Change in Europe: Theoretical Framework and Study Design." In *Developing Adaptation Policy and Practice in Europe: Multi-level Governance of Climate Change*, ed. E. Keskitalo. Umeå, Sweden: Springer, 1–38.

———. 2010b. *Developing Adaptation Policy and Practice in Europe: Multi-level Governance of Climate Change*. Dordrecht: Springer.

King, D. 2004. "Climate Change Science: Adapt, Mitigate, or Ignore?." *Science* 303 (5655): 176–7.

Klein, R., S. Huq, F. Denton, T. Downing, R. Richels, J. Robinson, and F. Toth. 2007. "Inter-relationships between Adaptation and Mitigation." In *Climate Change 2007: Impacts, Adaptation and Vulnerability*, ed. M.L. Parry, O.F. Canziani, J.P. Palutikof, P.J. van der Linden, and C.E. Hanson. Cambridge: Cambridge University Press, 745–77.

Knill, C., K. Schulze, and J. Tosun. 2012. "Regulatory Policy Outputs and Impacts: Exploring a Complex Relationship." *Regulation & Governance* 6 (4): 427–44.

Lachapelle, E., and M. Paterson. 2013. "Drivers of National Climate Policy." *Climate Policy* 13: 547–71.

Lechtenböhmer, S., and H. Luhmann. 2013. "Decarbonization and Regulation of Germany's Electricity System After Fukushima." *Climate Policy* 13 (01): 146–54.

Lederer, M. 2011. "From CDM to REDD+—What Do We Know for Setting Up Effective and Legitimate Carbon Governance?" *Ecological Economics* 70 (11): 1900–7.

Lesnikowski, A., J. Ford, R. Biesbroek, L. Berrang-Ford, and S. Heymann. 2016. "National-level Progress on Adaptation." *Nature Climate Change* 6 (3): 261–4.

Levin, K., B. Cashore, S. Bernstein, and G. Auld. 2012. "Overcoming the Tragedy of Super Wicked Problems: Constraining Our Future Selves to Ameliorate Global Climate Change." *Policy Sciences* 45 (2): 123–52.

Lipscy, P., and L. Schipper. 2013. "Energy Efficiency in the Japanese Transport Sector." *Energy Policy* 56: 248–58.

Maor, M., J. Tosun, and A. Jordan. 2017. "Proportionate and Disproportionate Policy Responses to Climate Change: Core Concepts and Empirical Applications." *Journal of Environmental Policy & Planning* 1–13. doi: 10.1080/1523908X.2017.1281730.

Marcinkiewicz, K., and J. Tosun. 2015. "Contesting Climate Change: Mapping the Political Debate in Poland." *East European Politics* 31 (2): 187–207.

Marshall, A. 2005. "Europeanization at the Urban Level: Local Actors, Institutions and the Dynamics of Multi-level Interaction." *Journal of European Public Policy* 12 (4): 668–86.

Martens, P., D. McEvoy, and C. Chang. 2009. "The Climate Change Challenge: Linking Vulnerability, Adaptation, and Mitigation." *Current Opinion in Environmental Sustainability* 1 (1): 14–8.

Massey, E., R. Biesbroek, D. Huitema, and A. Jordan. 2014. "Climate Policy Innovation: The Adoption and Diffusion of Adaptation Policies Across Europe." *Global Environmental Change* 29: 434–43.

Matthews, H., T. Graham, S. Keverian, C. Lamontagne, D. Seto, and T. Smith. 2014. "National Contributions to Observed Global Warming." *Environmental Research Letters* 9 (1): 014010.

Moser, S. 2012. "Adaptation, Mitigation, and Their Disharmonious Discontents: An Essay." *Climatic Change* 111 (2): 165–75.

Nachmany, M., S. Fankhauser, J. Davidová, N. Kingsmill, T. Landesman, H. Roppongi, P. Schleifer et al. 2015. *The 2015 Global Climate Legislation Study—A Review of Climate Change Legislation in 99 Countries* [Online]. Seacourt Ltd. http://www.lse.ac.uk/GranthamInstitute/wp-content/uploads/2015/05/Global_climate_legislation_study_20151.pdf. Accessed June 28, 2016.

Nachmany, M., S. Fankhauser, T. Townshend, M. Collins, T. Landesman, A. Matthews, C. Pavese, K. Rietig, P. Schleifer, and J. Setzer. 2014. *The GLOBE Climate Legislation Study: A Review of Climate Change Legislation in 66 Countries* [Online]. Carbon Copy Communications Ltd. http://www.lse.ac.uk/GranthamInstitute/wp-content/uploads/2014/03/Globe2014.pdf. Accessed March 29, 2017.

Nalau, J., B. Preston, and M. Maloney. 2015. "Is Adaptation a Local Responsibility?" *Environmental Science & Policy* 48: 89–98.

Negro, S., F Alkemade, and M. Hekkert. 2012. "Why Does Renewable Energy Diffuse So Slowly? A Review of Innovation System Problems." *Renewable and Sustainable Energy Reviews* 16 (6): 3836–46.

Nilsson, M., and Å. Persson. 2012. "Can Earth System Interactions be Governed? Governance Functions for Linking Climate Change Mitigation With Land Use, Freshwater and Biodiversity Protection." *Ecological Economics* 81: 10–20.

Obergassel, W., C. Arens, L. Hermwille, N. Kreibich, F. Mersmann, H. Ott, and H. Wang Helmreich. 2017. *Setting Sails for Troubled Waters. An Assessment of the Marrakech Climate Conference* [Online]. Wuppertal Institute for Climate, Environment and Energy. http://wupperinst.org/a/wi/a/ad/3795. Accessed March 28, 2017.

Oberthür, S., and C. Roche Kelly. 2008. "EU Leadership in International Climate Policy: Achievements and Challenges." *The International Spectator* 43 (3): 35–50.

Pacala, S., and R. Socolow. 2004. "Stabilization Wedges: Solving the Climate Problem for the Next 50 Years with Current Technologies." *Science* 305 (5686): 968–72.

Parker, C., and C. Karlsson. 2010. "Climate Change and the European Union's Leadership Moment: An Inconvenient Truth?" *Journal of Common Market Studies* 48 (4): 923–43.

Pielke, R., G. Prins, S. Rayner, and D. Sarewitz. 2007. "Climate Change 2007: Lifting the Taboo on Adaptation." *Nature* 445 (7128): 597–8.

Rajamani, L. 2016. "Ambition and Differentiation in the 2015 Paris Agreement: Interpretative Possibilities and Underlying Politics." *International and Comparative Law Quarterly* 65 (02): 493–514.

Rayner, J., and M. Howlett. 2009. "Introduction: Understanding Integrated Policy Strategies and Their Evolution." *Policy and Society* 28 (2): 99–109.

Rayner, T., and A. Jordan. 2013. "The European Union: The Polycentric Climate Policy Leader?" *Wiley Interdisciplinary Reviews: Climate Change* 4: 75–90.

Rezessy, S., K. Dimitrov, D. Urge-Vorsatz, and S. Baruch. 2006. "Municipalities and Energy Efficiency in Countries in Transition: Review of Factors That Determine Municipal Involvement in the Markets for Energy Services and Energy Efficient Equipment, or How to Augment the Role of Municipalities as Market Players." *Energy Policy* 34 (2): 223–37.

Schaffrin, A., S. Sewerin, and S. Seubert. 2014. "The Innovativeness of National Policy Portfolios—Climate Policy Change in Austria, Germany, and the UK." *Environmental Politics* 23 (5): 860–83.

———. 2015. "Toward a Comparative Measure of Climate Policy Output." *Policy Studies Journal* 43 (2): 257–82.

Schipper, E. 2006. "Conceptual History of Adaptation in the UNFCCC Process." *Review of European Community & International Environmental Law* 15 (1): 82–92.

Selin, H., and S. VanDeveer. 2015. *European Union and Environmental Governance*. New York, NY: Routledge.

Shipan, C., and C. Volden. 2012. "Policy Diffusion: Seven Lessons for Scholars and Practitioners." *Public Administration Review* 72 (6): 788–96.

Smith, P., D. Martino, Z. Cai, D. Gwary, H. Janzen, P. Kumar, B. McCarl et al. 2008. "Greenhouse Gas Mitigation in Agriculture." *Philosophical Transactions of the Royal Society B: Biological Sciences* 363 (1492): 789–813.

Somanathan, E., T. Sterner, T. Sugiyama, D. Chimanikire, N. Dubash, J. Essandoh-Yeddu, S. Fifita et al. 2014. National and Sub-national Policies and Institutions. Climate Change 2014: Mitigation of Climate Change. Contribution of Working Group III to the Fifth Assessment Report of the Intergovernmental Panel on Climate Change.

Steurer, R., and C. Clar. 2015. "Is Decentralisation Always Good for Climate Change Mitigation? How Federalism has Complicated the Greening of Building Policies in Austria." *Policy Sciences* 48 (1): 85–107.

Termeer, C., A. Dewulf, and G. Breeman. 2013. "Governance of Wicked Climate Adaptation Problems." *Climate Change Governance*, ed. J. Knieling, and W. Leal Filho. Berlin, Heidelberg: Springer, 27–39.

Tol, R. 2005. "Adaptation and Mitigation: Trade-offs in Substance and Methods." *Environmental Science & Policy* 8 (6): 572–8.

Tosun, J., and I. Solorio. 2011. "Exploring the Energy-Environment Relationship in the EU: Perspectives and Challenges for Theorizing and Empirical Analysis." *European Integration Online Papers* 15 (1): 1–7.

Touza, L., and E. López-Gunn. 2011. "Climate Change Policies-Mitigation and Adaptation at the Local Level: The Case of the City of Madrid (Spain)." In *Sustainable Systems and Energy Management at the Regional Level: Comparative Approaches*, ed. M. Tortora. Hershey, PA: IGI Global Publishers, 261–87.

Townshend, T., S. Fankhauser, R. Aybar, M. Collins, T. Landesman, M. Nachmany, and C. Pavese. 2013a. "How National Legislation Can Help to Solve Climate Change." *Nature Climate Change* 3: 430–2.

———. 2013b. *The GLOBE Climate Legislation Study—A Review of Climate Change Legislation in 33 Countries*. Croydon: CPI Group (UK).

Townshend, T., S. Fankhauser, A. Matthews, C. Feger, J. Liu, and T. Narciso. 2011. "Legislating Climate Change on a National Level." *Environment: Science and Policy for Sustainable Development* 53 (5): 5–17.

Tsebelis, G. 2002. *Veto Players: How Political Institutions Work*. Princeton, NJ: Princeton University Press.

UN Climate Change Newsroom. 2016. *Nations Take Forward Global Climate Action at 2016 UN Climate Conference* [Online]. http://newsroom.unfccc.int/unfccc-newsroom/nations-take-forward-global-climate-action-at-2016-un-climate-conference/. Accessed December 8, 2016.

UNFCCC. 2016. *Green Climate Fund* [Online]. http://unfccc.int/cooperation_and_support/financial_mechanism/green_climate_fund/items/5869.php. Accessed December 8, 2016.

Urpelainen, J. 2009. "Explaining the Schwarzenegger Phenomenon: Local Frontrunners in Climate Policy." *Global Environmental Politics* 9 (3): 82–105.

Van Buuren, A., P. Driessen, M. van Rijswick, P. Rietveld, W. Salet, T. Spit, and G. Teisman. 2013. "Towards Adaptive Spatial Planning for Climate Change: Balancing Between Robustness and Flexibility." *Journal for European Environmental & Planning Law* 10 (1): 29–53.

Wälti, S. 2004. "How Multilevel Structures Affect Environmental Policy in Industrialized Countries." *European Journal of Political Research* 43 (4): 599–634.

Ward, H., and X. Cao. 2012. "Domestic and International Influences on Green Taxation." *Comparative Political Studies* 45 (9): 1075–103.

Watts, N., W. N. Adger, P. Agnolucci, J. Blackstock, P. Byass, W. Cai, S. Chaytor et al. 2015. "Health and Climate Change: Policy Responses to Protect Public Health." *The Lancet* 386 (10006): 1861–914.

Webler, T., S. Tuler, K. Dow, J. Whitehead, and N. Kettle. 2016. "Design and Evaluation of a Local Analytic-Deliberative Process for Climate Adaptation Planning." *Local Environment* 21 (2): 166–88.

Wibowo, A., and L. Giessen. 2015. "Absolute and Relative Power Gains Among State Agencies in Forest-related Land Use Politics: The Ministry of Forestry and its Competitors in the REDD+ Programme and the One Map Policy in Indonesia." *Land Use Policy* 49: 131–41.

Widmer, A. 2014. *The Governance of Climate Change Adaptation in Switzerland: Issues, Actors, and Processes at the National and Cantonal Level and in Land-use Relevant Policies*. Dissertation No. 22144, ETH Zürich.

European Policy Analysis, Vol. 3, No. 1, 2017

Equal Treatment, Labor Promotion, or Social Investment? Reconciliation Policy in Finnish and Dutch Coalition Programs 1995–2016

Minna van Gerven and Mikael Nygård

This article investigates government-level intentions on work/family reconciliation policies in Finland and the Netherlands. By analyzing the coalition programs between 1995 and 2016, it traces three dominant ideas of equal treatment, employment promotion, and social investment in the reconciliation policy discourses in these countries. The content analysis shows a general tendency toward labor promotion in both countries and weak steps toward social investment have been taken. The dominant ideas seem, however, reasonably stable over time.

KEY WORDS: reconciliation policy, equal treatment, employment promotion, social investment, coalition agreements, Finland, the Netherlands

平等待遇、劳动促进还是社会投资？ 1995-2006年间芬兰和荷兰两国联盟计划之和解政策

本文调查了芬兰和荷兰两国政府使用“工作家庭和解政策”的意图。通过分析*1995-2016*年间的联盟计划，追溯了两国和解政策论述的三大主导性观点：平等待遇、就业促进和社会投资。内容分析显示：两国采取的措施总体上都倾向于劳动促进，社会投资方面则较少。主导性观点似乎随着时间的推移一直相当稳定。

关键词: 和解政策, 平等待遇, 就业促进, 社会投资, 联盟协议

Introduction

European family policy is currently undergoing major transformations. One specific area of change is reconciliation policy—a policy area addressing work–family balance or, differently put, the harmonization of paid and unpaid work (Lewis, 2006). The European Union has taken a coordinating role in this field and made it a part of the Lisbon strategy and its social investment focus (Jenson, 2009; Saraceno, 2015). Moreover, the Commission has launched several initiatives for enhancing work–family balance (e.g., European Commission, 2015). However, initiatives such as these can be conceptualized or implemented in varying ways depending on national institutions and policy legacies, and there is also debate on what ideas actually underpin reconciliation as a family policy tool. It has been argued, for instance, that the idea on gender equality has lost ground in favor of

doi: 10.1002/epa2.1007

a focus on employment imperatives specially directed at women (Daly, 2011; Jenson, 2009; Lewis, 2006; Stratigaki, 2004). Moreover, the social investment perspective has widened the focus of reconciliation policy also to children, human capital and early childhood education and care (Morel, Palier & Palme, 2012). As a consequence, there is little consensus on what the policy domain of work/family reconciliation actually entails in different countries and how it changes over time.

This article discusses how this policy field has been conceptualized on a national level and what ideas have been used in these constructions. The aim is to investigate government-level intentions on work/family reconciliation policy in Finland and the Netherlands since the mid-1990s by analyzing coalition programs. The main research questions are (1) How have governments in these two countries constructed the meaning of work/family reconciliation and to what extent are these constructions underpinned by ideas pertaining to equal treatment, employment promotion, or social investment? (2) How have these constructions and their ideational structure changed between 1995 and 2016?

The article contributes to the literature on European work/family reconciliation in at least three ways. First, it expands the theoretical discussion of gender equality by showing how gender equality objectives interplay with labor market–related policy objectives. Second, it contributes to the understanding of policy change by empirically deconstructing diverse ideas relating to work/family reconciliation. Third, it compares political agendas in two European countries (Finland and the Netherlands) for over 20 years (1995–2016).

These two countries constitute an interesting case for comparison for several reasons. Due to their high rates of female labor market participation and fertility, Finland and the Netherlands have often been praised as good examples of efficient work/family reconciliation (e.g., European Commission, 2015). The two countries, however, differ with respect to their cultural values concerning reconciliation of motherhood and work as well as their labor market conditions (Pfau-Effinger, 1998). On one hand the Netherlands has witnessed a rise in female employment after launching its one-and-half-male breadwinner model in the mid-1990s (Visser, 2002). Finland, on the other hand, nurtures a strong dual breadwinner model—adopted decades ago—that manifests a strong full-time work norm for all women.

The time frame 1995–2016 captures longitudinal trends and is long enough to cover among others the launch of the Amsterdam Treaty (1997), the Lisbon Strategy (2000), and the Europe 2020 (2010)—strategies that have constituted external pressures for member states to encourage female labor market participation as well as to promote gender mainstreaming objectives. This article will not, however, trace the causal link between the EU and Member state policies due to methodological problems of such an approach. Instead it uses the time period for capturing shifts in political discourse and ideational emphasis on a national level.

Ideas, Discursive Institutionalism, and Reconciliation Policy

This article uses theories on how ideas influence policy change (Béland & Cox, 2010), discursive institutionalism (Schmidt, 2008), and discursive politics

(Fischer, 2003) as its starting points. A common denominator of these theories is that ideas matter in politics, since they exercise cognitive and normative influence on how the social world is constructed and create discourses on how this world needs to be changed. According to Schmidt (2008, p. 306) three main categories of ideas can be distinguished: specific policy ideas, general ideas or programs, and "public philosophies" or "world views." While specific policy ideas offer a recommendation or solution in relation to a certain problem, the more general ideas and "world views" entail larger constructions and offer normative justifications for specific policy ideas. This article focuses primarily on policy ideas, but it also relates these ideas to the more general ideas and world views that give them normative power. As stated in the introduction, the aim of this article is to discuss how governments in Finland and the Netherlands have constructed policy ideas relating to work/family reconciliation, and to assess whether these recommendations are underpinned by more general ideas pertaining to gender equality, (female) labor promotion, and social investment. In the following, we therefore discuss these three ideational perspectives more in detail.

Although work/family reconciliation is commonly couched in a gender-neutral language, it embeds the meaning of harmonization of paid and unpaid work and the sharing of work and family responsibilities between men and women (Lewis, 2006). To this end, reconciliation policies generally aim at increasing women's labor supply, fertility, and child well-being, but they do so based on different ideas and theoretical perspectives.

The first ideational approach is in line with the feminist literature suggesting that the way in which public policies are framed is underpinned by normative assumptions regarding the gender order and gender differences (Lewis, 2006; Walby, 2005). An underlying assumption is that gender (in)equality is derived from disparities that exist among individuals solely based on their gender instead of their skills, abilities, or other characteristics (Hakim, 1995). Due to the biological uniqueness for women to give birth and the traditionally important role of women in raising children makes women different to men in preferences, lifetime labor patterns, and associated social rights (Orloff & Palier, 2009). Welfare state institutions may perpetuate these social divisions of gender, as well as those of class and race, affecting men and women in different ways (Esping-Andersen, 1990, 2009). These realizations have led way to vivid discussion of gendered nature of welfare states and the gendered division of labor (e.g., Pascall & Lewis, 2004). From this debate, we construct two contrasting ideational frames that are applicable when analyzing reconciliation policies and practices. First, reconciliation policies can be advocated as a matter of *social justice* (Sen, 1992, 1995) and the corresponding welfare state task is to promote *equal treatment of women* and men (in the labor market) and enable women to make use of their capabilities freely. Following Rees (2005), this perspective is based on the perception of ultimate goal of sameness that should be fostered. In the context of the labor market, women enter previously male-dominated terrains with existing male standards. State interventions, in the field of labor and care, should therefore make sure that women have the same equal rights and they are provided equal opportunities.

Second, reconciliation policies can be promoted as a matter of *economic empowerment of women*. Based on the prevailing differences, this perspective suggests that women are different to men, for instance, due to their biological and cultural features. The state interventions should, therefore, aim at equal valuation of the existing and different contribution of women and men in a gendered segregated society. A twofold strategy to achieve such economic-based goal can be established. On one hand, similar to Rees's (2005) positive action perspective, an *employment promotion strategy* aims at facilitating women's entry to (secondary) labor market and enables transitions between work and care (Knijn & Smit, 2009). On the other hand, a *social investment strategy* aims at changing the economic behavior of women (and men) and weakening the traditional male breadwinner model (Saraceno, 2015, p. 1). Following Saraceno (2015), the social investment "ideology" redraws the boundaries between family, market, state, and the gender arrangements that underpin these boundaries. Paid work is the basis of social citizenship and state interventions support the various life time transitions and avoid individuals (not just women) to fall outside of the labor market (Saraceno, 2015, p. 4). From this discussion, we construct a theoretical model for understanding of the three ideational perspectives on reconciliation policy (Table 1).

The reconciliation policies coined in the *equal treatment perspective* promote the gender-based equality within the primary labor market (Stratigaki, 2004, p. 50; Rees, 2005). Following the theory on segmentation on the dual labor market, labor markets are split into primary and secondary labor markets (e.g., Boeri & Van Ours, 2013). These segments differ with respect to job characteristics such as stability of employment, salary, and contents of work. The primary labor market consists of quality jobs providing equal rights and access to (generous) social security arrangements. The ambition is to achieve an equal sharing of family and domestic tasks between women and men according to an equal treatment perspective, and it hinges on egalitarian arrangements that make parental leave transferable between parents, increases the quality of care provision (and access to it), and prevents discrimination based on gender or family status. Such ambitions are also engraved in anti-discrimination laws, and policies about quotas, affirmative actions, and other forms of interventions that aim at protecting equal presence of and opportunities for women at the labor market.

The *employment promotion perspective* stems from a mounting public need to increase the capacity of women to work, often in the secondary labor market (Knijn & Smit, 2009; Schmid, 2006). The secondary labor market, an avenue aimed predominantly for policies devoted to employment promotion perspective consists of precarious jobs, limited job-mobility, and limited access to social protection. A dominance of economic priorities and higher labor market flexibility to reconcile work and family responsibilities is a central feature in such arrangements. Policy solutions no longer include measures providing equal chances for male and female nor extending rights (e.g., for family leaves); rather they advocate accessible and affordable care (implicitly emphasizing the criteria of enough quantity of care places) and flexible working conditions to activate the women and therefore, allow them to reconcile family and work responsibilities.

Table 1. Different Models for the Theoretical Understanding of Reconciliation Policy (Goals and Instruments)

Theoretical Perspectives		Reconciliation Policies Though		
		Equal Treatment	Employment Promotion	Social Investment
Key concepts		Equal treatment and opportunities of women and men	(Equal) opportunities of women *at the labor market*	Equal opportunities of women *at the labor market, supplemented with* child-oriented perspective, (targeted) investments for future and *opportunity to care*
Main arena		Private (individual/ household)	Public (labor market)	Private (individual/ household) and public (labor market)
Main policy approach		Egalitarian	Work promotion and activation	Activation, targeted inclusion, and distribution of life chances and income over the life cycle for children by emphasizing human capital formation and choice
Family leave	Goals	Equal treatment in sharing work and family responsibilities	Support of working mothers during (limited) absence from work	Support of (choice of) working mothers during (limited) absence from work, the human capital maintenance (lifelong learning) of adults/ parents
	Policy instruments	Equal sharing of family responsibilities (anti-discrimination goal): option to (compulsory) sharing of paid parental leave and new leave arrangement for fathers	Create leave arrangements without disincentives for return to employment	Leave arrangements, with strong emphasis on transition to early childhood education and child care facilities, support of families, life-long learning for parents
Childcare	Goals	Mother liberated from care (if preferred), supportive quality care provided	Women liberated for employment. Supportive care provided, emphasis on quantity of women make use of this	Support female labor market participation, good quality child(hood) care, and public and private investment in early childhood education
	Policy instruments	(Full) Child care provision	Childcare provision, flexible working times	Investments in childcare provision, flexible working times
Working conditions	Goals	Equal pay, equal employability, and chances at primary labor market	Job opportunities for women (at secondary labor market)	Job opportunities for women at primary labor market, with a goal of social inclusion and poverty (prevention or cure), life-ling learning
	Policy instruments	Gender fairness through antidiscrimination measures	Activation and flexible forms of employment	Activation, flexible forms of employment, targeted measures to families at risk, training/retraining

The *social investment perspective* focuses on equality of opportunity through increased investments in human capital as well as more preventive social protection systems. This perspective is proposed to be more child-oriented than oriented toward mothers (Jenson, 2009; Saraceno, 2015). It focuses on distributing life chances and income over the life by emphasizing human capital formation and advocating human capital maintenance (lifelong learning). The return of a full-employment "ideology" is central since both men and women expected to participate and be adequately prepared for participation in paid labor. The imperative of female employment is inherent, but the social investment perspective highlights women's human capital by promoting not only participation but also improvement of wages and career opportunities (Saraceno, 2015, p. 6). Critics suggest that real choice of parents to care may be undermined through such a quasi-paternalistic approach, especially if it prioritizes public care for the (very) young children above informal care, and female labor market participation. This school of thought advocates a more "neo-conservative" view of social investment in the sense of "optional familialism" (Leitner, 2003). In this stream, employment and family care are considered equally respected choices, as are parental choices are prioritized as when and how they want to reconcile various needs. Policy measures attained to the social investment perspective are preventive and targeted policies against social exclusion and (state) led support to early childhood education and/or childcare services for the families (Hemerijck, 2013; Morel et al., 2012). It can be argued that social investment builds on the employment promotion perspective, or is a kind of "employment promotion plus" discourse. It has, however, a distinct emphasis on human capital investment throughout the life cycle that can be at least ideationally and discursively reconstructed.

The analytical perspectives sketched above are archetypes, complementary rather than mutually exclusive (see also Walby, 2005, p. 326), especially when analyzed with empirical data. As reflected above already, the models overlap with respect to (in)direct goals of employment promotion as well as avenues of action (public and/or private). We acknowledge that listing, for example, equal opportunities as being merely about private relations and egalitarianism minimizes gender quality to be about gender roles in the private sphere (for a theoretical debate on sameness/difference, see, e.g., Hobson, Lewis & Siim, 2002). Furthermore, social investment is not one single perspective that stands alone. Nevertheless, the three ideational perspectives can fruitfully serve as heuristic tools for analyzing national government discourses and allow us to make sense of the ideas underpinning governments' constructions of work/family reconciliation.

Research Design

The article compares two countries that differ in some ways, such as gendered family and work divisions (Lewis, 2006; Pfau-Effinger, 2005; Sainsbury, 1999), but that also share some similarities, such as high female employment. While the Netherlands is often considered a member of the continental, or conservative, welfare regime, Finland is generally considered a member of the Nordic, or social democratic, welfare regime (Esping-Andersen, 1990). The placement of the Netherlands in the conservative regime, however, is not entirely unproblematic due to many similarities with Nordic countries, which is why Whelan and Maitre (2008) choose to place the country in the social democratic regime instead. The Dutch welfare state is built around a strong continental insurance regime with comprehensive worker protection. The male breadwinner was strongly rooted in the conservative society up to the 1980s, but from mid 1990s onward, the Dutch one-and-a-half-earner model family has been praised at home and abroad. The high female labor market participation rates (69.7 in 2014 by Eurostat 2016) are predominantly credited to the female working part time. This debate, however, rarely recognizes the institutional challenges in reconciliation of (full-time) work and family responsibilities. Knijn and van Oorschot (2008) show that in many respects the Netherlands lags behind in public investments in families in Europe. They find that mothers' (full-time) employment is strongly hindered by the relatively high costs and low quality of privatized childcare. The maternity leave period is short (16 weeks; parental leave 26 weeks) and the parental leave is non-paid, causing many parents, predominantly mothers, to either stop working or to work (much) less hours after the maternity leave. According to national statistics, 60 percent of Dutch women has a job of more than 12 hours a week, but only 18 percent of women work over 35 hours a week in 2012 (CBS, 2013). In addition, as Thevénon (2011, p. 72) has observed, the Dutch tax system is not designed to encourage full labor market participation of both parents. In addition, Knijn and van Oorschot (2008) and Portegijs, Cloïn, Ooms & Eggink (2006) found that the Dutch uphold the strong cultural idea that parents should care for their children themselves and prefer combining care with a part-time job. These factors, although promoting (part-time) employment of women, defer the societal legitimacy for public social investment and hamper the political room for adjustments in reconciliation policies.

By contrast, Finland has nurtured a "Nordic" dual-earner model since 1970s, and the publicly financed childcare services effectively facilitate parental employment and reconciling work and family. Since the Mid-1990s, universal childcare service system covers all children under school age, and is topped up with a system of child home care (for children under three) and a system of publicly supported private childcare (STM, 2013). The parental leaves are longer than in the Dutch system, with 105 days of maternity leave, 158 days of parental leave, and 54 days of paternal leave. In 2014, the female labor market participation rate was 72.1 percent (Eurostat 2016). The participation rate of parents with children under seven is approximately 70 percent of mothers and 95 percent of fathers belonged to the work force in 2007 (Lammi-Taskula & Salmi, 2010). Part-time employment is not common among Finnish parents: in 2008, only 17 percent of women and 7 percent of men worked part time, and among mothers with small children, the part-time labor participation was little over 20 percent in 2005 (Lammi-Taskula & Salmi, 2010).

Even though Finland and the Netherlands differ in some respects, we choose to follow Whelan and Maitre (2008) in treating these two countries as rather similar cases, since there are more similarities than differences between the two. By using a "method of difference" (Mill,1961), we search for differences in government discourses on work/family reconciliation constructions and seek to identify any differences in outcome. For example, on the basis of the policy legacies discussed above, we expect ideas of labor promotion to be more salient in the Netherlands, and equal treatment and child-centered social investment perspective to be more prevalent in Finland. We also expect a trend toward more social investment in both countries from 2000 (start of the Lisbon Strategy), albeit to a different degree (and perhaps to different directions).

The focus of the analysis is the policy recommendations and policy instruments of work/family reconciliation policies as portrayed in the coalition programs 1995–2016. Previous research on reconciliation policies has shown that this policy area is rich in variety of meaning, orientation, and evolution (Lewis, 2006). Reconciliation policies traditionally include a wide range of policy instruments, from maternity leave arrangements, cash transfers (e.g., child allowance), and recently in-work tax benefits to early childhood education and care services. For reasons of analytical clarity, we focus on three main areas of reconciliation policies: family-related leave, childcare and provision of childcare services (formal or informal care), and working conditions.

In order to investigate country-level intentions on reconciliation, all coalition programs (*Regeerakkoord* in Dutch, *Hallitusohjelma* in Finnish) between 1995 and 2016 were collected and analyzed. Coalition programs are results of the information phase of the new cabinet and they codify the political goals and objectives for the forthcoming cabinet period (cf. Moury, 2013; Strøm, Müller & Bergman, 2008). The documents include governments' plans regarding to the budget, legislation plans, and their shared viewpoint to the most challenging social problems. The content of the programs varies from coalition to coalition, but they generally list sections for the most crucial area of policy (e.g., public administration, international relations, economy and finances, health, immigration and integration, infrastructure, education, elderly care, security, work and social security, housing). We collected eight Finnish and six Dutch coalition programs between 1995 and 2016. The length of the analyzed documents was on average 62 pages for the Dutch documents and 41 for the Finnish documents. For the analysis, we looked for the sections where the reconciliation policies were addressed: mostly discussed under the headings employment and social security, but sometimes within other sections, that is, sections on education, health care, and social care, or in a separate section on emancipation. The method applied was qualitative content analysis, which Hsieh and Shannon (2005) define as a "research method for the interpretation of the content of text data through the systematic classification process of coding and identifying themes or patterns" (Hsieh & Shannon, 2005, p. 1278). We analyzed textual contents of the documents and used a deductive variant of the method. This means that the documents were coded by using the three ideational approaches described in Table 1 as starting points. On the basis of these three categories, the qualitative assessment focused on policy recommendations (policy ideas) and policy instruments proposed, as well as more general justifications (general ideas and/or world views). In the analysis, we retrospectively linked these policy intentions to policy outcomes derived from national policy documents and scholarly work. The analysis allows us to conduct a general assessment of the potential ideational change over time in line with the theory of discursive institutionalism (Schmidt, 2008). Although we place the government's plans retrospectively in the context of the reforms implemented in this time period, the analysis can say little of causal links between intentions and effects, but analysis of coalition programs adds to the knowledge of the agenda setting of the government (e.g., Moury 2013) and the institutionalization of policy ideas (Schmidt, 2008).

The Reconciliation Approaches and Perspectives in the Dutch Coalition Programs

In a decentralized unitary state, such as the Netherlands, politics and governance are characterized by a common strive for a broad consensus within the political community and society as a whole. Most governments in the analysis period were coalition governments with a majority (with the exemption of Rutte I minority cabinet in 2010–2012) and therefore often considered to be better able to have its legislation passed than minority governments. During the whole period of analysis, the Dutch coalition programs (Table 2) across-the-board put forward the employment promotion as the prominent idea. In line with reforms introduced, the uttermost attention in the coalition agreements was directed toward an elimination of the structural bottlenecks hampering women's job entry and creating a labor market for women. Yet, the documents indicate clear shifts in the government's perspective to female employment over time. For most part, the explanatory factor for these shifts is the composition of the new cabinet and presence of certain parties with specific viewpoint on gender equality (see also Morgan, 2013). The coupling of the Social Democratic party and the equal treatment perspective is evident. The coalition programs of 1994 and 1998 strongly framed the policy plans from the equal treatment perspective. In the 1994 coalition program, for instance, the governing parties (Social Democrats (PVdA), Liberals (VVD), and Progressive Liberals (D66)) recognized men and women to need to have equal rights to be economically independent (1994, p. 28). Similar undertones were found in the coalition programs of 1994, 1998, and 2007, all written by coalitions including the Social democrats. In these documents, emancipation is framed more broadly than just a catch-up of women on men in the labor market: emancipation is seen to necessitate changes in division of tasks between men and women (1998, p 70.) With a reference to the UN Women's treaty, and the report by Commission Groenman, 1998 coalition program, for example, called for gender equality by remarking that the increasing labor market participation of women has not been compensated with increasing participation of men in the unpaid caring tasks (p. 70).

The out-of-tradition extension of the childcare facilities in the Netherlands is often credited to the Social democrats (Morgan, 2013; van Hooren & Becker,

Table 2. An Overview of Main Discursive Threads in Dutch Coalition Agreements 1994–2016

Agreement	Coalition Parties	Main Perspective to Gender Equality	Specifics of the Period
1994 "Choices for future" keuzes voor de toekomst'	PvDA, VVD, D66	Equal treatment and Employment promotion in primary labor market	Encouragement female employment (primary labor market)
1998 "Power" "kracht"	PvDA, VVD, D66	Equal treatment and Employment promotion in primary/part-time labor market, social investment	Economic growth, investments in childcare
2002 "Work for trust" "werken aan vertouwen"	CDA, LPF, VVD	Employment promotion in part-time labor market, neo-conservative social investment	Decreasing economic growth, participation at part-time employment, freedom to choose
2003 "work together, more jobs, less rules" "meedoen, meer werk, minder regels"	CDA, VVD, D66	Employment promotion in part-time labor market, neo-conservative social investment	Lowering economic growth, self-responsibility, freedom to choose
2007 "Work together, live together" "samen werken, samen leven"	CDA, PvDA, CU	Employment promotion in part-time labor market, neo-conservative social investment, equal treatment	Millennium goals, participation, freedom to choose
2010 "Freedom and Responsibility" "vrijheid en verantwoordelijkheid"	CDA, VVD (PVV)	Employment promotion in part-time labor market, neo-conservative social investment	Participation and responsibility, freedom to choose
2012 "Crossing Bridges" "bruggen slaan"	VVD, PvDA	Employment promotion in part-time labor market, neo-conservative social investment, some elements of (general) equal treatment and social inclusion	

Note: CDA = Christen Democrats, PvDA = Labor, VVD = Liberals, D66 = progressive democrats, CU = Christen Union, PVV = Party for Freedom, LPF = List Pim Fortyin.

2012). Largely as an answer to the increasing entry of women into the labor market (see also Lewis, Knijn & Martin, 2008; Visser, 2002), a formalization of the childcare provision was consolidated in the PVdA-led coalition programs of 1994 and 1998. Setting up the urgency for modernization of gender relations between men and women, the coalition program of 1998 introduced the new Combination Scenario and the launch of its main legislative source law on Work and Care Act (p. 27). By 2001, this law came to effect and promoted greater equality between men and women, by positioning a policy goal of both men and women engaging in paid work and unpaid work (coalition agreement 1998, 27). It extended (unpaid) parental leave and was considered a success since the take-up among fathers has been reasonably high (19 percent in 2005 in Lewis et al., 2008, p. 273), at least in continental European standards.

The growing prevalence of part-time work is also credited to the Social democrats (Morgan, 2013, p. 92). The old breadwinner model was given a kiss goodbye in the coalition program of 1994, when new bright future was sketched for women as emancipated and economically independent citizens (p. 28). Under their siege, a 1996 law was passed that banned discrimination against workers based on their hours of work. Later this law was followed by the Working Hours Adjustment Act 2000 that gave all workers the right to reduce working hours to part-time work or increase to full-time hours. Partially to respond the need of accommodating women (with special preferences to work part time) in the primary labor market, but in line with their party ideological preferences to provide women with equal rights (coalition program, 1998, p. 28), Liberal-Social Democratic coalition gave rise to Dutch female employment promotion perspective, based on more or less equal terms with men. The law was extended in 2000s.

From 2002, the Dutch politics moved toward a more conservative direction (Morgan, 2013, p. 92), and the importance of the "neo-conservative" view of social investment (Leitner, 2003) where employment promotion and family care are equally valuable options, while mothers/fathers' choices are maximized how do they (mothers) will reconcile various needs. Flexible labor markets were seen to allow citizens to adapt their labor market participation in different phases of life. Although the labor market created in late 1990s was made intentionally flexible, one should not confuse the part-time work with the more general term "precarious work" at the secondary labor market. In the Netherlands, part-time work is regarded as work that is carried out regularly and voluntarily, where working hours are shorter than the working hours generally customary in the sector (i.e., the normal working hours for full-time workers). Employees with a fixed-term contract, temporary employment agency workers, and on-call workers—except when they actually work part-time—are not considered part-time workers. Under Christian Democratic-Liberal rule labor market participation *vis-à-vis* protection of traditional family norms became the norm from 2002 onward. For example, the coalition program of 2002 posited that men and women should have the freedom to choose different roles in life cycle, especially in relation to paid and unpaid work (p. 19). This policy approach driven by Christian Democrats proposes that the family is the corner stone of society and consequently that, in sake of the children, women should be able choose whether to work or not. Although the 2002 coalition program is gender neutral in its tone, the silence of equal equality objectives hints that the Dutch male breadwinner family has made a strong return under the cabinets reigned by the CDA. Similar message is expressed by the coalition program in 2003: emancipation of women serves no function here, rather cabinet pleads for extending freedom and self-responsibility of all citizens. Noteworthy is the emphasis on participation, not only on the labor market but also in civil society activities and the emphasis on informal care provision (2003: 44). The plan of the Liberal-Christen democratic coalition governments (2002: 19, 2003: 44) to maximize the choice of the parents materializes later under the Life-course saving scheme (LCSS). Under the LCSS of 2006 parents could save a part of their wages to care for their children. In theory, the LCSS was a social innovation coining the virtues of equal treatment: it treated men and women equally as individualized workers on the flexible labor markets. In practice, the take-up of the program was low from the start (Lewis et al., 2008, p. 274), and despite good intentions, it failed after one and half years of its existence. It is questionable whether this "dragonfly" meant a shift toward equal treatment: the coalition program of 2002 is gender neutral in its description of goals behind the new scheme, but it apprises the LCSS scheme of its ability to guarantee women's employability and higher job productivity (2003: 19). In wisdom of hindsight, this hints to prioritizing the labor promotion of women and emphasizes government's intentions to remove bottlenecks of women's employment on the labor market.

From 2003 onward, self-responsibility of families is highlighted. The coalition program of 2007, where Social Democrats were a part of drafting it, raises the issue of gender inequality on the labor market (with respect to income gap, lack of women in top position p. 30 see coalition agreement, 2013: 19). Yet, the main attention goes to promotion of participation (in and out of labor market, p. 23–26) and advocating parents' freedom to choose between formal and informal care (p. 25). Strengthened by the declining economic growth and the surmounting Eurozone crisis, the former Christen democratic-Liberal and the current liberal-Social Democratic governments have strengthened these arguments. In the midst of cuts in childcare provision as part of a larger budget-trimming effort, the 2010 coalition program (p. 44), for instance, posited that childcare supplements (by state to parents) should not weaken parents' own responsibility. It calls for more responsibilities for parents (also financially) to improve the language proficiency of their children (coalition program, 2010, p. 31) and emphasizes flexible working times and working forms. For example, work flexibility in terms of telework and home work was seen essential for helping parents to combine work and care responsibilities (coalition agreement, 2010, p. 44). Not only gainful employment, but also civic participation (e.g., of parents in schools and grandparents in provision of informal childcare) are examples of how to strike a balance between paid work, care responsibilities, voluntary work, training, and free time (coalition agreement, 2010, p. 44).

The intentions expressed in the Dutch coalition programs suggest that child-centered social investment discourse has not (yet) found its way to the political agendas. During the mid-1990s when economy was still flourishing, governments announced several measures of "early" social investment: increases in childcare services, improvements in the quality of childcare, and attempts to liberate women for employment in line with human capital perspective. For instance, in 1998, with Social democrats and Liberals in government, an intensification program was announced to improve the quality of education and increase the number of childcare and after-school care facilities (p. 12). With a fourfold growth of the day-care capacities, and with focus on after-school care supply, the coalition program (1998, p. 27) claimed to have taken an important step toward a better response to the current need as well as the need in the future of day-care services. Although full-fletched child-centered social investment remains silent in the Dutch cabinet plans thereafter, education remains as one of the focal points of the governments, even after the decline of economic growth. For example, in the coalition program of 2003, straight references were made to the importance of education for society and economy at large, but no references were made to investments in early childhood education. In 2007, investments in quality are highlighted, yet their interpretations stem from freedom to choose (by parents) and from freedom of schools to choose substance and ways of teaching. Only in the document of 2012, direct references to early childhood education and its importance for society as a whole are included in the government strategy. The child-centered approach, however, is posited toward the goal of social inclusion through more stringent testing of preschool children's language proficiency and the allocation of more resources to schools to improve the language education. In many cases, these are targeted measures toward poor families, and especially those with migration background. The rhetoric of targeting is nothing new. It started already in 2002, when the populist *Pim Fortyin* party changed the political climate toward more stringent migration policies. For example, in the coalition program of 2007, children (of migrant families) with lacking language proficiency are suggested to be guided to preschool play schools (before the preschools starting at the age of 4). These measures were to be integrated with measures that aim at parents' integration (2007, p. 28).

As a whole, the Dutch governmental-level reconciliation perspective is firmly anchored in the employment promotion perspective and maintaining the choice to parents to care or to work (or combine both). A part-time labor market provides mothers (and fathers) with flexible working time arrangements including reasonable social protection and facilitates reconciliation of work and family. In the Dutch case, the labor market where women have entered is not secondary labor market, but neither do women work equally long hours as men. The Dutch part-time labor market is creation to improve to liberating women working, without emancipating them from family obligation. Although the strong care culture is prevalent, partisan politics seems to linger behind the changes in the last decades. The promotion of gender equality was strongest under the social democratic-led governments. After the change of political power in the early 2000s, the emphasis of (Christian democrats and Liberal) governments has been on the promotion of informal care, under the buzzword of freedom to choose. This manifests a birth of optional familialism (Leitner, 2003) or strengthening of "neo-conservative" view of social investment. Under the notion of individual responsibilities, governments with Christian democrats and Liberals in charge have introduced some social inclusion measures. These predominantly target the migrant families but otherwise, the social investment paradigm with full-employment for male and female focus has not undertaken the Dutch reconciliation politics.

The Reconciliation Approaches and Perspectives in the Finnish Coalition Programs

Finnish politics is known for its long-standing tradition of broad consensus. In the field of reconciliation policy, the social partners play a visible role for agreements on, for example, family leaves. Moreover, there is a strong tradition of majoritarian coalition governments, which is the case with the governments included in this analysis. As can be seen in Table 3, since the mid-1990s until the outbreak of the international finance crisis in 2008, the Finnish government approach on reconciliation policy was primarily framed by an employment promotion perspective as a means for generating higher growth and securing financial sustainability, but as a way of achieving higher levels of gender equality both in family life and working life in accordance with the "equal treatment"

Table 3. An Overview of Main Discursive Threads in Finnish Government Programs 1995–2015

Agreement	Coalition Parties	Main Perspective to Gender Equality	Specifics of the Period
1995 Government of Employment and joint responsibility, "Työllisyyden ja yhteisvastuun hallitus"	SDP, KOK, LW, GRE, SPP	Employment promotion through gender equality in working life and family life	Activation through a more spurring social protection scheme
1999 A fair and supportive Finland, "Oikeudenmukainen ja kannustava—sosiaalisesti eheä Suomi"	SDP, KOK, LW, GRE, SPP	Employment promotion through gender equality, social inclusion and anti-discrimination policies (equal treatment of women and men)	Parents' right to choose with regard to childcare
2003 Through work, entrepreneurship and joint responsibility toward a new rise, "Työllä, yrittämisellä ja yhteisvastuulla uuteen nousuun"	CEN, SDP, SPP	Employment promotion through gender equality in working life and family policy, social inclusion through anti-poverty measures and social investment (human capital)	Introduction of "fathers' month" within the parental leave system
2007 A responsible, caring and supportive Finland, "Vastuullinen, välittävä ja kannustava Suomi"	CEN, KOK, GRE, SPP	Employment promotion though gender equality, social inclusion (anti-poverty measures), social investment (human capital)	More flexibility and incentives in family transfers and welfare services
2011 An open, just and bold Finland, "Avoin, oikeudenmukainen ja rohkea Suomi"	KOK, SDP, CHR, GRE, LW, SPP	Employment promotion through gender equality, social investment (human capital)	Flexibility in childcare services, extension of father's leave, accentuation of sound public finances and austerity
2014 A new boost for Finland: growth and employment, "Suomi uuteen nousuun—kasvua ja työllisyyttä"	KOK, SDP, CHR, GRE, SPP	Employment promotion (activation)	Accentuation of sound public finances and austerity measures, activation and workfare measures prevalent
2015 Finland, a land of solutions, "Ratkaisujen Suomi"	CEN, KOK, TRUE	Employment promotion, activation, social investment (human capital)	Accentuation of sound public finances and austerity measures, activation and workfare measures prevalent

Note: SDP = Social Democrats, KOK = Conservatives, CEN = Centre Party, GRE = Greens, SPP = Swedish People's Party, LW = Left-Wing Party, CHR = Christian Democrats, TRUE = True Finns.

perspective described in Table 1. During the first half of the 2010s, the social investment perspective gained increasing importance in Finnish coalition programs, most notably in relation early childhood education and care, and other investments in human capital, but also in terms of extended paternal leave and stronger inducements for fathers to take-up family leave (Lammi-Taskula & Salmi, 2010).

The Finnish public childcare system was expanded in 1996 to cover all children under school age, and the motives behind this expansion were to facilitate mothers' employment in accordance with the European Employment Strategy, but also to curb the tendencies of rising child poverty among families with children (Nygård, 2010). The strong accentuation of public childcare as a means for higher gender equality as well as favorable child outcomes has been more or less univocal across political parties ever since the 1990s. All of the governments, irrespective of ideological composition, have expressed its support for this system. Accordingly, social investment instruments have deep roots in Finland, similar to most Nordic countries. As a result of shortage in labor supply and women's movement public childcare was introduced in Finland in the 1970s and, has since then been a beacon for "women-friendliness" and the dual-earner model. High female employment has been seen as an important prerequisite for the small and export-oriented Finnish economy.

The strong reconciliation discourse that can be found in the Finnish coalition programs since the 1990s, and that is anchored in ambitions related to employment promotion, gender equality, and investments in childcare, has not only been an influential and ideologically exceeding theme, but it has constituted a path-dependent institutional characteristic for Finnish social policy irrespective of the ideological composition of coalitions. However, the Finnish reconciliation system consists of other policy instruments than public childcare and early childhood education. Finnish parents can opt for home childcare (for children under three) instead of public childcare through the child home care leave/allowance system instituted in 1985. Originally this benefit was advocated by the Centre Party as a "mothers wage" compensating mothers for their domestic work, but in the 1990s it was increasingly seen as a way of relieving municipalities in their responsibility of providing public childcare to parents (Hiilamo & Kangas, 2009). On top of this, Finnish parents can care for their children under school age privately and get compensation from the state through the private care allowance for children (STM 2013).

Of the eight coalition programs under scrutiny, the first two (from 1995, 1999) focused strongly on restoring economic growth and reducing unemployment when the Finnish economy hit one of its most severe economic crises in the beginning of the 1990s with souring unemployment as a consequence (van Gerven, 2008). The government program launched by the broad five-party coalition led by the Social Democrats in 1995, for instance, firmly set on economic growth as well as structural reforms of the social protection schemes, notably unemployment benefits, to make the system more activating (see also van Gerven, 2008). At the same time the need to make family policies and working life more "family friendly" was emphasized through, for example, flexible working arrangements and flexible parental leaves. There was, however, a strong accentuation of gender equality in terms of equal rights for women and men in both working and family life and an ambition to reduce gender discrimination.

This discursive thread was followed up in the following coalition program from 1999. Equal rights equality in working life as well as in family life were put forth as an objective for the government, but the role of public welfare services for the overall employment rate and for the social inclusion of (poor) families (considered work as the best remedy for child poverty) was emphasized. The 1999 coalition program entailed a stronger emphasis on social inclusion than its predecessor, since day-care services and active labor market policies were not only seen as important for the labor market participation of parents but also for fighting family-related poverty.

The 1999 coalition program was the first one to openly acknowledge child poverty as a national social problem (Nygård & Krüger, 2012). The program also acknowledged the role of the antidiscrimination directive enacted through the Amsterdam Treaty as a way of preventing gender inequality. The parental leave system was seen as one of the areas where the objective toward gender equality should be put to test by granting fathers a "daddy quota" and thereby shifting care responsibilities more evenly between parents.

In 2003, the coalition base shifted in Finland as the Centre Party regained office after 8 years in opposition. By and large, this Centre-left government followed in the footsteps of its predecessor by emphasizing employment promotion and by pinpointing the role of reconciliation policies when parental employment was concerned. The agreement accentuated the importance of gender equality in working life and saw the enactment of a new anti-discrimination law as one major step toward this goal. In family life, the need to accomplish gender equality was seen as central, and the way to achieve this was seen to induce fathers to take longer leaves with their children and to redistribute the financial burdens of the parental insurance system more evenly between female- and male-dominated employment branches.

Notwithstanding the fact that preschool education had been introduced already in 2001, the creation of human capital among children through welfare services and educational services were now seen as ways of achieving social inclusion and better life chances for children over the life cycle. Furthermore, piecemeal improvements of the child benefit and home care allowance systems as well as the parental insurance allowance were seen as central for curbing poverty among families, notably lone-parent households. The reforms conducted in the family transfer system, notably the parental insurance and the child benefit system, have largely aimed at two objectives; to increase the level of gender equality within the parental leave system through a larger up-take of fathers' leave and to enhance the social inclusion of (poor) families with children, notably single-parent and multi-child families, through improvements of child benefits and child benefit supplements for single parents (Lammi-Taskula & Salmi, 2010). The Centre-left coalition formed in 2003, reacted to the increasing number of poor family households by launching a series of "poverty packages" consisting of piecemeal improvements of family transfers in 2004 and 2005. Alongside these improvements there was a prolongation of the father's leave to 30 weekdays under the condition that the father used 12 days of the mutual parental leave (Kuivalainen & Niemelä, 2010).

The Centre-right government taking office in 2007 drew heavily on reconciliation as an instrument for employment promotion, gender equality, and poverty reduction, but the focus on human capital formation in terms of preschool education and childcare, as well as activation through more flexible and effective family transfers, was somewhat more accentuated. This government saw the exclusion of poor families as devastating to society as a whole and the economy in particular, which is why piecemeal improvements of the family transfer system were called for. The public childcare system needed to be reformed: not only should the system allow parents to choose the form of childcare, but the flexibility of part-time care should facilitate a smooth balance between work and family life.

The Conservative-led six-party coalition taking office in 2011 strongly set out to strengthen the financial sustainability of the Finnish welfare state in the wake of the financial crisis by increasing the overall employment level and prolonging working lives of Finns. Accordingly the accentuation of reconciliation policy is stronger in the 2011 coalition program than in any of the previous programs, but this theme is linked most squarely to the aim of promoting employment, and only secondary to creating equal rights for women and men. An important step toward a more equal parental leave system was taken in 2010, and again in 2013, when the paternal leave was extended from 36 to 54 days, with an ear-marked leave period for daddies.

Early childhood education and care were seen as crucial not only for the combination of work and family life but also for raising the overall employment levels and thereby securing the long-term financial sustainability of the welfare system. Although the legal right to public childcare was defended, there were claims for making the system more flexible, notably when it comes to part-time care. The use of child home care was seen in a more critical light than before as the agreement called for flexibilization of the system and encouraged parents to take-up part-time jobs. Allegedly, the system was thought of as a potential obstacle to parental employment, although this was not said out loud in the program. Due to the wide popularity of the child homecare system, the government, however, refrained from direct cuts; instead the existing part-time child home care allowance was replaced with a flexible care allowance (effective January 1, 2014). But simultaneously, in its structural reform program from August 2013, it proposed to divide the child homecare leave between the parents, and that the negligence to take-up these leaves would shorten the overall leave period.

The two governments that followed in 2014, and in 2015, criticized the child homecare system and proposed a partial reduction in the universal whole-day childcare right for families. The policy ideas on work/family reconciliation in these coalition programs were framed primarily through the lenses of employment promotion, and there are almost no mentions of gender rights, gender equality, or social investment, save some occasional mentions on the importance of education. The most probable reason for the one-sided accentuation of employment promotion is the overall focus on austerity measures and the governments' foremost ambition to restore balance in public finances.

As a whole, although being considered important to employment and gender equality already in the 1990s, reconciliation policies became increasingly and explicitly emphasized as drivers of economic growth, gender equality, social inclusion, and family friendliness in the 2010s. Finnish reconciliation policy has mostly been underpinned by ideas of employment promotion and gender equality, whereas ideas pertaining to social inclusion became visible only in the 2010s. The ideological composition of governments seems to have had little impact on the construction of work/family reconciliation policy, instead the discursive thread and the general ideas underpinning the policy recommendations have been quite stable over time and conditioned more by contextual factors such as soaring poverty rates or sluggish growth.

Conclusion and Discussion

This article set out to investigate government intentions in the field of work/family reconciliation in two European countries, Finland and the Netherlands, since 1995. On the basis of our research questions and the theoretical framework, the following conclusions can be made. Based on the national discourses relating to perspectives on gender equality, employment promotion, and/or social investment, we found out, by and large, employment promotion to be the main discursive thread dominating reconciliation discourses across countries as well as across time. Although the cases analyzed gave a rise to many similarities in this respect, there were also clear differences between Dutch and Finnish reconciliation perspectives. Close to our initial expectation, we found out that the governmental approach seemed to uphold (part-time) labor promotion for women and optional familialism (Leitner, 2003) in the Netherlands, whereas the equal treatment on the (full-time) labor market and child-centered social investment perspectives were more prevalent in Finland. We found no evidence on labor promotion on the secondary labor market, since both of countries analyzed have labor generous labor market rights, even in the Netherlands where women work mostly part-time. We captured a weak general trend toward more social investment over the life cycle in both countries over time but the extent of attention was, as expected, stronger in Finland than in the Netherlands. The gender equality objectives were more deeply institutionalized in the Finnish social democracy than in the Netherlands (Christian) social democracy.

On the basis of these three categories, the qualitative assessment focused on policy recommendations (policy ideas) and policy instruments proposed, as well as more general justifications (general ideas and/or world views), the general conclusion where we arrived is that Finnish documents make a stronger case for including women to the labor market by promoting equal treatment objectives for women, whereas the Dutch documents in the recent decade endorse the freedom of choice of parents by advocating for flexible working arrangements and (part) time care. The discursive framing remains rather stable over time which provides evidence for the well-known claim of the Institutionalist school that paradigms behind public policies remain path-dependent and resilient to change. The observed (temporal) shifts in governmental rhetoric may be explained by partisan politics and coalition structure (inclusion of Social Democrats or Christian democrats in the government in the Netherlands) and/or contextual factors such as soaring poverty rates and sluggish economic growth (as was found for Finland). Our research design was, however, not explanatory, and therefore these assumptions require appropriate testing.

It is, however, clear that the current social investment debate is *de facto* labor promotion 2.0. Both countries have adopted ideas and policy ambitions close to those of the EU's agenda regarding higher labor market participation rates and more human capital investments. A child-centered approach, central to the theorization of social investment, is well institutionalized in Finland. The Netherlands, however, lags considerably behind in this European ambition. As argued earlier, the onset of the full-fledge agenda on social investment is hampered by the strong belief of family being the best care-giver for the children in the society and political arena. In The Netherlands, the social investment discourse is in line with the prevailing political (conservative, Christian Democratic) parties, where employment promotion and family care are equally valuable options and where parental choices are prioritized.

What is striking, however, is that under the social investment ethos, national policies are implemented that seem to go against the philosophy of social investment. Examples from Finland and the Netherlands show clear evidence of social investment perspective culminating into selective policies: giving rise to a social inclusion through extra investments targeted to low-income families. This supposes that the concept social inclusion and investment contains a double loading, on one hand a broader social investment and on the other hand more narrow social inclusion. Despite its good intentions of social investment agenda to bring more "social" into economic-driven policies, social investment promotion may further marginalize social policy goals.

Minna van Gerven is Assistant Professor in Sociology of Governance at the Department of Public Administration of University of Twente, the Netherlands. Her research interests include European welfare state change and comparative public policy reform.
Mikael Nygård is professor of Social Policy at Åbo Akademi University (Vaasa), Finland. His research interests include welfare state reform, societal participation and health-related research.

Note

The authors thank the two anonymous reviewers and the editor of EPA for their constructive comments. The usual disclaimer applies.

References

Béland, D., and R. H. Cox. 2010. "Introduction: Ideas and Politics." In *Ideas and Politics in Social Science Research*, ed. D. Béland & R. H. Cox. New York: Oxford University Press, 1–17.

Boeri, T., and J. Van Ours. 2013. *The Economics of Imperfect Labor Markets*. Princeton: Princeton University Press.

CBS. 2013. *Statline Database* [Online]. http://statline.cbs.nl. Accessed June 2, 2013.

Daly, M. 2011. "What Adult Worker Model? A Critical Look at Recent Social Policy Reform in Europe from a Gender and Family Perspective." *Social Politics* 18 (1): 1–23. doi: 10.1093/sp/jxr002.

Esping-Andersen, G. 1990. *The Three Worlds of Welfare Capitalism*. Princeton, New Jersey: Princeton University Press.

———. 2009. *Incomplete Revolution: Adapting Welfare States to Women's New Roles*. Cambridge: Polity Press.

European Commission. 2015. *New Start to Address the Challenges of Work-Life Balance Faced by Working Families. Comminicaiont 2015/JUST/012* [Online]. ec.europa.eu/smart-regulation/roadmaps/docs/2015_just__maternity_leave.en.pdf. Accessed November 1, 2015.

Eurostat. 2016. *Labour Force Survey* [Online]. http://ec.europa.eu/eurostat/data/database. Accessed November 1, 2016.

Fischer, F. 2003. *Reframing Public Policy: Discursive Politics and Deliberative Practices.* Oxford: Oxford University Press.

Hakim, C. 1995. "Five Feminist Myths About Women's Employment." *The British Journal of Sociology* 46 (3): 429–55.

Hemerijck, A. 2013. *Changing Welfare States?*. Oxford: Oxford University Press.

Hiilamo, H., and O. Kangas. 2009. "Trap for Women or Freedom to Choose. The Struggle Over Cash for Child Care Schemes in Finland and Sweden." *Journal of Social Policy* 38 (3): 457–75.

Hobson, B., J. Lewis, and B. Siim. 2002. *Contested Concepts in Gender and Social Politics.* Cheltenham: Edward Elgar.

Hsieh, H.-F., and S. Shannon. 2005. "Three Approaches to Qualitative Content Analysis." *Qualitative Health Research* 15 (9): 1277–88.

Jenson, J. 2009. "Lost in Translation: The Social Investment Perspective and Gender Equality." *Social Politics* 16 (4): 446–83. doi: 10.1093/sp/jxp019.

Knijn, T., and A Smit. 2009. "Investing, Facilitating, or Individualizing the Reconciliation of Work and Family Life: Three Paradigms and Ambivalent Policies." *Social Politics: International Studies in Gender, State & Society* 16 (4): 484–518. doi: 10.1093/sp/jxp020.

Knijn, T., and W. van Oorschot. 2008. "The Need for and the Societal Legitimacy of Social Investments in Children and Their Families: Critical Reflections on the Dutch Case." *Journal of Family Issues* 29 (11): 1520–42. doi: 10.1177/0192513X08319477.

Kuivalainen, S., and M. Niemelä. 2010. "From Universalism to Selectivism: The Ideational Turn of the Antipoverty Policies in Finland." *Journal of European Social Policy* 20 (3): 263–76.

Lammi-Taskula, J., and M. Salmi. 2010. "Lapsiperheiden toimeentulo lamasta lamaan." In *Suomalaisten hyvinvointi*, ed. Ma. Vaarama, Pa. Moisio, and S. Karvonen. Helsinki: THL, 198–214.

Leitner, S. 2003. "Varieties of Familialism: The Caring Function of the Family in Comparative Perspective." *European Societies* 353–75.

Lewis, J. 2006. "Work/Family Reconciliation, Equal Opportunities and Social Policies: The Interpretation of Policy Trajectories at the EU Level and the Meaning of Gender Equality." *Journal of European Public Policy* 13 (3): 420–37. doi: 10.1080/13501760600560490.

Lewis, J., T. Knijn, and C. Martin. 2008. "Patterns of Development in Work/Family Reconciliation Policies for Parents in France, Germany, the Netherlands, and the UK in the 2000s Patterns of Development in Work/Family Reconciliation Policies for Parents in France, Germany, the Netherlands." *Social Politics* 15 (3): 261–86.

Mill, J. S. 1961. *A System of Logic, Ratiocinative and Inductive: Being a Connected View of the Principles of Evidence and the Methods of Scientific Investigation.* White Plains, NY: Longman. (Original work published 1843)

Morel, N., B. Palier, and J. Palme, ed. 2012. *Towards a Social Investment Welfare State? Ideas, Policies and Challenges.* Bristol: Policy Press.

Morgan, K. J. 2013. "Path Shifting of the Welfare State: Electoral Competition and the Expansion of Work-Family Policies in Western Europe." *World Politics* 65 (01): 73–115. doi: 10.1017/S0043887112000251.

Moury, C. 2013. *Coalition Government and Party Mandate: How Coalition Agreements Constrain Ministerial Action.* London: Routledge.

Nygård, M. 2010. "Family Policy in the Context of Social Change and Post-industrialism—A Study of Family Policy Positions among Finnish Parties 1970–2007." *Social and Public Policy Review* 4: 57–80.

Nygård, M., and N. Krüger. 2012. "Poverty, Families and the Investment State. The Impact of Social Investment Ideas on Family Policy Discourses in Finland and Germany." *European Societies* 14: 755–77.

Orloff, A. S., and B Palier. 2009. "The Power of Gender Perspectives: Feminist Influence on Policy Paradigms, Social Science, and Social Politics." *Social Politics* 16 (4): 405–12. doi: 10.1093/sp/jxp021.

Pascall, G., and J. Lewis. 2004. "Emerging Gender Regimes and Policies for Gender Equality in a Wider Europe." *Journal of Social Policy* 33 (03): 373. doi: 10.1017/S004727940400772X.

Pfau-Effinger, B. 1998. "Culture or Structure as Explanation for Differences in Part-time Work in Germany, Finland, and the Netherlands." In *Part-time Prospects*, ed. J. O'Reilly, and C. Fagan. London: Routledge, 177–98.

———. 2005. "Welfare State Policies and the Development of Care Arrangements." *European Societies* 7 (2): 321–47. doi: 10.1080/14616690500083592.

Portegijs, W., M. Cloïn, I. Ooms, and E. Eggink. 2006. *Hoe het werkt met kinderen: moeders over kinderopvang en werk*. The Hague: No. SCP publikatie 2006/5.

Rees, T. 2005. "Reflections on the Uneven Development of Gender Mainstreaming in Europe." *International Feminist Journal of Politics* 7 (4): 555–74.

Sainsbury, D. 1999. *Gender and Welfare State*. Oxford: Oxford University Press.

Saraceno, C. 2015. "A Critical Look to the Social Investment Approach from a Gender Perspective." *Social Politics* 22 (2): 257–69. doi: 10.1093/sp/jxv008.

Schmid, G. 2006. "Social Risk Management through Transitional Labour Markets." *Socio-Economic Review* 4: 1–33.

Schmidt, V. A. 2008. "Discursive Institutionalism: The Explanatory Power of Ideas and Discourse." *Annual Review of Political Science* 11: 303–26.

Sen, A. 1992. *Inequality Examined*. New York: Harvard University Press.

———. 1995. "Gender Inequality and Theories of Justice." In *Women, Culture and Development*, ed. M. Nussbaum, and J. Glover. Oxford: Clarendon Press, 259–71.

STM. 2013. *Child and Family Policy in Finland*. Helsinki: Social and Health Ministry of Finland.

Stratigaki, M. 2004. "The Cooptation of Gender Concepts in EU Policies: The Case of "Reconciliation of Work and Family." *Social Politics: International Studies in Gender, State & Society* 11 (1): 30–56. doi: 10.1093/sp/jxh025.

Strøm, K., W. C. Müller, and T. Bergman. 2008. *Cabinets and Coalition Bargaining: the Democractic Life Cycle in Western Europe*. Oxford: Oxford University Press.

Thevénon, O. 2011. "Family Policies in OECD Countries: A Comparative Analysis." *Population and Development Review* 37 (1): 57–87.

van Gerven, M. 2008. *The Broad Tracks of Path Dependent Benefit Reforms. A Longitudinal Study of Social Benefit Reform in Three European Countries, 1980–2006. Yhteiskuntapolitiikka*, Vol. 10. Vammala: Social Security Institution.

van Hooren, F., and U. Becker. 2012. "One Welfare State, Two Care Regimes: Understanding Developments in Child and Elderly Care Policies in the Netherlands." *Social Policy & Administration* 46 (1): 83–107.

Visser, J. 2002. "The First Part-time Economy in the World: A Model to be Followed?" *Journal of European Social Policy* 12 (1): 23–42.

Walby, S. 2005. "Gender Mainstreaming: Productive Tensions in Theory and Practise." *Social Politics* 12 (3): 321–43. doi: 10.1093/sp/jxi018.

Whelan, C. T., and B. Maitre. 2008. "Poverty, Deprivation and Economic Vulnerability in the Enlarged EU." In *Handbook of Quality of Life in the Enlarged European Union*, ed. J. Alber , T. Fahey, and C. Saraceno. London: Routledge, 201–17.

European Policy Analysis, Vol. 3, No. 1, 2017

The Construction of a New Policy Domain in Debates on German Internet Policy

Abel Reiberg

Within the past two decades, the emergence of a new policy domain has become evident in several countries. One example is Germany, where the political parties appointed spokespeople for Internet policy and a standing parliamentary committee for a "digital agenda" has been established. In this paper, the question of how political actors are constructing the new domain of Internet policy is addressed with an empirical analysis. While briefly describing the underlying theoretical framework, it is argued that the development of the new policy domain can be understood as a process of "collaborative meaning making" (Fligstein & McAdam, 2012). During this process, networks of political actors settle for a shared understanding regarding the societal problems that give reason to state intervention and the form this intervention may take. The empirical study is focused on the first debates on German Internet policy. Two text corpora containing parliamentary minutes and articles of five major newspapers are analyzed using close as well as distant reading techniques. The results show how political actors established a shared understanding regarding the policy domain and how this resulted in its particular governmental institutionalization.

KEY WORDS: policy subsystems, policy fields, field theory, Internet policy, Internet governance

关于德国互联网政策的辩论—新政策领域的建构

过去二十年里，数个国家都明显觉察到了新政策领域的出现。以德国为例，建立了以“数字化议程”为主的长期性国会委员会，各政党也指派了互联网政策发言人。本文通过一项实证分析处理了政治参与者如何构建互联网政策新领域的问题。在简要描述潜在理论框架的同时，本文还提到，新政策领域的发展可以被理解为一种“协作意义建构”(*Fligstein & McAdam, 2012*)的过程。在此过程中，多个政治行为者网络勉强共享同一个关于社会问题的看法，该社会问题解释了国家干预和可能的干预形式。实证研究聚焦于德国互联网政策的首次辩论，并通过运用细读法和远距离阅读法分析了两个包含国会会议记录和五大主流报纸文章在内的文本语料库。结果表明了政治行为者是如何建立关于新政策领域的共同看法，以及该看法的建立如何造成了相关政府的制度化。

关键词： 政策领域，领域理论，互联网政策，网络治理，网络政策

doi: 10.1002/epa2.1001

Introduction: The Emergence of a New Policy Domain

While the Internet is, by definition, a border-spanning network, most political decisions affecting its development are still made on a national level. In several nation states Internet policy develops into an independent domain of politics, in the sense that new specialized actors and institutions emerge on different levels of the political system. One example is Germany, where parties appointed spokespeople for "Internet policy",[1] a standing parliamentary committee for a "Digital Agenda"[2] has been established, and several administrative bodies were created.[3] The range of issues these actors and institutions are concerned with reaches from protection of minors from inappropriate content to the regulation of telecommunication markets. With continuing institutionalization, the specific form the field currently has is increasingly taken for granted.

In the following, however, it is pointed out that Internet policy, like any other policy domain, does not have a specific form *per se*. There is no subject that naturally belongs in the realm of Internet policy nor could any of the political actors claim a natural legitimacy. Instead, the political problems and the form of state intervention to solve them are defined by political actors. It is the political actors who gave (and still give) the policy field its specific form and thereby define the spectrum of possible political outcomes for long periods. Thus, the emergence of the new policy domain is not determined by factors external to the political system but by the political actors.

The details of the process in which policy domains emerge are yet not fully understood. This can be related to a lack of research in the past, with rare exceptions.[4] More recently however, several studies on the emergence of policy fields were presented,[5] some of which are focused on the field of Internet policy.[6] The basis for this new line of studies is a social constructivist perspective. In accordance with these approaches, it is assumed in this study that the emergence of a policy domain is an act of social construction. As will be shown, the details of this process can be understood by making use of field theory, institutional theory, and a decisionist notion of the political. Based on this theoretical framework, the process of field emergence can be studied empirically by focusing past interactions of political actors in the emerging domain.

For this paper the first years of German Internet policy were studied in order to understand how a new domain was constructed in debates on Internet policies for the years 1994 to 1998. The analysis focuses on parliamentary minutes and newspaper articles and shows how actors settled on a shared understanding regarding problems in the domain of Internet policy and the form of intervention deemed necessary to solve them. Furthermore, it shows how the shared understanding was established by making extensive use of the concept of information society. Finally, it is explained how the shared understanding influenced governmental institutionalization and therefore the current form of the Internet policy field in Germany. In the following, the results of the analysis mentioned will be described, after briefly explaining its theoretical basis and design.

Theoretical Basis: Combining Field Theory and Institutional Theory

As a concept for describing a specific part of the political system, consisting of specialized actors and institutions, the "field" (Massey & Huitema, 2013) competes with concepts like the "domain" (Burstein, 1991) or "subsystem" (Sabatier, 1988). One advantage which the term "field" has over its competitors is its rich theoretical foundation. As John Martin (Martin, 2003) points out, field theory has a long tradition not mainly but also in social sciences. Especially, the field-theoretic approaches of Pierre Bourdieu[7] were widely recognized, and still provide a thorough basis for the conceptualization of meso-level social order. A work that heavily relies on Bourdieu's ideas and is suited for the analysis of policy domains was presented in 2012 by Neil Fligstein and Doug McAdam. More consistent than for example Paul Sabatier with his concept of subsystems, Fligstein and McAdam followed a social constructivist path. This allowed the development of a concept of field emergence. In contrast, Sabatier's Advocacy Coalition Framework still lacks such a concept.[8] Fligstein and McAdam (2012) describe the process of field emergence as a result of "collaborative meaning making." In this process, actors reach a common understanding concerning the key aspects of a field. This "settlement" is then reestablished in future interactions (Fligstein & McAdam, 2012, pp. 86–108).

As Fligstein and McAdam explain, they drew heavily from Bourdieu's work (2012, p. xiii). They also declare to have "borrowed elements" (2012, p. 8) from different institutionalist approaches. However, the particular concept of institutionalization used is not explained in detail. This is unfortunate, since the concept of institutionalization can be used for a theoretical microfoundation of the process of field emergence. In the following, it is assumed that the elements of the field are institutions and actors. The establishment and reestablishment of a field is achieved through institutionalization. Based on these assumptions, the process of emergence can be explained in more detail with regard to the concept of institutionalization.

For this purpose, it can be drawn upon one of Fligstein's and McAdam's main references: In "the social construction of reality" Berger and Luckmann (1967) theorized extensively on the subject of institutionalization, explaining it as a process of social construction of reality in general. To summarize their extensive work in very few words, institutionalization can be described as consisting of two main steps: the externalization of typifications of interaction and the internalization of such typifications. What is important for empirical analysis, and shall be stressed here, is that the sequencing of the two steps mentioned presupposes "objectivation." Objectivation is described as an act in which the typifications of interactions take on a physical form (Berger & Luckmann, 1967, p. 49). As Berger and Luckmann explain, objectivation can occur in many forms. The form of objectivation which is focused on in this study is language. As Berger and Luckmann point out, language is not only an important means for first-order objectivation, but also for second-order objectivation. With "second-order objectivation" or "legitimation," Berger und Luckmann refer to the integration of institutions of different levels (1967, p. 110). The integration of institutions of a policy field into the existing institutions of a political system can be seen as a typical example for such a nested institutionalization. Therefore, language, or in other words, political discourse is the area of objectivation which is studied in order to understand the process, in which political actors establish shared beliefs regarding "their" policy field. Since political discourse can be studied in regard to numerous aspects, a clarification is needed regarding the aspects that are considered most relevant for the construction of a new policy field.

For this study two aspects were focused on: the first of those being descriptions of societal problems, the second being demands for state intervention. The focus on these two aspects results from a decisionist perspective on the political (Greven, 2008; Mouffe, 2005; Schmitt, 2015). Seen from this perspective, the political process is a process in which binding decisions for society are produced. The possible subjects that are decided on are forms of behavior, which are present in society and which, in the course of the decision, are labeled positive behavior that should be fostered or negative behavior that should be hindered. It is not assumed that political action is caused by societal problems, but that, at least in democratic political systems, political actors have to be able to point to such problems in order to legitimate and realize political activity. Thus, political actors need a shared understanding regarding the problems addressed by their decisions. Furthermore, the decisions have to be made binding for society as a whole, which is achieved by establishing a form of state intervention.[9]

To summarize the theoretical assumptions mentioned: The existence of a policy field presupposes that a common understanding between political actors is achieved through discourse. This common understanding includes answers to the questions of which societal problems are addressed with the actors' decisions and in which form of intervention these decisions are realized. Accordingly, the goal of the empirical analysis was to show which problem descriptions and demands of state interventions were established during the first years of German Internet policy and how this common understanding influenced the form of the field of Internet policy. In the following section, the setup of this analysis will be explained.

Methods of Analysis: Combining Close and Distant Reading

As explained above, the type of objectivation studied for this paper is objectivation through language. This objectivation, or (in other words) discourse, mostly takes the form of verbal utterance. However, for the analysis of longer, past periods, text is a more utile type of data. Therefore, an analysis of texts was conducted. To describe this analysis, it will be distinguished between "close" and "distant reading"[10] of textual data. In contrast to the explanation of Franco Moretti, close and distant reading will be understood here as two ends of a continuum representing all possible modes of text analysis. The more an analysis is based on representations of specific features of text, instead of the text itself, the more it resembles "distant" instead of "close reading." According to this simple typology, the analysis carried out for this study can be defined as an analysis for which mostly "close reading" was performed following very basic techniques of "distant reading." The "sequential" (Stulpe & Lemke, 2016) combination of techniques is based on the assumption that these have a varying utility for the three main steps of analysis made. These three steps are described in the following, whereby the mode of text analysis they resemble is named.

In the first step of analysis, texts which incorporated parts of discourses on Internet policy were selected. Here a challenge lay in the amount of data which had to be handled. With digitalization, the availability of textual data in general has risen significantly. The amount of data that can and should be considered is particularly high, if the object of study is a policy field; this field, as argued above, is created in numerous interactions by large numbers of actors in various parts of the political system over a long period of time. Therefore, this study was based on a large set of textual data selected from two corpora: The first of these two corpora includes the minutes of all debates held in the German Bundestag between the years 1996 and 1998.[11] This corpus was considered assuming that parliament is the central arena where perceptions of societal problems and demands for state intervention are translated into binding law. The second corpus consists of most articles of five major German newspapers published between 1994 and 1998.[12] The articles were considered based on the assumption that they constitute a valid source of political discourse as it takes place also outside parliament. The parliamentary minutes and the newspaper articles were considered objectivations of political discourse in general. Since the political discourse on Internet policy was the subject of study, only those debates and articles that concerned Internet policy had to be identified. Since the content of the two corpora practically could not have been determined by close reading, a simple distant reading was performed in the sense that instead of the text itself, the frequencies of the terms constituting it were analyzed: The single documents were checked for the presence of keywords and documents in which keywords appeared significantly often, compared to the rest of the corpus, were selected. This not only allowed the processing of the extensive initial data, but, due to the necessary formalization involved, warranted careful reflection on the formulation of criteria used for the selection of sources.[13]

In the second step of analysis, the previously selected sources were analyzed according to the descriptions of societal problems used and forms of state intervention demanded by political actors of the policy process in question. For the identification of the broad themes of the texts, a distanced look was considered appropriate. However, in order to gain an understanding of the specific reasoning of single political actors, a close reading was deemed more applicable. This close reading was carried out largely following the principles of qualitative content analysis.[14] Therefore, a codebook describing the features of statements that were considered to constitute problem descriptions and demands for state intervention was created. Additionally, typical examples were selected for both aspects. Samples[15] of the previously selected sources were then imported into software for qualitative content analysis.[16] Using this software, the samples were read and statements were categorized as representing types of "problem description" or "demands for state intervention."

In the final step of analysis, the problem descriptions and demands for state intervention present in the discourses on policies of the studied period were analyzed in order to identify their similarities and therefore possible aspects of an understanding shared by the political actors in the policy field. This procedure was derived from Philip Mayring's description of a "summarizing content analysis" (Mayring, 2015). It consists of two main steps: a paraphrasing of statements and the summarizing of paraphrases. In the first step, a set of rules for creating paraphrases, a formal generalization of the problem description and demands for intervention, was defined. According to those rules, each previously identified problem description and demand for state intervention was then paraphrased. In the second step, a set of rules to summarize the paraphrases was defined. Following these, the list of paraphrases was reduced and summarized under more general paraphrases. Thus a general description of problems and demands for intervention present in the studied period was gained.

The setup of analysis can again be summarized naming the steps of analysis described above. At first, documents which represent discourse on Internet policy were selected from two corpora, consisting of newspaper articles and parliamentary minutes. The documents were then analyzed in order to identify problem descriptions and demands for state intervention used in the discourse. The results of the analysis will be described in the following section. In doing so, an overview on the field of German Internet policy in the thirteenth legislative period will be provided.

Results of the Analysis: The First Years of Germany Internet Policy

Before turning to the first years of the field, the form it currently has shall be described briefly. Unsurprisingly the level of institutionalization which the field has reached until today does not compare to the level of institutionalization of older policy fields like security, health, or environmental policy. In contrast to the aforementioned cases, there is no department on the highest level of government in the case of Internet policy. Instead, a large set of administrative bodies was established on lower levels of government. This set of administrative bodies spreads mainly over the Departments of the Interior, Traffic and particularly Commerce. Following Andreas Blätte (2012), the field can be described as "decentered": "It lacks actors with an identity orienting them exclusively to the [...] field." In the case of Internet policy, most actors are also active in the fields of economic policy or security policy. For this study, the decentralized form, the field currently has, was not considered as a more or less adequate reaction to factors outside the political system, but as a product of the interaction of political actors. In the empirical analysis, the first years of Internet policy were studied in order to understand how the specific form of the field was determined by the "collaborative meaning making" (Fligstein & McAdam, 2012), taking place in the first discourses on Internet policy. The period chosen for analysis is the thirteenth legislative period, which lasted from 1994 to 1998 and involved two of the first major discourses on Internet policy in Germany.

Like in many other countries, the rise of the WWW in the year 1993 meant an important breakthrough in Internet development in Germany; however, it was not until the year 1995 that legislation resembling "the first important framework" for "the new services"[17] was established. This framework took the form of two pieces of legislation, the Information and Communication Services Act[18] (IUKDG) and the Telecommunications Act[19] (TKG). Those two laws not only included binding rules for the use and provision of the Internet, but also defined competence for the formulation of policies in the future. Furthermore, in the course of the thirteenth legislative period, specialized organizations for Internet policy were created in the executive and legislative branch as well as in the private sector. These included units in several departments, a temporary parliamentary committee on the "future of media",[20] and private associations like the "Association of the Internet Industry".[21] The compromise which these actors reached during the discourse of the two policies mentioned can be seen as a first settlement in the emerging field of Internet policy. The contents of this settlement will be described in the following. As explained above, the focus lies on two aspects of the discourses which are considered relevant for the construction of a common basis for long term political action: First, a description concerning problems of society, and second, a demand for state intervention for the solving of the problems described.

The Stated Reasons for Political Action

As stated within the parliamentary proposals for legislation, the goal pursued in the case of the TKG was to "implement the decision [...] to liberalize telecommunication markets" (Bundesregierung 1996). It can be considered as a "final" step in the process of liberalization that took place in Germany during the 1980s and 1990s. By previous acts, the state-run telecom was turned into a private corporation whose shares were held by the state. With the TKG the legal requirements for listing the new telecommunications corporation on the stock markets were met. The privatization of core parts of the physical infrastructure for the Internet was thereby completed.

At the same time, a first "reliable basis" for "the provision of new information and communication services" was created in the form of the IuKDG.[22] The IuKDG was supposed to be a comprehensive legal framework for the emerging Internet. The law included very specific rules concerning among other things data protection and the protection of minors, as well as very basic definitions concerning users' responsibilities for content on the one hand, and state competence for further regulation on the other.

In the discourses the two policies were legitimatized using various descriptions of problems. In the case of the IuKDG the regulation concerning protection of minors and data protection, respectively, for example were legitimatized in parliament by the Minister of Education and Technology who stated:

> Regarding Multimedia: In the course of this legislation all that is necessary for the protection of youth and children has to be warranted. The new

communication systems and data networks – such as the Internet – cannot be the playground of sex offenders.[23] (Meister, 1996)

Concerning the problem of data protection, as another example, the Minister declared:

Me too – when I arrange a bank transaction using a computer, I want to be sure that some hacker cannot move the decimal one digit further to the right. We have to create security here.[24] (Rüttgers, 1997)

While various descriptions of problems of Internet use were brought forward in the discourses of the two policies in order to legitimatize the new legislation, one form of description was most present. Following this description, a perceived general lack in the use and provision of online services was the main challenge to be solved by both policies. The IuKDG for example was legitimated accordingly in the Frankfurter Allgemeine Zeitung:

With the new law, the conditions for the development, commercialization and use of multimedia are created, which are deemed absolutely necessary by all political parties.[25] (FAZ 1997)

The Süddeutsche Zeitung explained similarly:

"Make multimedia possible," postulated the Minister of Education and Technology [...] Rüttgers urges to create a clear and consistent framework that would give optimal conditions for the deployment of modern information and communication technologies in Germany.[26] (SZ 1996a)

The lack in use and provision of online services was not only the problem most intensively described in the legitimations of the new policies. It was also perceived as a problem of greater importance. This becomes apparent in statements in which other problems described are subsumed under the overarching problem of a lack in use and provision of online services. The Minister of Education and Technology stated in regard to the rules for protection of minors from inappropriate content:

For me it is important that we have those rules – due to the general insight that every technology requires acceptance. If it doesn't receive acceptance, it won't have a market. Therefore, it is necessary that the one or the other legitimate reservation against information garbage is addressed with the proposal.[27] (Rüttgers, 1997)

In similar fashion, Edzard Schmidt-Jortzig from the liberal party (FDP[28]) explained:

> Ladies and Gentlemen, the clear regulation regarding responsibilities for criminal and private content creates trust in the German "Informations-standort."[29] Another important means of promoting trust in the new services is the protection of data and the private sphere in the Internet. Trust in the protection of intellectual property is needed as well for those who create works accessible through the Internet.[30] (Schmidt-Jortzig, 1997)

To summarize, the problem descriptions used in the two discourses studied here can be generalized as mainly stating a perceived lack in use and provision of online services. It is this lack in provision and use of online services that was seen as the societal problem which, in the eyes of the political actors, called for solving, or, in other words, political action.

The Forms of Intervention Demanded

Based on the problem descriptions explained above, the political actors of the field argued for specific forms of state intervention. The interventions demanded and finally realized by the Internet policies of the 1990s are described in the following, using Theodore Lowi's classical typology for policies (Lowi, 1972). Using Lowi's terms, the interventions can be characterized as regulative, instead of distributive or redistributive policy.

The IuKDG had a regulative character, insofar as the use and provision of the Internet, the stated goal of the intervention, was not pursued mainly through public investments or the provision of public services. Instead a "clear framework", and "legal certainty for corporations" (Yzer, 1996) thus a regulative intervention was the desired outcome. This becomes visible in the newspaper articles on the debate,[31] as well as the parliamentary protocols. In the parliament, the governing conservative party, for example, explained:

> In this area, it is much more important to get the framework right and to leave room for innovation than to constantly call for state money. Private money is needed here; entrepreneurial courage must be shown here.[32] (Mayer, 1997a)

The many statements with which it was argued for a regulative intervention were supplemented with statements specifying the degree of regulation expected. Mayer, for example, continued his above cited speech by saying:

> The government must restrict itself to setting the basic rules of the game and to enforce them. Every attempt to meddle in the private companies' business will inevitably lead to failure.[33] (Mayer, 1997b)

Most statements were mentioned in regard to what the Minister of Education and Technology termed the "main question" answered by the IuKDG: the legal requirements for the provision of online services. Concerning those requirements, controversies arose between the federal government and the state governments. While the state governments initially asked for a regulation under their oversight, they also pointed out that the absolute level of regulation in the field of online services should be moderate.

While with the IuKDG a regulative framework was defined, the TKG brought a major change from a distributive to a regulative role of the state in telecommunications. The TKG meant the third and final step for the dissolving of the state monopoly. All major parties[34] perceived this as a necessary step to ending inefficient provision of telecommunication services. While the provision of telecommunication was seen as a task best fulfilled by private companies, the task that remained for the state was to create conditions for functioning markets. The Minister for Telecommunication and Post accordingly stated:

> The TKG is the suitable frame for the transition from monopoly to competitive conditions. We have to create the conditions in which the huge potential for innovation in communication and information technology is used in competition.[35] (Bötsch, 1996)

The question of how this task was supposed to be achieved caused controversies. The major opposition party of that period, the Social Democratic Party (SPD[36]), for example, opposed the governing parties' initial drafts of the bill, arguing for a regulation that would include more qualitative requirements for the services provided by telecommunication companies. However, even when opposing the bill, the social democrats supported the general shift to a regulative instead of a distributive or redistributive role of the state in telecommunications.

In short, the understanding shared by the actors of the thirteenth legislative period can be generalized as follows: The main societal problem to be solved in the field of Internet policy was seen to be a lack in use and provision of online services; accordingly, the goal for political action was a fostering of the provision and use of such services. To achieve this, a regulative instead of distributive or redistributive intervention was deemed appropriate. More precisely, a basic framework of rules for the competition in the evolving markets was perceived as the most promising way to reach the goal mentioned. In the following section, it will be explained how these shared ideas were promoted in discourse, making use of a specific version of the concept of information society.

Information Society—A Discursive Means

Analyzing the descriptions of societal problems and the demands for state intervention, it became clear that the term "information society" was used frequently by the political actors. A comparison of the parliamentary debates on Internet policy in the thirteenth period, with all debates held in later periods, shows that "information society" is among the ten words most typical for the debates in Internet policy of the thirteenth period.[37] The term information society is not only very present in discourse but also in the names of events,[38] organizations,[39] and documents.[40]

In the discourses studied,[41] information society refers to an inevitable, positive change societies in general are undergoing at different speeds. The actors contradict each other and sometimes themselves by either explaining that Germany has already reached the state of information society or that it is still moving toward that end. However, they share the understanding that the process is promoted by private companies. The actors see their own task in setting the basic rules for the competition of companies. What is striking is the fact that the benefits of reaching the state of information society are mainly seen as economic benefits and that these benefits are expected to be higher if the political actors are to act faster than their counterparts in other countries.

This use of the concept can be found not only in the debates on the national level. A brief look at the international discourse shows that "information society" was a term frequently used by actors on the international level as well. For its meeting on 24 and 25 June 1994, the European Council requested a report on "the measures to be taken into consideration by the Community and the Member States for infrastructures in the sphere of information." The report, which is better known under the name of the council's chairman Martin Bangemann, starts with a chapter titled "the global information society" where it is explained:

> All revolutions generate uncertainty, discontinuity - and opportunity. [...] How we respond, how we turn current opportunities into real benefits, will depend on how quickly we can enter the European information society. [...] The first countries to enter the information society will reap the greatest rewards. (European Council 1994: 5)

Which measures should be taken is explained previously, in an executive summary:

> This report urges the European Union to put its faith in market mechanisms as the motive power to carry us into the Information Age. (European Council 1994: 4)[42]

The report was used as a basis for the G7 summit which the European Commission hosted from February 25 to 26, 1995. The final report of the summit, which was named "Summit on the Information Society" explains on its first page:

> The smooth and effective transition towards the information society is one of the most important tasks that should be undertaken in the last decade of the twentieth century. (G7 1994: 1)

Regarding this task, it is clarified:

> The rewards for all can be enticing. To succeed, governments must facilitate private initiatives and investments and ensure an appropriate framework aiming at stimulating private investment and usage for the benefit of all citizens. (G7 1994: 1)

The term "information society" in the above described notion finally appears in the discourse on the TKG and IuKDG. In the first parliamentary debate on the IuKDG, in which the term "information society" appears 28 times, it is intensively discussed how well the country is "prepared for the information society" compared to others (Thierse, 1997a,b). While the parties have different answers to that question, all seem to agree that it is their task to enable the change:

> If Germany wants to keep up with the international development, we should get it done and create a framework for a successful transition to the information society.[43] (Thierse, 1997b)[44]

In the newspaper articles on the two policies, the specific use of the term "information society" is adopted:

> By approving the IuKDG the parliament has created the conditions for continuing the path to the information and knowledge society. The law, which from the first of August onward will regulate the use of new information and communication services in worldwide data networks like the Internet, was approved on in third reading by the governing coalition.[45] (taz 1997)

In short, the concept of information society is used to describe the provision of online service as a goal or a problem that needs to be solved. A solution to the problem is described as well: Private companies are considered the driving force of the change and the state is seen in the role of creating a "reliable framework" for these companies as well as "trust" in the "new services" on the consumer side. The concept of information society therefore was a means to achieve the settlement in the field of Internet policy. This settlement had effects not only in the thirteenth legislative period but, as is pointed out in the next section, also in the following periods.

Constitutive Effects of the Policies

As Lowi explained in reaction to criticism on his typology, some policies can be assigned to more than one type. The TKG and the IuKDG are two examples for such policies. As explained above, both policies can be categorized as regulative policies. At the same time, they had constituting effects, namely the "setting up and reappointing of agencies" (Lowi, 1972). Not only from an organizational perspective, but also from a broader decisionist perspective, the policies had a constituting effect in the sense that they defined which actors would be eligible for making binding decisions in the field of Internet policy. In other words, the policies defined particular competences and therefore gave the field a particular form.

With the IuKDG it was determined on which level of the political system, the state or federal level, competencies for Internet Policy would mainly reside. When presenting his draft for the IuKDG, the Minister of Education and Technology claimed the "domain of multimedia" for the federal government. The state governments reacted to this by announcing plans for an interstate agreement by which they would be regulating the "new services." According to these plans, providers of online services would have had to register at the state-level authorities. The state governments backed their claims by pointing to their competence for the regulation of broadcasting. This competence included among other things the issuing of licenses for radio or TV stations, film funding, and the setting of standards for the protection of minors. The federal government, on the other hand, based its claims on its competence in the area of telecommunications. Since from a technical perspective the "new services" were to a certain degree similar to both broadcasting and telecommunication, a decision could not be made on the existing legal basis. Instead, the conflict was finally resolved in direct negotiations between the state governments and the federal government.

In the preceding discourse, the actors in the field argued on the basis of the above described shared beliefs regarding the main problem in the area of Internet policy and the optimal solutions to it. As was explained, the actors saw a lack in use of online services as the pressing societal problem to be solved. A solution to this problem was seen in the promotion of economic development in the telecommunications sector. The Minister for Education and Technology, as the federal government's representative, relied on this shared beliefs, with two lines of argument. With the first, he explained, that Internet regulation would belong in the field of economic policy. By the German constitution, economic policy is assigned to the federal level of the political system. With the second line, the minister argued that, in contrast to the federal government, the state governments would plan to establish a high level of regulation as known from broadcasting and that this high level of regulation would impede economic development. In reaction to these argumentations, the state governments neither questioned the economic perspective on Internet policy nor the preference for a moderate regulation. Instead, while still backing their claims by pointing to their competence for broadcasting regulation, the state governments asserted not to plan for a level of regulation as known from broadcasting regulation. The Prime Minister of Northrine Westphalia for example was cited accordingly by the Süddeutsche Zeitung:

> The states would not seek to establish the same level of regulation for the new multimedia services as in broadcasting, Clement asserted. Instead it would be about a "liberal and clear" authorization procedure, that would

> not impede the dynamics of the market and at the same time would create transparency in this often blurry field. (SZ 1996b)[46]

Such assertions, however, were mostly discounted. The Frankfurter Allgemeine Zeitung for example explained:

> Apparently with an eye on the plans of the state governments to deeply regulate contents and to define liabilities for access providers by making use of a broad notion of the term broadcasting, Rüttger's draft determines that regulation should not impede the development of the markets; therefore, the principle of free service provision and open access for all participants would apply.[47] (FAZ 1996b)

In the negotiations between the federal government and state governments, the latter finally refrained from their initial claims. The key agreement, reached on September 1, 1996 did not include a registration of online services providers at the state level authorities. Therefore, the federal government, particularly the Minister for Education and Technology, circumvented a strong presence of the state governments in the field of Internet policy.

While with the IuKDG it was decided that new competence for Internet policy would mainly reside on the federal level, the TKG defined in which particular organizational form the competence would be created.

As explained, the federal government had backed its claims for competence in the field of Internet policy mainly by pointing to its competence for telecommunication regulation. Before the TKG was implemented this competence resided in the federal government's Department for Post and Telecommunication. In the decades of its existence, the Department's task was seen in the provision of communication infrastructure, with the notion of infrastructure constantly changing according to technological development. In the 1990s, the emerging Internet was seen as part of such infrastructure. However, the provision of information infrastructure in general and the Internet in particular was no longer seen as a task best fulfilled by the state but by private companies. The states' task was seen in the creation of a regulatory framework for the new markets. Accordingly, the privatization of the post and telecommunications markets was decided. The TKG of 1994 was intended to be the "final" step of this privatization. While the previous steps resulted in the restructuring of the Department for Post and Telecommunication, the consequence of the TKG was the complete disestablishment of it. To fulfill the newly defined regulatory role of the state, the TKG prescribed the creation of a "regulatory agency for Post and Telecommunication."

The decision to disestablish the Department for Post and Telecommunication was consensual between the main political actors. However, the form and scope of activity of the new agency was intensively debated. One[48] of the key questions in these debates was the question to which department of the federal government the new agency would be subordinated. Both the Department of Commerce and the Department of Education and Technology were considered as candidates. The line of conflict in the debate lay within the federal government. The participating actors can roughly be assigned to two separate groups: The first group was represented by the Minister of Commerce, a member of the liberal party (FDP[28]). The second group was represented by the Minister of Post and Telecommunication and the Minister of Education and Technology, both members of the conservative parties (CSU[49] and CDU[50]). In the conflict, the first group argued for a moderate intervention in markets with a focus on establishing competition. The second group, particularly the Department for Post and Telecommunication, advocated a slightly stronger intervention with a focus on ensuring quality of service.[51] In the said debates, the Department of Commerce and the liberal party finally succeeded in establishing their perspective by referring to the ideas shared by the actors of the field. With statements like the following, it was argued for a focus on competition, by describing it as the most promising way to solve the problem of a lack in use and provision of online services.

> Effective competition in telecommunications is the best foundation to build up and strengthen new media at the business location Germany.[52] (Meister, 1996)

The actors further argued that the Department of Commerce was best suited to create competition in the new markets.

> The establishing of a new agency on the highest—not high—administrative level and its subordination under the department of commerce are appropriate. With that, it is made sure that the rules of market economy apply for this market of the future.[53] (Stadler, 1996)

In accordance with the preferences of the Minister of Commerce and the liberal party, it was finally decided to subordinate the new regulatory agency under the Department of Commerce. As a head of the new agency, the candidate preferred by the liberal party was established. In addition to the new agency, a new unit for "telecommunication and post" was created in the Department for Commerce. The Department for Education and Technology, on the other hand, was not able to gain competence in the course of the conflict. This relative loss of competence finally resulted in an absolute loss of competence. At the end of the legislative period, the units for "media policy" and "multimedia," which had just been created in the Department of Education and Technology, were also integrated in the Department of Commerce. The established perspective on Internet policy as economic policy therefore led to a loss of competence for the Department of Education and Technology. This can be considered almost ironic, since the establishment of the said economic perspective had previously helped the Department to secure competence for the federal government.

To summarize, the IuKDG and the TKG had a lasting effect on the form of the Internet policy field in Germany. The Department for Education and

Technology successfully claimed major competence for the federal government in the domain of Internet policy. This competence was not centered in a specialized department, which the Department of Post and Telecommunication could have become. Instead, it was assigned to one of the long established departments. Of the two candidates, the Department for Education and Technology and the Department of Commerce, the latter established itself as the key administrative player in the field of Internet policy.

Conclusion

In this study, the emergence of a new policy domain was viewed from a social constructivist perspective. Based on field theory, institutional theory, and decisionist democratic theory, the political actors were seen as the driving force of policy field emergence. In the empirical analysis, which was based on close and distant reading of textual data, the first years of German Internet policy were studied in order to understand how political actors constructed a new policy field.

It was shown that the political actors participating in early debates on Internet policy settled for a shared understanding regarding the new policy field. This shared understanding included a specific notion of societal problems addressed and the form of state intervention deemed necessary for the solving. The understanding was established in discourse by the extensive use of a specific version of the concept of information society. In this version, the concept of information society was introduced in debates on the international level and later used in the discourses on two major German Internet policies, the TKG and IuKDG. In its particular form, the ideational basis of the field influenced the outcome of the two Internet policies. These policies in turn had a constituting effect for the field, in the sense that they defined competence that prevailed not only for the thirteenth but also the following legislative periods. The federal government successfully claimed competence in the evolving field. This competence however was not assigned to a specialized department. Therefore, the field did not take on a centralized form. In contrast, the competence was assigned to one of the established Departments, the Department of Commerce. Until today it remains a key political actor. However, other Departments of the federal government increased their influence on Internet policies. Among those are the Department of the Interior and the Department of Transport as well as the Department of Education and Technology and the Department of Foreign Affairs. Furthermore, state level actors remain active in the evolving field. The field therefore still lacks an administrative body on the highest level of federal government, whose competence solely concerns Internet policy. In contrast, it continues to be institutionalized in a decentralized form.

The analysis described in this article has, like any analysis, specific limitations. Some of these stem from the particular selection of sources and methods of analysis. As a source of data, newspaper articles and parliamentary minutes were selected. These are viable sources in regard to beliefs shared by the majority of actors in the field, as well as major controversies. However, to precisely estimate the degree of influence of specific single actors, particularly those outside the parliamentary arena, a more specific selection of sources would be necessary. Furthermore, close reading techniques were mainly used for the analysis. This was possible because a relatively small period in the development of the policy field was studied. If, in contrast, a complete process of policy field emergence is studied, the amount of relevant textual data will be significantly higher and may (dependent on the field in question) prove unmanageable by close reading. However, a distant reading procedure which could replace the close reading procedure described in this article is yet a desideratum.

Abel Reiberg is a researcher at the Institute for Political Science at the University of Münster. His research interests include Internet governance, policy theory and text mining.

Notes

An earlier version of this article was presented at the IPSA World Conference on Political Science 2016. I want to thank Andreas Blätte (Universität Duisburg-Essen) for his comments on the text.

1. Official title as used by the conservative Party (CDU): "Sprecher für Internetpolitik"
2. Official title (German): "Ausschuss Digitale Agenda"
3. Two examples are the units for "media policy" and "multimedia" in the Department of Education and Technology.
4. Two of these exceptions are Döhler and Manow (1997) and Mai (2003). These pieces are extensive empirical studies on the emergence of two specific policy fields. They include only limited theoretical work on the general issue of policy field emergence. An early theoretical piece on the issue was presented by Knoke (2004). In an eclectic fashion, Knoke identifies categories for the study of field emergence. These categories however are not integrated in a causal model of the process.
5. Some of the recent works on policy field emergence are Noweski (2011), Töller and Böcher (2012), Blätte (2012, 2015) and Massey and Huitema (2013). In these works, the authors theorize mainly on elements of policy fields, criteria for emerging fields and, in the case of Blätte (2015), also on the variety of forms of policy fields. The causality of the process, which is the main topic of this study, is covered only to a limited extent.
6. The works of Haunss and Hofmann (2015) and Hösl and Reiberg (2016) mainly address the question as to whether the field fulfills the criteria of an established policy field. The two pieces also entail assumptions regarding the causal mechanisms of the process of field emergence. However, they do not include an in-depth study of the actual working of these mechanisms.
7. See for example: Bourdieu (1996)
8. Based on the ACF, the emergence of a policy field could be explained by referring to, for example, "external events" or "policy beliefs," two main theoretical components of the ACF. However, the reference to "external events" would only mean an incomplete conceptualization, since the concept is mostly used to capture such phenomena that are "external" to the general analysis. In other words, the "external event" usually resembles a factor that was introduced *ad hoc* and not fully integrated in the theoretical framework and/or empirical analysis. Conceptualizing policy beliefs as a cause of subsystem emergence is problematic as well, since the beliefs are understood to be stable and a dynamic process could not be deduced from the stable factor of beliefs.
9. This might also be a nonintervention.

10. The term "close reading" was mainly coined in literature studies at the beginning of the 20th century, describing forms of analysis through which a relatively small sample of text is intensively studied, in respect to many of its features (Jänicke, Franzini, Faisal Cheema & Scheuermann, 2015). "Distant reading" is described by Franco Moretti (2013) as a set of techniques, which may be applied to great samples of text, for example "all the mystery stories" of a specific period (Moretti, 2013: pp. 219–220). With "distant reading," representations of specific aspects of the text are focused on, which are usually created on the basis of statistical methods.
11. See Blätte (2016) for details on the creation and features of this corpus.
12. The newspapers selected were the five non-tabloid national newspapers with the highest print run in 2014 according to IVW e.V.: Süddeutsche Zeitung, Frankfurter Allgemeine Zeitung, Die Welt, Frankfurter Rundschau, taz - Die Tageszeitung. The corpus consists of 38,037 articles.
13. The complete process for the formulation of keywords cannot be laid out in detail here, but shall be described briefly: At first, articles from one single newspaper were selected using the term "Internet" and its synonyms as keywords. The selected articles were then read and classified as either representing discourse on Internet policy or not. The 129 articles that (at least partially) included discourse on binding rules for the use and provision of the Internet were compared to all articles of the same newspaper. Thus the words most typical for articles on Internet policy were identified. The list of keywords was then reduced, leaving such terms that constitute either synonyms of Internet policies or names of organizations focusing specifically on Internet policy. With this list, articles of other newspapers were selected and processed. The resulting corpus was then analyzed according to names of Internet policies. After identifying those Internet policies that were enacted during the period under analysis, synonyms for the specific policies were gathered on the basis of a keyword in context analysis. Using the synonyms, a sample of articles was then selected for the second step of analysis.
14. See Krippendorff (2013) for an overview.
15. After identifying Internet policy processes of the period, 30 articles for each process as well as all protocols relating to the processes were analyzed.
16. The software used was MaxQDA 12.
17. Original text (German): "Das Gesetz führt erstmals die wichtigsten gesetzlichen Rahmenbedingungen für eine freie Entwicklung neuer Dienstleistungen im Multimedia-Sektor auf" (Rüttgers, 1996)
18. Original title (German): "Informations- und Kommunikationsdienste Gesetz" (IuKDG); The interstate agreement "Staatsvertrag für Mediendienste" also resulted from the same process and is here also referred to with the abbreviation "IuKDG."
19. Original title (German): "Telekommunikationsdienste-Gesetz"
20. Enquette Komission Zukunft der Medien – Deutschlands Weg in die Informationsgesellschaft
21. eco – Verband der Internetwirtschaft e. V.
22. Original text (German): "Ziel des Gesetzes ist es, im Rahmen der Bundeskompetenzen eine verläßliche Grundlage für die Gestaltung der sich dynamisch entwickelnden Angebote im Bereich der Informations- und Kommunikationsdienste zu bieten" (Bundesregierung 1997).
23. Original text (German): "Ich nenne Multimedia. Im Rahmen der Gesetzgebung muß alles getan werden, um Kinder- und Jugendschutz zu gewährleisten. Die zunehmend genutzten neuen Kommunikationssysteme und Datennetze - wie zum Beispiel das Internet dürfen - nicht Spielwiese von Sexualverbrechern sein."
24. Original text (German): "Auch ich will, wenn ich in Zukunft meine Banküberweisungen per Computer ausstelle, sicher sein, daß nicht irgendein Hacker das Komma auf meiner Banküberweisung eine Stelle weiter rechts setzen kann. Hier müssen wir Sicherheiten schaffen."
25. Original text (German): "Durch das neue Gesetz sollen die Rahmenbedingungen für die Entwicklung, die Vermarktung und die Nutzung von Multimedia geschaffen werden, die von allen Parteien für dringend notwendig gehalten werden."
26. Original text (German): "'Multimedia möglich machen', postulierte der Forschungsminister [...] Rüttgers forderte, überschaubare und einheitliche Rahmenbedingungen zu schaffen, unter denen

die modernen Informations- und Kommunikationstechnologien in Deutschland optimale Entfaltungsbedingungen finden können."

27. Original text (German): „Mir ist [...] wichtig, daß wir diese Regelungen haben; [...] aus der allgemeinen Erkenntnis heraus, daß jede Technologie Akzeptanz benötigt. Wenn sie keine Akzeptanz erhält, findet sie auch keinen Markt. Von daher ist es notwendig, daß der eine oder andere Vorbehalt, den es mit Recht gegenüber manchem Informationsmüll gibt, im Gesetzentwurf aufgenommen worden ist.„
28. Freie Demokratische Partei
29. The term mentioned is a neologism created by the speaker. It appears to be a modification of the term "Wirtschaftsstandort"/"business location" (with the term "business" being replaced by "information").
30. Original text (German): "Meine Damen und Herren, die klare Regelung der Verantwortlichkeit für straf- und zivilrechtliche Inhalte schafft Vertrauen in den Informationsstandort Deutschland. [...] Ein weiterer wichtiger Mosaikstein zur Förderung des Vertrauens in die neuen Dienste ist der Schutz der Daten und der Privatsphäre in den Netzen. [...] Vertrauen in den Schutz ihres geistigen Eigentums brauchen auch die Urheber der im Internet verfügbaren Werke."
31. One example is this comment in the Franfurter Allgemeine Zeitung regarding the IuKDG: With that, the Minister of Education and Technology tries to create clear regulation for the plurality of possibilities that are summarized under the term multimedia. Until now the new multimedia services, to which belong telebanking and teleshopping as well as the use of the Internet, are developing only with difficulties, since there is no legal certainty. (FAZ 1996a)Original text (German): "Damit unternimmt der Forschungsminister den Versuch, für die Vielzahl neuer Möglichkeiten, die unter dem Sammelbegriff Multimedia zusammengefaßt werden, eine klare rechtliche Regelung zu schaffen. Bisher entwickeln sich die Multimedia-Dienste, zu denen beispielsweise das Telebanking und Teleshopping, aber auch die Nutzung des Internet gehören, zum Teil nur unter Schwierigkeiten, weil es keine rechtliche Klarheit gibt."
32. Original text (German): "In diesem Bereich ist es viel wichtiger, die Rahmenbedingungen richtig zu setzen und der Innovation Spielraum zu lassen, als ständig nach staatlichem Geld zu rufen. Hier muß privates Geld hinein; hier muß letztlich unternehmerischer Mut greifen."
33. Original text (German): "Die Spielregeln, die der Staat festlegen muß, beziehen sich auf die Verfolgung strafbarer Handlungen, auf den Jugendschutz, auf den Datenschutz, auf die Gewährleistung der allgemeinen Sicherheit, auf die Regelungen für das Urheberrecht und den Wettbewerb und auf einiges andere mehr."
34. The only party arguing against a liberalization was the socialist party—Partei des Demokratischen Sozialismus (PDS). All other parties in the Bundestag were arguing in favor of liberalization. The speaker of the green party for example proclaimed: "for these reasons, I explicitly welcome the objectives set out for this law. Cost-efficient provision as well as optimal customer orientation are not created by monopolies, but most likely by competition" (Kiper, 1996). Original text (German): "Aus diesem Grunde begrüße ich die Zielsetzung dieses Gesetzes ausdrücklich. Kostengünstige Versorgung wie auch optimale Kundenorientierung werden nicht durch Monopole, sondern am ehesten durch Konkurrenz erreicht."
35. Original text (German): "das Telekommunikationsgesetz bildet einen geeigneten Rahmen für den Übergang vom Monopol zu wettbewerblichen Verhältnissen. Wir müssen die Voraussetzung dafür schaffen, daß das große Innovationspotential bei kommunikations- und informationstechnischen Anwendungen im Wettbewerb ausgeschöpft werden kann."
36. Sozialdemokratische Partei Deutschlands
37. The term occurred 119 times in the debates on Internet policy of the thirteenth legislative period and 476 in all debates held in the fourteenth to sixteenth legislative period.
38. Example: The G7 summit "on the Information Society"
39. Example: The temporary parliamentary commission "future of media" which was also titled "Germany's way into the information society."

40. Example: The federal governments report "Info 2000" which, like the parliamentary commission, was also titled: "Germanys way into the information society."
41. The notion of information society obviously differed to that of authors like Manuel Castells or Daniel Bell, who mainly coined the term.
42. What "that means" is clarified further in three points: "it means fostering an entrepreneurial mentality to enable the emergence of new dynamic sectors of the economy; it means developing a common regulatory approach to bring forth a competitive, Europe-wide, market for information services; it does NOT mean more public money, financial assistance, subsidies, dirigisme, or protectionism." (European Council 1994: 4)
43. Original text (German): "Wenn Deutschland den Anschluß an die internationale Entwicklung nicht verlieren will, sollte es uns doch gelingen, angemessene Rahmenbedingungen für einen erfolgreichen Übergang in die Informationsgesellschaft zu schaffen."
44. Similarly, the term "information society" is used also in the debates on the TKG: "Dear ladies and gentlemen! With the TKG the road to the information society of the twenty-first century has been cleared in Germany. To what extent multimedia applications and multimedia services have a chance in Germany and to what extent Germany can be competitive internationally in this sector is determined by the TKG." (Meister, 1996)
45. Original text (German): "Mit der Verabschiedung des Multimedia-Gesetzes hat der Bundestag am Freitag die rechtlichen Rahmenbedingungen für den weiteren Weg Deutschlands in die Informations- und Wissensgesellschaft geschaffen. Das Gesetz, das mit Wirkung vom 1. August die Nutzung neuer Informations- und Kommunikationsdienste über weltweite Datennetze wie das Internet regelt, wurde in Dritter Lesung mit den Stimmen der Regierungskoalition beschlossen."
46. Original text (German): "Die Bundesländer strebten bei den neuen multimedialen Diensten keinesfalls eine Regulierungsdichte wie beim traditionellen Rundfunk an, stellte Clement fest. Es gehe vielmehr um ein 'liberales und leicht nachvollziehbares 'Genehmigungsverfahren, das die Dynamik des Marktes nicht bremse und zugleich Transparenz in diesem oft unübersichtlichen Bereich schaffe."
47. Original text (German): "Offensichtlich mit Blick auf die Planungen der Bundesländer, über eine breitere Auslegung des Rundfunkbegriffs weit in die Inhalte hineinzuregulieren und den Anbietern von Online-Zugängen Verantwortlichkeiten zuzuweisen, stellt der Rüttgers-Entwurf fest, die Reglementierung dürfe die Entwicklung der Märkte nicht behindern; deshalb gelte der Grundsatz der Zulassungs- und Anmeldefreiheit für Anbieter und des freien Zugangs für alle Beteiligten."
48. The subjects of the dispute also included the form of the new regulatory agency, the procedure for the election of the head of the agency, and finally the election itself.
49. Christlich Soziale Union
50. Christlich Demokratische Union
51. It shall be noted that a stronger intervention was also advocated by the social democrats, who at that time were not part of the governing coalition, but who nevertheless were a veto player, due to their majority in the second chamber and who therefore took part in the conflict.
52. Original text (German): "[E]in funktionierender Wettbewerb in der Telekommunikation [ist] das beste Fundament für den Aufbau und Ausbau der neuen Medien am Standort Deutschland."
53. Original text (German): "Die Einrichtung einer Bundesoberbehörde und nicht etwa einer obersten Bundesbehörde sowie die Zuordnung der Regulierungsbehörde zum Bundesministerium für Wirtschaft sind sachgerecht. Dadurch ist sichergestellt, daß auf diesem Zukunftsmarkt die Regeln der Marktwirtschaft gelten."

References

Berger, Peter L., and Thomas Luckmann. 1967. *The Social Construction of Reality: A Treatise in the Sociology of Knowledge*. New York: Anchor.

Blätte, Andreas. 2012. "Unscharfe Grenzen von Policy-Feldern im parlamentarischen Diskurs: Messungen und Erkundungen durch korpusunterstützte Politikforschung." *Zeitschrift für Politikwissenschaft* 22 (1): 35–68.

———. 2015. "Grenzen und Konfigurationen politischer Handlungsfelder. Skizze einer typologischen Theorie." *der moderne staat – Zeitschrift für Public Policy, Recht und Management* 8 (1): 92–112.

———. 2016. *The PolMine Project: Corpus Analysis for Political Science.* http://polmine.sowi.uni-due.de/polmine/ Accessed January 10, 2017.

Bourdieu, Pierre. 1996. *The Rules of Art: Genesis and Structure of the Literary Field.* Stanford: Stanford University Press.

Burstein, Paul. 1991. 'Policy Domains: Organization, Culture and Policy Outcomes.' *Annual Review of Sociology* 17: 327–50.

Döhler, Marian, and Philip Manow. 1997. *Strukturbildung von Politikfeldern: Das Beispiel bundesdeutscher Gesundheitspolitik seit den 50er Jahren.* Opladen: Leske & Budrich.

Fligstein, Neil, and Doug McAdam. 2012. *A Theory of Fields.* Oxford, NY: Oxford University Press.

Greven, Michael. 2008. *Die politische Gesellschaft: Kontingenz und Dezision als Probleme des Regierens und der Demokratie,* 2nd ed. Wiesbaden: VS Verlag für Sozialwissenschaften.

Haunss, Sebastian, and Jeanette Hofmann. 2015. 'Entstehung von Politikfeldern – Bedingungen einer Anomalie.' *Der moderne Staat - Zeitschrift für Public Policy, Recht und Management* 8 (1): 29–49.

Hösl, Maximilian, and Abel Reiberg. 2016. 'Netzpolitik in statu nascendi.' In *Text Mining in den Sozialwissenschaften.*, ed. Matthias Lemke, and Gregor Wiedemann. Wiesbaden: Springer, 315–42.

Jänicke, Stefan, Greta Franzini, Muhammad Faisal Cheema, and Gerik Scheuermann. 2015. *On Close and Distant Reading in Digital Humanities: A Survey and Future Challenges.*

Knoke, David. 2004. "The Sociopolitical Construction of National Policy Domains." In *Interdisziplinäre Sozialforschung. Theorie und empirische Anwendungen. Festschrift für Franz Urban Pappi,* ed. Christian Henning, and Christian Melbeck. Frankfurt: Campus Verlag, 81–96.

Krippendorff, Klaus. 2013. *Content Analysis: An Introduction to Its Methodology,* 3rd ed. Los Angeles: Sage.

Lowi, Theodore J. 1972. 'Four Systems of Policy, Politics, and Choice.' *Public Administration Review* 32 (4): 298–310.

Martin, John Levi. 2003. "What Is Field Theory?" *American Journal of Sociology* 109 (1): 1–49.

Mai, Manfred. 2003. "Medienpolitik: Genese und Ausdifferenzierung eines Politikfeldes." In *Politische Steuerung im Wandel,* eds. Katharina Holzinger, Christoph Knill and Dirk Lehmkuhl. Wiesbaden: Springer, 219–39.

Massey, Eric, and Dave Huitema. 2013. "The Emergence of Climate Change Adaptation as a Policy Field: The Case of England." *Regional Environmental Change* 13 (2): 341–52.

Mayring, Philip. 2015. *Qualitative Inhaltsanalyse: Grundlagen und Techniken.* Weinheim: Beltz.

Moretti, Franco. 2013. *Distant Reading.* New York: Verso.

Mouffe, Chantal. 2005. *On the Political.* New York: Routledge.

Noweski, Michael. 2011. "Ausreifende Politikfelder: Perspektiven einer Theorie." *Der moderne Staat* 4 (2): 481–94.

Sabatier, Paul A. 1988. "An Advocacy Coalition Framework of Policy Change and the Role of Policy-Oriented Learning Therein." *Policy Sciences* 21 (2/3): 129–68.

Schmitt, Carl. 2015. *Der Begriff des Politischen: Text von 1932 mit einem Vorwort und drei Corollarien,* 9th ed. Berlin: Duncker & Humblot.

Stulpe, Alexander, and Matthias Lemke. 2016. "Blended Reading." In *Text Mining in den Sozialwissenschaften.,* ed. Wiesbaden: Springer.

Töller, Annette Elisabeth, and Michael Böcher. 2012. *Reifung als taugliches Konzept zur Konzeptualisierung langfristigen Wandels von Politikfeldern? Überlegungen anhand des Politikfeldes Umweltpolitik.* Hagen: FernUniversität Hagen.

Cited Documents

Bötsch, Wolfgang. 1996. Redebeitrag. In Plenarprotokoll des Deutschen Bundestages. 13th Bundestag 83th sess.

Bundesregierung. 1996. Entwurf eines Telekommunikationsgesetzes vom 23.04.1996

Bundesregierung. 1997. Entwurf eines Gesetzes zur Regelung der Rahmenbedingungen für Informations- und Kommunikationsdienste vom 09.04.1997

European Council. 1994. "Report on Europe and the Global Information Society." In Bulletin of the European Union 2/94.

FAZ. 1996a. *Frankfurter Allgemeine Zeitung vom* 12.11.1996: 17.

FAZ. 1996b. *Frankfurter Allgemeine Zeitung vom* 27.04.1996: 13.

FAZ. 1997. *Frankfurter Allgemeine Zeitung vom* 14.06.1997: 13.

G7. 1994. "Conclusions from the Information Society Conference".

Kiper, Manuel. 1996. Redebeitrag 283.1In *Plenarprotokoll des Deutschen Bundestages*. 13th Bundestag, 110th sess.

Mayer, Martin. 1997a. Redebeitrag 8.9. In *Plenarprotokoll des Deutschen Bundestages*. 13th Bundestag, 170th sess.

Mayer, Martin. 1997b. Redebeitrag 8.11. In Plenarprotokoll des Deutschen Bundestages. 13th Bundestag, 170th sess.

Meister, Michael. 1996. Redebeitrag 289.1. In Plenarprotokoll des Deutschen Bundestages. 13th Bundestag, 110th sess.

Rüttgers, Jürgen. 1996. Redebeitrag 2.1. In Plenarprotokoll des Deutschen Bundestages. 13th Bundestag, 147th sess.

Rüttgers, Jürgen. 1997. Redebeitrag 2.21. In Plenarprotokoll des Deutschen Bundestages. 13th Bundestag, 170th sess.

Schmidt-Jortzig, Edzard. 1997. Redebeitrag 36.5. In Plenarprotokoll des Deutschen Bundestages. 13th Bundestag, 170th sess.

Stadler, Max. 1996. Redebeitrag. In Plenarprotokoll des Deutschen Bundestages. 13th Bundestag, 83th sess.

SZ. 1996a. *Süddeutsche Zeitung vom* 14.03.1996: 25.

SZ. 1996b. Süddeutsche Zeitung vom 22.04.1996: 22.

taz. 1997. *taz - die Tageszeitungvom* 14.06.1997.

Thierse, Wolfgang. 1997a. Redebeitrag 6.1. In Plenarprotokoll des Deutschen Bundestages. 13th Bundestag, 170th sess.

Thierse, Wolfgang. 1997b. Redebeitrag 6.10. In Plenarprotokoll des Deutschen Bundestages. 13th Bundestag, 170th sess.

Yzer, Cornelia. 1996. Redebeitrag 142.6. In Plenarprotokoll des Deutschen Bundestages. 13th Bundestag, 95th sess.

European Policy Analysis, Vol. 3, No. 1, 2017

Learning Processes in Hungarian Health Policy 1990–2004: A Case Study of Health Resource Allocation[1]

Balázs Babarczy and László Imre

Hungary became a democracy and market economy in 1989–1990. As a result of the transition process, new ideas and solutions were adapted to the various problems of public policy. This paper analyzes the policy and political learning processes of Hungarian health policy within an advocacy coalition framework. We focus on a case study of health resource allocation reforms, and use it as a proxy for wider health policy analysis, given the pivotal importance of this field in health policy reforms, particularly at the beginning of the period observed. When defining the right principles and solutions, it appears stakeholders were influenced to a large degree by trial-and-error learning processes: this may be at least partially attributable to the technical nature of the policy problems.

KEY WORDS: policy learning, health policy, resource allocation, diagnosis-related groups, Hungary

1990-2004年间匈牙利卫生政策的学习进程关于卫生资源分配的案例分析

匈牙利在*1989-1990*年间实现了民主和市场经济。作为过渡阶段的结果，新观念和措施都被用于适应公共政策的不同问题。本文分析了倡议联盟框架下匈牙利卫生政策的政治学习进程。考虑到卫生资源分配改革在卫生政策改革中 (尤其在观察期间开始时) 的关键重要性，本文对其进行了案例分析，并将其作为测量“更广泛卫生政策分析”的指标。在定义正确的原则和措施时，利益相关者似乎都在很大程度上受到了试错法学习进程的影响：这可能至少要部分归因于政策问题的技术性质。

关键词: 政策学习，卫生政策，资源分配，诊断相关组，匈牙利

Introduction

Over the past 25 years, the countries of Central and Eastern Europe have gone through substantial social and economic change. In an historic setting such as this, learning processes play an important role in most areas of social life, and the development of health policy is no exception. This paper focuses on health policy learning processes in Hungary, as reflected in health resource allocation reforms introduced throughout the period following the change of regime, i.e., from 1990 until 2004 when these reforms came to a halt. The analysis is supplemented by an overview of the transition process itself, concentrating on the years immediately preceding the 1989–1990 turning point.

doi: 10.1002/epa2.1004

Resource allocation mechanisms have a particular importance because, as will be seen in the case study, they were considered by many stakeholders, especially at the beginning of health reform processes, as a cornerstone, and that changing them would trigger widespread positive evolution.

Within a very wide range of literature on transition politics and economics —an overview of which would exceed the limits of this contribution—Haggard and Kaufman (2001) analyze public policy reforms according to three main axes: (1) whether the reforms in question are carried out in a situation of acute crisis or in a more relaxed environment, (2) whether the political architecture of the given country supports swift executive decisions or consultative procedures, and (3) whether the nature of the problem to be solved is a coordination one, i.e., a relatively wide-shared goal to be achieved via new methods, or whether a whole new set of institutions and procedures will have to be created.

In Hungary, the crisis element seems to have played an important role. The country went through an acute economic crisis, and was therefore in need of immediate reform between 1989 and 1996.

On an institutional level, however, the situation has been relatively calm and supportive to centralized decision making. The Hungarian political landscape is characterized by a strong government, answering to a unicameral assembly, which has served through the entire duration of each of its mandates since 1990. This has given the executive substantial leverage for reform, though this was often perceived as limited by, among other things, the existence of multiparty governmental coalitions.

As for the nature of the problem in hand, i.e., health resource allocation reform, it appears to be less a coordination issue, but requires, first and foremost, the creation of a complex institutional system. Because the solution itself is complex, it is relatively difficult to reach a consensus on its detail and, ex-post, to evaluate precisely its effects.

This paper builds on May's (1992) distinction between political learning and policy learning, the latter comprising instrumental and social policy learning. It tries to answer the question: What was the respective role of political and policy learning processes in Hungarian health resource allocation reforms after the change of regime?

As will be seen, substantial policy learning processes have taken place both before and during the introduction and refinement of a resource allocation system based on diagnosis-related groups (DRG). They helped this technical solution emerge as a rational choice at the time of transition to a market economy. Later, they also contributed to the acknowledgement that health resource allocation reform was no panacea, and that its incentives alone could not transform the whole healthcare sector. Meanwhile, political learning guided stakeholders' behavior within the newly created system. May's (1992) article also draws attention to the importance of trial-and-error—as opposed to systematic evaluation—in the policy learning process, which is commonly observable in the case treated here.

The paper is organized as follows. The next section describes in more detail the concepts and methods used to answer the question. Third section gives a brief overview of the Hungarian health system. Fourth and fifth sections present the different phases treated within the case study of health resource allocation policy in Hungary between 1990 and 2004. Sixth section concludes.

Concepts and Methods

This paper builds, first and foremost, on the theoretical grounds laid by Sabatier and Jenkins-Smith (1993), when defining their advocacy coalition framework (ACF). Although the framework has gone through some revisions, e.g., in Weible, Sabatier and McQueen (2009), these do not concern the concepts to be used here. Indeed, as Jenkins-Smith, Nohrstedt, Weible and Sabatier (2014) point out, those concepts have been used throughout the last 20 years to analyze different policy areas in a wide variety of countries.

The main concepts to be used here relate to coalitions, beliefs, and learning. The paper takes the ACF's approach of focusing on long-term (more than one decade long) evolution in given policy subsystems. It also stakes its epistemological position, in the sense that it wishes to analyze the policy arena as one of competing beliefs and world views—though it does not exclude considerations as to the stakeholders' pursuit of self-interest.

Within this context, advocacy coalitions are built around common beliefs regarding the positive or negative consequences of a given policy. Beliefs can be arranged into three categories. Deep core beliefs relate to basic values and the way one looks at the world. They separate optimists from pessimists and progressives from conservatives, but are rarely manifested directly in policy subsystems.

Conversely, policy core beliefs determine the fundamental orientation of actors relative to the issues of a given subsystem. For example, as Sabatier and Jenkins-Smith (1993) put it, the preference between economic growth and job creation on the one hand, and the protection of the environment on the other, may orient the stances taken and actions pursued by different stakeholders within the air pollution policy subsystem. One of the ACF's key hypotheses even affirms that the members of an advocacy coalition have to have similar policy core beliefs relative to the given issue. Though this hypothesis is not tested in this paper, policy core beliefs are regarded as constitutive of advocacy coalitions.

Finally, secondary beliefs relate to the technical details of a policy programme, i.e., what instruments best serve the pursuit of a policy goal inspired by policy core beliefs. Secondary beliefs are concrete, therefore easier to identify than deep core or policy core beliefs. They can also be the subject of policy learning: what May (1992) conceptualizes as instrumental learning. But policy learning can concern policy core beliefs, too. In this case, the interpretation of common good within the policy subsystem is altered. May (1992) calls this process social policy learning.

Within the ACF, policy learning—in connection with both secondary and policy core beliefs—can happen within and across coalitions. However, the alteration of stakeholders' beliefs is not the only factor that leads to policy change: external factors, such as a change of government, or the rise of one coalition to a key position (e.g., ministry), play an equally important role. Although trial-and-error learning itself may perform an important function, the availability of good quality information on the policy issue can potentially lead to more intensive learning and more rapid policy change. Finally, policy forums and policy brokers may also have paramount importance as catalysts in the debate.

Political learning happens when stakeholders' beliefs stay the same, but they evolve in their methods and behavior in order to pursue their interests. Political learning typically comprises within-coalition learning on how best to act in favor of the given coalition's policy beliefs. However, in this paper, it is extended to the adaptation of stakeholders to the incentives created by a given policy instrument, and all their actions in order to gain power and resources within the predefined rules.

The health policy case study is based on: (1) the full bibliography of István Bordás, one of the chief architects of the health resource allocation system, complemented by (2) a full title scan of three major Hungarian health policy journals —Egészségügyi Gazdasági Szemle, Informatika és Menedzsment az Egészségügyben and Kórház—for the period 1998–2013.[2]

Against this background, it was subsequently deemed necessary to carry out interviews with a targeted sample of healthcare decision makers, managers, and technical experts. A total of six interviews were carried out: three with former policymakers, and one each with a technical expert later turned hospital manager, a key technical expert of the health financing system, and a former healthcare specialist at the Ministries of Health and Finance (see the list at the end).

The interviews were tape-recorded: three have been fully transcribed and three summarized. The transcriptions and summaries were then coded via the method of directed content analysis (see Hsieh & Shannon, 2005). The coding categories were derived from the above mentioned terminology of the ACF in order to identify coalitions, belief systems, learning patterns, and policy change. ATLAS.ti (trial version) was used to process the material.

The number of interviews this study is based on limits the robustness of its conclusions. Further research is needed to understand better the belief systems present in both policy arenas, and to be able to draw more generalizable conclusions.

Overview of the Hungarian Healthcare System

The following brief overview of the Hungarian health system is based on the WHO health system model presented on Figure 1.

The healthcare system of Hungary operates under thorough state control, although one of the main objectives of transition reforms was to ease this. Resource generation has been tightly overseen by central government throughout the entire period from 1990 to this day. Service delivery was first substantially decentralized, and then later re-centralized. Since the change of regime, revenue

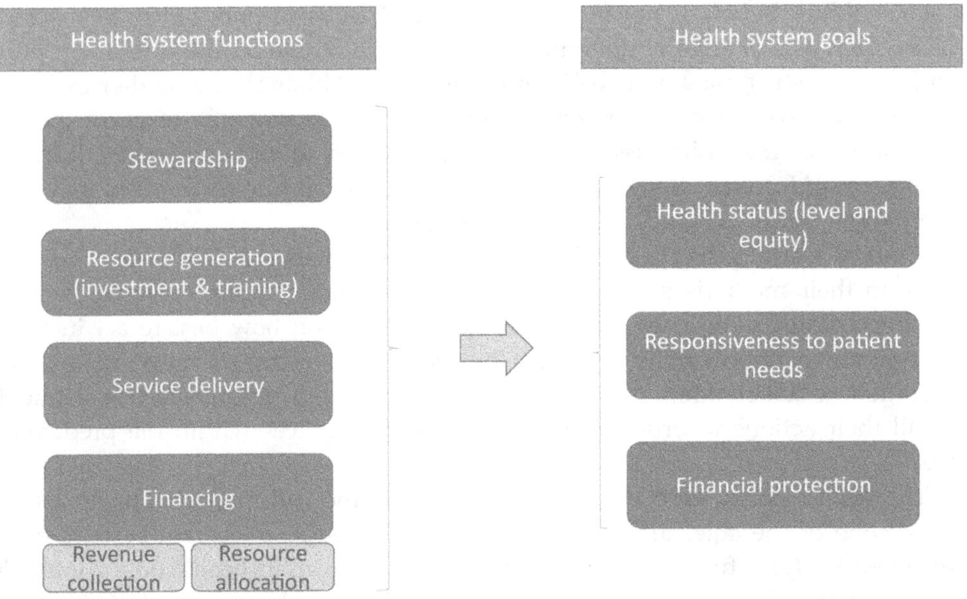

Figure 1. A health system model.

Source: Kutzin et al. (2015), based on WHO (2000).

collection has taken place in a single-insurer social health insurance (SHI) model. Finally, resource allocation has also been the subject of various reforms in different directions, some of which will be detailed in this case study.

Resource generation in healthcare has been under strong state control throughout the period. Central government makes detailed decisions concerning medical and allied health specialist training, as well as relating to investment in buildings and equipment. In an early move of decentralization, the ownership of healthcare provider infrastructure was transferred from the state to local and county authorities as early as 1990 (Orosz, 2001, p. 238–39). However, from 1996 onwards, hospital and outpatient capacity (measured by bed numbers and consultation hours) has been determined by law (Orosz, 2001, p. 77–78). The National Health Insurance Fund also pursues a strategic buyer function, triggering important changes in the provider infrastructure (Dózsa, 2010, p. 28–29). Since 2012, all hospitals and a substantial number of outpatient clinics have again belonged to the state, with a central administration responsible for their management (National Healthcare Service Center 2016, p. 8; hereafter: NHSC). In 2014, the share of centrally funded investment (European Union and central government funds) in inpatient care—building and equipment in hospitals and hospital-integrated outpatient clinics—amounted to 71% (NHSC 2014). European Union funds are attributed via flagship projects and open calls, the latter enabling municipalities with healthcare providers to realize their own investment initiatives. Since 2012 however, municipal ownership of health providers has been only marginal (Figure 2).

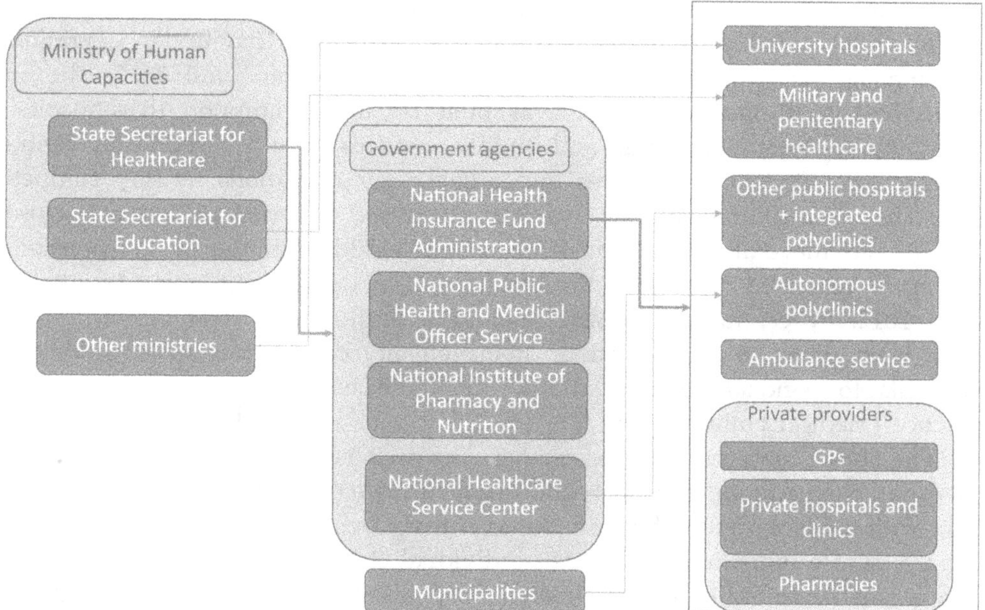

Figure 2. Governance structure of the Hungarian publicly financed health system[2].

Source: National Healthcare Service Center (2016).

Health service provision is divided among the distinct subsystems of primary care, outpatient and inpatient healthcare. Primary care is the responsibility of local authorities who create GP practices and assign a territorial obligation for them to care for. However, patients are free in their choice of provider, and may change once a year, provided they can find a non-obligated doctor to take them on (MoH Decree 4/2000). GP practices are operated by individual enterprises or small companies, and financed by the Health Insurance Fund through—principally age-weighted—capitation. GP out-of-hours services are often provided through different contracts. In addition to GPs, primary care also includes dental services and a system of maternity and childcare nurses. Currently, the government is planning to introduce group practices (NHSC 2016). Primary care officially has a gatekeeper role; however, outpatient clinics are accessible without referral in a number of important medical specialties, e.g., surgery and ophthalmology (Gov. Decree 217/1997).

Outpatient specialist care is, for the most part, provided by polyclinics employing their own personnel, including doctors. The majority of polyclinics operate independently from hospitals. Some of these are overseen by the state's hospital holding, but most belong to local authorities. Seventy-five percent of the outpatient cases treated and interventions performed take place in hospital-integrated polyclinics, which are under central government control (National Health Insurance Fund 2015).

Though inpatient care capacities and service profiles have always been subject to close central government scrutiny and regulation, day-to-day operations and management were organized in a decentralized way until 2012. The so-called "managed market model" was built on the assumption that hospitals belonging to local authorities and county councils would respond to central government's financial incentives and adjust their operations to stay competitive. The 2012 centralization move has given the government a much closer insight into the daily management of hospitals, although the key responsibilities have remained with the director general of each institution (designated, since 2012, by central government, not local authorities). Most recently, there have been plans to shift financial management competences from individual hospitals to regional administrations, but these have not yet been put into practice (Medical Online 2016).

The above concerns only the publicly financed health system. Providers who choose to charge more than the reimbursement price of social security cannot contract with the latter and so operate on an entirely free-market basis. These include mostly private outpatient providers—individual doctors or clinics—but there are also a small number of non-contracted hospitals. Other privately owned providers, e.g., GPs, private diagnostics and dialysis providers, etc., are contracted with the Health Insurance Fund, and their services are entirely reimbursed to the patients using them.

Concerning revenue collection and pooling, a compulsory single-payer health insurance model has been in place since the beginning of the transition period. Every citizen with a permanent residence is required by law to be part of the health insurance system, either through the payment of contributions proportional to their earnings, or the remittance of a fixed monthly amount for those without formal income, or through a settlement paid by the central budget for certain groups (students, pensioners, etc.).

In practice, the proportion of salary-based contributions and budgetary transfers within the revenues of the Health Insurance Fund vary considerably from one year to another, due to the frequent modification of the legal framework governing the different transfers. In addition to this, a fraction of public health spending—most notably capital expenditure—does not pass through the Fund, but is channeled through the central and local budgets, as described above (Gaál et al., 2011, p. 67–69).

The National Health Accounts in Figure 3 suggest that in 2014 compulsory health insurance added up to only a little more than 57% of total health spending. A further almost 10% came from government sources distinct from statutory health insurance, and the rest from—mainly out-of-pocket—private payments. Nevertheless, as the bulk of these private payments are spent on drugs co-payment, it can still be claimed that the health system is driven predominantly by providers under state control and/or state financing. How this financing is allocated is, therefore, of pivotal importance. The aim of the following case study is to shed some light on the evolution of this public resource allocation system.

Figure 3. Distribution of healthcare revenues by financing agents (National Health Accounts, 2014).

Source: OECD Statistics.

Initial Reforms

Within the framework of Kutzin, Evetovits, Jakab and Thomson (2015), based on the established terminology of the World Health Organisation (WHO), health resource allocation encompasses all the functions and mechanisms of a health system responsible for paying healthcare providers from an insurance pool of funds. As a consequence of this, the incentives provided by health resource allocation systems determine the behavior of most health system actors, and therefore have a potential influence on the quality, quantity, and distribution of healthcare supply (see Moreno-Serra & Wagstaff, 2010).

At the end of the socialist era, health resource allocation was decentralized and arbitrary: local and county councils were responsible for the allocation of most funds, and they were using the block contract method, i.e., providers received a predetermined budget, intended to cover all expenses, unrelated to the number and severity of cases treated.

Within a general context of economic reform (see Adam, 1987), efforts were made to rationalize these mechanisms. There was a general move away from central planning and rationing, and toward a better remuneration of actual performance. Its first target was industry: in Hungary, the so-called "New Economic Mechanism" of 1968 allowed the management of corporations more control over the way they spent profits and invested resources (For an assessment of the reform, see, e.g., Bauer, 1983). After some hesitation, as well as a period of counter-reform (see Verbászi, 2004), in the 1980s the government sought to extend this form of reorganization to the institutions of the welfare sector. There was a search for measures capable of reconciling the control and allocation mechanisms of state and market.

In this context, an expert coalition arose, composed of technocrats from both the Ministry of Health and the Ministry of Finance, with a double aim of creating a centralized system of resource allocation (independent of local councils) and of introducing performance-related payment instruments. Advice received from various international organizations pointed in a similar direction, as one of the interviewees recalls (Interview A). Policy core beliefs of this coalition included a need for more transparency and accountability, also the superiority of decentralized, market-based incentives above central planning and administrative measures, but equally a need for strong state regulation and universal coverage in healthcare (Bordás, 1990).

The superiority of performance-related financing has indeed become a key policy core belief of this technocratic coalition, and has been exercised, from 1987 onwards, principally within the Reform Secretariat of the Ministry of Social Affairs and Health. Secondary beliefs on what payment instruments would best fit the new model varied within the Reform Secretariat. But a powerful wing of young experts advocating the hospital financing method of diagnosis-related groups (DRG), utilized in the United States since the mid-1980s, finally prevailed (Interview B). Although their composition and beliefs have changed in many ways over time, this line of thinking will hereafter be referred to as the DRG coalition.

According to this coalition's secondary belief, a DRG system would promote free competition of providers for patients, with revenues allocated as a function of the number and severity (resource-intensity) of cases treated. Given that the DRG system sets unit prices of healthcare interventions at the average level observed across all providers, it was also envisaged less efficient providers would need to refine their management techniques, or, if they failed to compete with the cost level of others, to shut down their given services. The system was designed to promote transparency, cost-efficiency and competition among hospitals.

These secondary beliefs extended over the strict boundaries of resource allocation: the coalition believed resource allocation would be a trigger for a series of other reforms, brought about by the incentives created in the new, competitive environment for healthcare providers. Accordingly, the coalition aspired to realize most of its policy core through the DRG instrument (and the related financing system). Some of the most important goals were the following (after Nagy, Dózsa & Boncz, 2008):

- reducing or eliminating unneeded hospitalization
- focusing the care profile of hospitals on the diseases strictly requiring inpatient care
- streamlining patient pathways and assuring proximity care, where possible
- increasing the technical efficiency of hospitals (i.e., reducing the cost per case)

- balancing the territorial disparities of access to hospital care within the country
- keeping budgetary costs down.

Meanwhile, following the first democratically elected government taking office in 1990, power relations outside of the health policy subsystem underwent changes. The Hungarian Democratic Forum (MDF), the main center-right government party, had its own policy core beliefs, at the center of which stood the idea of independent, entrepreneurial doctors. To aid the development of such a model, it was planned to introduce a German model of social insurance. Apart from a multiple-insurer system, the German system would also have meant a fee-for-service method of resource allocation, perceived as being more advantageous than DRG, as far as the revenue of health providers and professionals was concerned.

Despite the apparent differences in their approaches, there were several factors that allowed a compromise of the two coalitions. First, as for the policy core belief of decentralized (market-like) control mechanisms and performance-related remuneration, there was relative consensus between the two sides. In fact, both were starkly opposed to the existing system of global budgets, deemed both inequitable and inefficient, and debate centered instead around the secondary belief of which payment method to employ.

Second, the policy core belief advocated by the Ministry of Finance that cost control mechanisms had to be put in place, was successfully opposed to the policy core of the MDF that doctors' pay needed an urgent rise. Given the difficult and rapidly deteriorating economic situation in the country—an outside factor that seems to have played an important role—the government leaned increasingly toward the more economical DRG model.

Third, the DRG model had already been elaborated in detail, and tested on data provided by several hospitals. The coalition advocating German-style health insurance did not have such detailed technical information at its disposal, a deficiency especially critical in matters relating to cost control. Political considerations and personal factors also played an important role, as certain MDF politicians supported the DRG model which, this way, appeared less like a "communist" invention (Interview C).

In the end, the DRG coalition took over, and an American DRG-based system was introduced for hospital financing, complemented by capitation in primary care—both in conformity with the secondary beliefs of the DRG coalition. For secondary outpatient care, the German fee-for-service method was introduced, via literal copying of the points system in use there (It was subsequently amended to reflect the Hungarian cost structure).

According to certain experts (Interview D), the introduction of fee-for-service in outpatient care corresponded to the policy core of the DRG coalition that aimed at shifting care volumes from the inpatient to the outpatient setting, deemed more cost-efficient. Nevertheless, this solution appears rather as a compromise of the circumstances, with plans to be fine-tuned afterwards.

Experiences with Performance-related Financing

The new system of health resource allocation was put in place in 1993. It was the first time in Europe that a full-scale DRG-based reimbursement system had been used for hospital financing, and was, in some ways, the anticipation of the general direction of later reforms elsewhere on the Continent (Nagy et al., 2008). It also created a coherent system, with, for the most part, a purposefully planned design.

The reform included the creation of an independent institutional structure for health insurance, under the control of union representatives (workers and managers). This reflected the German model, in accordance with the secondary beliefs of MDF health and social policymakers. It was also meant to establish a stricter, contract-based relationship between the insured and the institutions of social security, in order to increase the market element within the system. The state, with its redistributive powers deemed arbitrary and inequitable, was to take a step back (Orosz, 2001, p. 71–72). It also helped establish a complete purchaser–provider split, with the perspective of developing a strategic buyer function for health insurance (On this issue, see Dózsa, 2011).

The general line of reform was to increase the degree of responsibility—both of the insured for paying their contributions and of healthcare providers for reducing their costs. There was a strong belief that individual responsibility and market-like forces would help make the healthcare system more efficient and achieve better results. The question was how to balance these moves against the attempts for national solidarity and comprehensive healthcare services for all (Table 1).

Nevertheless, the new system soon had to face substantial problems—and opposing coalitions. First, providers started increasing the volume of their output at a very high pace. In fact, even if the DRG system is less inclined to funding an unlimited additional volume of services than a fee-for-service model (see Cots, Chiarello, Salvador, Castells & Quentin, 2011 for the economic consequences of the system), it still provides, by design, incentives for volume increase.

There appeared a coalition, based first and foremost on Ministry of Finance experts, which was in favor of stronger cost control in healthcare, and demanded a refinement of the DRG system to this end. One of their policy core beliefs—at least perceived by the actors in the health system—was that healthcare is, in a sense, a budgetary burden, which can only be paid for when "the economy" (in a sense restricted to private, market-based actors) has produced a surplus large enough to cater for its needs. In the words of one interviewee (Interview C): "We have to develop the economy first, and then we'll have the resources to develop healthcare." The second important belief attributed to this coalition was—and remains—that health providers were cheating when reporting their performance to the Health Insurance Fund.

Table 1. Coalitions and Beliefs Within the Health Resource Allocation Arena

Coalition	Policy core beliefs	Secondary beliefs	Principal measures suggested
DRG experts	Transparent and equitable resource allocation is needed. Market-based incentives work better than administrative control.	DRG is the most cost-efficient way to achieve the policy core. DRG introduction would also help solve other problems in healthcare.	DRG introduction Floating reimbursement values Volume caps (partly)
MDF health policy specialists	Transparent and equitable resource allocation is needed. More autonomy and more funding is to be given to doctors.	The German health insurance model is to be adopted in Hungary.	Fee-for-service reimbursement
Ministry of Finance representatives	Healthcare is costly and hinders economic growth. Healthcare providers are inclined to cheat.	Cost control and efficiency are to be put in place.	No special suggestion, but advocate all DRGs, floating reimbursement and volume caps.
Socialist health policy specialists	Market-based incentives do not work. The healthcare system needs administrative changes.	The DRG system is insufficient as healthcare reform.	Centrally planned capacity adjustments Volume caps (partly)

In fact, the original DRG idea included features to avoid cheating. Unlike the American version, the Hungarian DRG system was designed in such a way that it classify cases into resource groups automatically, based on the diagnosis written on the medical record. In the end, however, this solution was not applied by the National Health Insurance Fund. One of the interviewees—a senior policymaker of the time—considers that the management of the Fund was reluctant to develop the general IT support, and hence the anti-fraud features of the system. It might have been because some of its managers believed more in administrative control than in market-based incentives (Interview B—review).

Fortunately, though, for DRG advocates, the system was introduced in a progressive manner, continuously unifying the initially highly diverse payment/case ratios of providers. A degree of uniformity was thus created, gradually eliminating the reimbursement differences stemming from historic global budget negotiations. This benefited equity as well as efficiency, all providers being required—at least in theory—to operate at or below the average cost.

Before this unification process took place, discrete payment restrictions had been introduced, in a so-called floating manner. This means that the total budget allocated to hospital (and similarly to outpatient) care was announced, and unit reimbursement prices were calculated by dividing this budget by the volume of performance actually reported by providers. In this sense, the more volume reported by providers as a whole, the less unit reimbursement they received individually.

As a result of the above system, the healthcare budget was placed under effective control, but providers, and certain practitioners, developed a belief that the resource allocation system was fundamentally unjust. This belief was advocated, among others, by the Chamber of Medical Doctors. The floating of prices was finally discontinued in 1998, year when—after continuous technical refinement of the DRG system—the convergence of unit prices finally took place. After this, the same unit price was paid to all providers, and was no longer adjusted according to the volume reported.

Now, for a second time, cost containment became the key issue. The Ministry of Finance pushed continually for the introduction of new methods, which incited the DRG experts of the National Health Insurance Fund to come up with ever newer proposals. Finally, in 2003, the government convened an expert group composed of representatives of the Fund and of providers' organizations, and asked them to put forward a solution to the MPs' congress of the governing Socialist Party. The solution finally retained was a system of provider-level caps, limiting the DRG-based budget of each hospital to 95% of its 2003 level. Any excess in volume would, from then on, penalize the institution that produced it, through reduced reimbursement, and keep the rest of the providers safe.

The problem had now escalated to a high level of decision making, where there was a strong policy core belief in the necessity for cost containment. Compared to the time of DRG introduction, the decision this time was made quite swiftly, the technical details of the cost containment method—provider volume caps—having to be worked out in haste. Nevertheless, it marked the end of a longer period of trial-and-error experimentation with different methods.

Provider volume caps also proved to be a victory for another advocacy coalition, encompassing officials in the Ministry of Health, MPs and local politicians, predominantly from the Socialist Party, in power between 1994–1998 and from 2002 until 2010. Certain officials of the National Health Insurance Fund also took part in this group, hence the reluctance of the Fund to develop the DRG system. This coalition is basically what experts like referring to as "politicians"—even those experts who themselves are considered by some of their peers as being part of it.

The coalition of "politicians" was reported to have the policy core belief that market-based mechanisms were inappropriate for the regulation of healthcare, which, instead, deserved direct administrative control. The original idea of competition advocates—that under-performing services would be closed down for financial reasons—was refuted by the course of events. Competition advocates had to acknowledge that administrative capacity planning was needed, at least to a certain extent (Interview E).

After 2004, much less attention has been given to health resource allocation reforms, the health policy emphasis being placed instead on other issues and areas. This way, the system that had forged by then has remained largely in place.

Conclusion

From a learning point of view, the policy change period of 1989–1993 can be characterized as one of cross-coalition policy learning. The DRG coalition, though represented at several administrative and political posts, had fairly limited direct power. However, through the level of sophistication of its proposals and with the endorsement of the cost control advocates, it managed to persuade the leading political forces of the superiority of its beliefs. Technocratic information, collected through years of tests and analysis beforehand, seems to have played a key role in this process.

In contrast to this, the learning processes of subsequent years took place much more within coalitions. Despite the build-up of a very significant health intervention database, thanks to the DRG system, reliable information of actual hospital costs has become more and more scarce. This, along with the policy core belief that the health intervention database is highly biased by unfair reporting, may have contributed to the defensive position of DRG-minded health administration officials. As a response to the cost-containment pressure, they often had to improvise solutions, some of which lived on, while others gave way to new trial-and-error experiments.

Finally, it was the DRG coalition—or at least several members of it—which has exhibited policy learning when acknowledging that the DRG system was no panacea for goals beyond the strict boundaries of resource allocation. Perhaps most importantly, the closing down of (over) capacity in healthcare supply proved to be impossible without some kind of direct administrative intervention.

Political learning took place primarily via accommodation to the incentives offered by the different payment systems. Providers, their organizations and their political advocates rapidly understood how to present financing problems and anomalies as threats to the continuous treatment of patients, and therefore put pressure on successive governments to act in their particular interests. It would be difficult to claim that the political agenda was substantially responsible for shaping health resource allocation reforms. The health resource allocation reform process is rather one of continuous trial-and-error technical experiments, with compromises between the different stakeholder coalitions allowing new courses of action.

Hungary found itself in an entirely new situation after the change of regime in 1989–1990. Both political and policy learning processes began, in order to face the challenges of transition and create a new economic and social framework. In health resource allocation, a coherent initial system model evolved in a largely trial-and-error manner, ending up in something which is in many ways different from what featured in the original ideas, while the main underlying beliefs and assumptions stayed largely the same. The primary role was that of policy learning, presumably also because of the highly technical nature of the problems.

List of interviews

Interview A: High-ranking former Ministry of Health and Ministry of Finance official. Date: 14th November 2014

Interview B: High-ranking former administrative official and secretary of state of the Ministry of Health. Date: 16th January 2015

Interview C: Former MP and high-ranking health administration official. Date: 8th March 2016

Interview D: Leading DRG expert of the National Health Insurance Fund. Date: 18th February 2015

Interview E: Former minister of health. Date: 23rd May 2016

Relevant Legislation

Act No. CLIV of 1997 on healthcare

Act No. LXXXIII of 1997 on the services of compulsory health insurance

Government Decree No. 217/1997 on the execution of Act No. LXXXIII of 1997

Government Decree No. 43/1999 on the detailed rules of financing health services from the National Health Insurance Fund

Ministry of Welfare Decree No. 9/1993 on certain questions of the social security financing of specialist healthcare

Minister of Health Decree No. 4/2000 on the services of general practice, children's general practice and primary dental care

Balázs Babarczy is a Ph.D. candidate in the Faculty of Social Sciences at Eötvös Loránd University of Budapest. His research interests include health financing and evidence-based policy making.

László Imre is senior advisor at the National Healthcare Service Center of Hungary, responsible for healthcare planning and financing questions.

Notes

1. An earlier version of this paper was presented by Balázs Babarczy at the 24th World Congress of Political Science Poznań 2016.
2. Eötvös Loránd University, Budapest.
3. Állami Egészségügyi Ellátó Központ (National Healthcare Service Center), Budapest.
4. The main focus of the full title scan being other than health resource allocation, a limited level of omission is possible.
5. Subject to reorganisation in early 2017.

References

Government Decree No 217/1997 on the execution of Act No LXXXIII of 1997 on the services of compulsory health insurance.

Adam, J. 1987. "The Hungarian Economic Reform of the 1980s." *Soviet Studies* 39 (4): 610 27.

Bauer, T. 1983. "The Hungarian Alternative to Soviet-type Planning." *Journal of Comparative Economics* 7 (3): 304–16.

Bordás, I. 1990. "Az egészségügyi ellátás új rendszere" [The New Model of Healthcare]. *Egészségügyi Gazdasági Szemle* 28 (5–6): 323–42.

Cots, F., P. Chiarello, X. Salvador, X. Castells, W. Quentin. 2011. "DRG-based Hospital Payment: Intended and Unintended Consequences." In *Diagnosis-Related Groups in Europe*, ed. Reinhard Busse, Alexander Geissler, Wilm Quentin, and Miriam Wiley. Maidenhead: Open University Press and New York: Two Penn Plaza, 75–92.

Dózsa, Cs. 2010. A kórházak válaszai a változó stratégiai környezetre Magyarországon a 2000-es években [Hospitals' responses to a changing strategic environment in Hungary in the 2000s]. Ph.D.diss., Corvinus University of Budapest.

Dózsa, Cs. 2011. "Az OEP szolgáltatásvásárlói és biztosítói szerepének erősítése" [Stregthening the Purchaser and Insurer Functions of the National Health Insurance Fund Administration]. *Egészségügyi Gazdasági Szemle* 49 (4): 14–9.

Gaál, P, Sz. Sziget, M. Csere. et al. 2011. *Hungary: Health System Review*. Health Systems in Transition series Vol. 13. No. 5. Copenhagen: World Health Organisation.

Haggard, S., and R. R. Kaufman. 2001. "Introduction." In *Reforming the State: Fiscal and Welfare Reform in Post-Socialist Countries*, ed. J. Kornai, S. Haggard, and R. R. Kaufman. Cambridge: University of Cambridge, 1–22.

Hsieh, H-F., and S. E. Shannon. 2005. "Three Approaches to Qualitative Content Analysis." *Qualitative Health Research* 15 (9): 1277–88.

Jenkins-Smith, H., D. Nohrstedt, C. M. Weible, and P. A. Sabatier. 2014. "The Advocacy Coalition Framework: Foundations, Evolution and Ongoing Research." In *Theories of the Policy Process*, 3rd ed., ed. P. A. Sabatier, and C. M. Weible. Boulder, CO: Westview Press, 183–223.

Kutzin, J., T. Evetovits, M. Jakab, and S. Thomson. 2015. "Health Financing in the European Region: Objectives and Policy Instruments." Presented at The Barcelona Course on Health Financing, Barcelona.

May, P. T. 1992. "Policy Learning and Failure." *Journal of Public Policy* 12 (4): 331–54.

Medical Online. 2016. "Vétót emeltek a kancellária-rendszer ellen" [Veto against the chancellery system]. Budapest: Medical Online, July 4, 2016.

Minister of Health. Decree No. 4/2000 on the services of general practice, children's general practice and primary dental care. Minister of Health of the Republic of Hungary.

Moreno-Serra, R., and A. Wagstaff. 2010. "System-wide Impacts of Hospital Payment Reforms: Evidence from Central and Eastern Europe and Central Asia." *Journal of Health Economics* 29 (4): 585–602.

Nagy, J, Cs. Dózsa, and I. Boncz. 2008. "Experiences with the application of the DRG principle in Hungary." In *The Globalisation of Managerial Innovation in Health Care*, ed. J. R. Kimberly, de Pouvourville G., and T. D'Aunno. Cambridge (UK) and New York: Cambridge University Press, 284–319.

National Health Insurance Fund. 2015. *Statistical Yearbook 2014*. Budapest: National Health Insurance Fund.

National Healthcare Service Center. 2014. "*Beruházás-statisztika*" [Investment statistics]. OSAP 1576 Budapest.

National Healthcare Service Center. 2016. *Hungarian Health System Scan* 10 (1): 2014–5.

Orosz, É. 2001. "*Félúton vagy tévúton? Egészségügyünk félmúltja és az egészségpolitika alternatívái" [Midway or the wrong way? The semi-past of our health system and the alternatives facing health policy].* Budapest: Egészséges Magyarországért Egyesület.

Sabatier, P. A., and H. Jenkins-Smith. 1993. *Policy Change and Learning: An Advocacy Coalition Approach.* Boulder, CO/San Francisco, CA/Oxford, UK: Westview Press.

Verbászi, B. 2004. "A rendszer tragédiája. Az 1968-as gazdasági reform előzményei, beindítása és kudarca" [The Tragedy of the Regime. The Premises, Launch and Failure of the 1968 Economic Reform]. *Tudományos Közlemények* 11: 111–21.

Weible, C. M., P. A. Sabatier, and K. McQueen. 2009. "Themes and Variations: Taking Stock of the Advocacy Coalition Framework." *The Policy Studies Journal* 37 (1): 121–38.

WHO. 2000. *The World Health Report 2000: Health Systems: Improving Performance.* Geneva: World Health Organisation.

European Policy Analysis, Vol. 3, No. 1, 2017

Regulating Consumption for Sustainability? Why the European Union Chooses Information Instruments to Foster Sustainable Consumption

Jan Pollex

In light of ever increasing usage of natural resources, the global discourse on sustainable development is increasingly emphasizing the crucial role of sustainable consumption and thus the contribution of individual consumers—rather than the traditionally focused corporate producers—to the protection of ecosystems. This paper investigates how the European Union (EU) addresses and characterizes consumers and how the framing of the consumers' role impacts on the design of sustainable consumption policy. Thus, this paper analyzes the relevance of target groups and their discursive construction for policymaking. Based on the analysis of central EU policy agendas providing the frame for consumer-oriented environmental policy, the paper shows that the EU's sustainable consumption policy builds on an image of average-rational *consumers and a* weak sustainable consumption *perspective. Both constructions of reality subsequently frame the choice of* soft *policy instruments. The role of citizens (as opposed to only producers) and the image of average-rational consumers who can be activated through information measures or incentives gained prominence in the EU—and in OECD countries generally—at a time of dissatisfaction with the performance of regulatory policy in the 1990s, hinting at the significance of contextual factors in understanding discursive shifts with their policy implications.*

KEY WORDS: policy design, target groups, sustainable consumption, EU environmental policy, policy instruments

控制可持续消费？为何欧盟选择信息工具培养可持续消费

由于自然资源的使用日益增加，关于可持续发展的全球话语也越来越强调可持续消费的重要作用，以及个人消费者—而不是传统意义上所关注的企业生产者—对生态系统保护所做的贡献。本文调查了欧洲联盟（简称欧盟*EU*）如何称呼和描述不同类型的消费者，以及消费者角色框架的建立如何影响可持续消费政策的设计。由此，本文分析了目标群体的相关性和目标群体对决策的话语建构。欧盟中央政策议程为"以消费者为导向"的环境政策提供了框架，基于对此的分析，本文表明：欧盟的可持续消费政策建立在"一般理性的"消费者形象和"较弱的"可持续消费观上。这二者对现实的建构随后为"软"政策工具的选择提供了框架。公民（与之相反的是生产者）的角色和能从信息手段或其他激励方式中获得鼓舞的"一般理性"消费者形象在欧盟和绝大多数经合组织国家中都表现突出，与此同时，欧盟对*20*世纪*90*年代的监管政策表现并不满意。这也暗示了在理解话语转变及其政策意义时情境因素的重要性。

关键词： 政策设计，目标群体，可持续消费，欧盟环境政策，政策工具

doi: 10.1002/epa2.1005

Introduction

One of the main quests of policy analysis concentrates on the question how "exactly [...] problems and solutions are matched in the actual processes of policymaking [...] (Beland and Howlett, 2016, p. 393). This paper builds on the research on policy design (e.g., Howlett, Lejano 2015; Schneider, 2015) and focuses on the construction of target groups and its impact on the choice of policy instruments (Schneider & Ingram, 1993). The paper concentrates on the area of the European Union's sustainable consumption policy and investigates how certain assumptions about policy addressees facilitate the match of policy instruments with sustainable development goals.

Three research strands build the basis for this paper. Firstly, within research on sustainable development and environmental policy increasing relevance is assigned to individual behavior and consumption choices to preserve the environment and guarantee sustainability (John, Jaeger-Erben & Rückert-John, 2016; Spaargaren & Mol, 2008). The concept of sustainable development has especially steered environmental policymaking toward problems like the over-use of natural resources. But despite some political ambition, sustainable development remains a rather distant goal. Since the beginning of the industrial age, human development has "[...] been altering the Earth at an unprecedented and unsustainable rate [...]" (Hoekstra & Wiedmann, 2014, p. 1114). Thus, individual consumption is seen as a relevant factor for a turn toward a more sustainable development since societal change requires also individual change. Secondly, policymakers are expected to act more intensively to ensure this transformation toward sustainability regarding individual behavior (WBGU 2011). The importance of individual choices and consumption is discussed under the header of sustainable consumption and has led to a "consumerist turn" in environmental as well as political research (Spaargaren & Mol, 2008; p. 354). Thirdly, within policy research and among policymakers the notion of behavioral governance, especially the idea of nudging, is increasingly discussed (Strassheim & Korinek, 2015; Thaler & Sunstein, 2009). But the EU's sustainable consumption policy merely focuses on soft instruments (nearly exclusively information and education measures) to persuade citizens and consumers of more sustainable consumption behavior. Neither is there evidence of more ambitious policy goals in regard to sustainability nor do we find hints at the usage of coercion or authority to induce consumers of more sustainable consumption choices. The question therefore is: Why does the EU rely on information measures to promote sustainable consumption?

This paper concentrates on the European Union (EU) as one of the international frontrunners in environmental policymaking and as a globally relevant single market (Jordan & Adelle, 2013). Especially from a political science perspective, the focus on individual consumption is of interest. The targeting of consumers seems much more complicated than regulating the production of goods and services, which was the first and still is an important approach to foster sustainable development (Spaargaren & Mol, 2008, p. 353). Firstly, these complications are of a conceptual nature as there is "[...] little consensus [...] about the basic forms and general content" of the concept *sustainable consumption* and related policies (Spaargaren & Mol, 2008, p. 354). Secondly, consumption constitutes a rather complex issue influenced by social aspects and personal belief systems. Consumption acts are related to (perceived) personal needs and thus are impacted by "[...] different cultural, historical, and individual situations [...]" of consumers (Di Guilio & Fuchs, 2014, p. 187).[1] Thus, based on the complexity of consumption and manifold notions combined in the concept of sustainable consumption, research on how consumers are addressed and how the concept of sustainable consumption is translated into actual policies is necessary. Although research deals extensively with sustainable consumption or sustainability in general, the question why certain ways of influencing consumer behavior are used and others are neglected receives little attention.

Against the background of policy design research and the rise of behavioral aspects within policymaking, this paper investigates how specific characterizations of consumers favor the usage of certain instrument types as both aspects are discursively linked within policy. Thus, the paper wants to contribute to research on the relevance of target group constructions in policymaking. To answer this question, two contextual aspects must be considered. Firstly, the policy context also impacts the choice of instrument types. In the case of sustainable consumption, the policy area of environmental policy provides this context. Secondly, the concept of sustainable consumption itself and its translation into policy must be considered.

The paper builds on previous research on instruments in the area of sustainable consumption (e.g., Jordan, Wurzel, Zito & Brücker, 2009). Therefore, I concentrate on consumer-focused policies aiming to change individual behavior. Policies aiming at changes in production and services are not considered in this research since they primarily address producers not consumers.[2]

This paper proceeds as follows: First it provides the conceptual background regarding sustainable consumption, consumer, and environmental policy. Then, the paper elaborates on the research on policy design and instrument choice and deals with the research design. Following the presentation of the results of my analysis they are discussed against the background of policy design research. At last the paper provides a summary with concluding aspects.

Sustainable Consumption, Consumers & Policy in the EU

The concept of sustainable consumption links the goals of a sustainable (global) development to the relevance of individual, everyday consumption choices. Most importantly, the Oslo Symposium on Sustainable Consumption in 1994 has formulated a definition that still shapes the discussion about individual consumer choices and defines sustainable consumption as "[...] the use of services and related products which respond to basic needs and bring a better quality of life while minimizing the use of natural resources [...] as well as the emissions of waste and pollutants over the life-cycle so as not to jeopardize the needs of future generations" (Norwegian Ministry for the Environment, 1994).

Based on this (broad) definition, a variety of concepts address the issue of sustainable consumption, while the term functions rather as an "[...] umbrella concept for a heterogeneous set of [approaches]" (Geels, McMeekin, Mylan & Southerton, 2015).[3]

The idea to address consumer choices in order to enable a more sustainable development was popularized with the World Summit on Sustainable Development in 2002 and has shifted the policy-focus from aspects like pollution control toward everyday life consumption choices (Geels et al., 2015).[4] Basically, two versions of the concept can be identified: a weak and a strong version.[5] The weak version focuses on efficiency gains through technological improvements that lead to a reduction of resource consumption. Within this perspective, changes in the market are necessary to increase the number of environmentally friendly products and their uptake by consumers. But a fundamental change of consumption patterns or everyday life decisions is hardly addressed (Lorek & Fuchs, 2011). The strong version concentrates on an overall reduction of consumption, a change in individual behavior and consumer culture, and addresses the "social embeddedness of consumption decisions" as well as an active citizen-consumer role (Lorek & Fuchs, 2011, p. 39). While the weak perspective aims at a reform of consumption and economic activity, the strong version appears to be a rather revolutionary approach that advocates fundamental changes in market activity, political steering, and individual behavior (Geels et al., 2015).

Sustainable Consumption and Environmental Policy in the EU

In the European Union, "consumption-focused environmental legislation" already began in the early 1990's "as consumption-related environmental problems became more acute [...]" (Murphy, 2001, p. 43). Sustainable consumption policy is therefore mostly dealt with as an environmental issue and largely part of the environmental policy area in the European Union. The acknowledgement of consumption as one main factor to reduce environmental degradation essentially led to the EU's *Integrated Product Policy* (IPP) that incorporated a life-cycle-perspective on products and services and acknowledged the role of consumers and their choices (Murphy, 2001, p. 44). Following the IPP, the EU Commission further developed this approach with the *Sustainable Consumption and Production Agenda* (SCP) in 2008 and with the *Single Market for Green Products Agenda* (SMGP) in 2013 (Scholl, Rubik, Kalimo, Biedenkopf & Söebech, 2010; p. 40).

Looking at how the EU exactly targets the "act of consumption" (Murphy, 2001, p. 49), a focus on soft policy instruments (mainly information) imposing no coercion on the addressees is evident.[6] Following the goal of strengthening the single market, the Commission pursued the harmonization of national information labels with the introduction of the EU Eco-Label and thus the facilitation of the single market—since different schemes and requirements might hamper the free movement of products (Murphy, 2001, p. 45; Jordan et al., 2009, p. 172–73). Furthermore, educational approaches to enhance the knowledge of sustainable choices are used by the EU and the member states (Goldsmith & Piscopo, 2014, p. 52).

While in traditional environmental policy (e.g., pollution control in the industrial sector) command-and-control policy instruments dominate, they play a minor role in consumption-focused legislation. In this area, the EU concentrates on so-called "new environmental policy instruments" (NEPIs), especially information measures or non-binding instruments. Compared to traditional regulation, NEPIs characteristically are "relatively soft policy instrument[s]" using persuasion rather than coercion (Jordan et al., 2009, p. 163; Jordan, Wurzel, Zito & Brücker, 2003, p. 555–56.).[7] Especially with the fifth Environmental Action Program, the EU started focusing on shared responsibility among public and private actors (1993, p. 27), thus incorporating addressees beyond public authorities and industrial actors (Jordan et al., 2003, p. 563).

Consumer Policy & Consumers in Policy

The development of general European consumer policy can be dated back to the Treaty of Rome in which key objectives in regard to consumer policy were formulated. Although these provisions impacted consumer policy in the EU (and shaped it in the long run), they were not intended to establish a "[...] sophisticated structure of consumer rights [...]" (Weatherill, 2013, p. 4). First attempts to improve the consumer position in the single market were undertaken in the 1970's to protect consumers from wrongful information, health risks and to protect their economic interests (Joerges, 1979, p. 215). Especially, with the Maastricht Treaty "the constitutional status of the EU as an actor in the field of consumer protection has been secured" (Weatherill, 2013, p. 4). Consumer policy has become an integral part of the European single market, in which "consumer policy regulates the relationship between consumption and production" (Rauh, 2016, p. 33) and is "rooted in the process of market integration" (Weatherill, 2013, p. 4).

From an analytical perspective, two ideal types of *the consumer* can be differentiated. These two ideal types will guide the analysis of policy documents in regard to the characterization of consumers and underlying assumptions within the policies. The first ideal type can be called *average-rational consumer*. This consumer is a rational, reasonable, and information-seeking consumer who makes purchasing decisions based on information and cost-value ratio assessments (Albers, 2016, p. 172–73; Rauh, 2016, p. 37; Cseres, 2005, p. 322). The second ideal type is the *vulnerable-weak consumer*. This type is vulnerable because it is prone to being manipulated (e.g., advertising, creation of status symbols) and its decisions are based on habituated consumption patterns. Furthermore, this type tends to be overburdened by the supply of products and services on the market and opportunities provided within the market (Rauh, 2016, p. 37; Cseres, 2005, p. 322).

Policy Analysis—Theoretical Background

This paper builds on the literature on policy design and focuses four central elements policies contain of: (1) goals or problems to be solved; (2) target

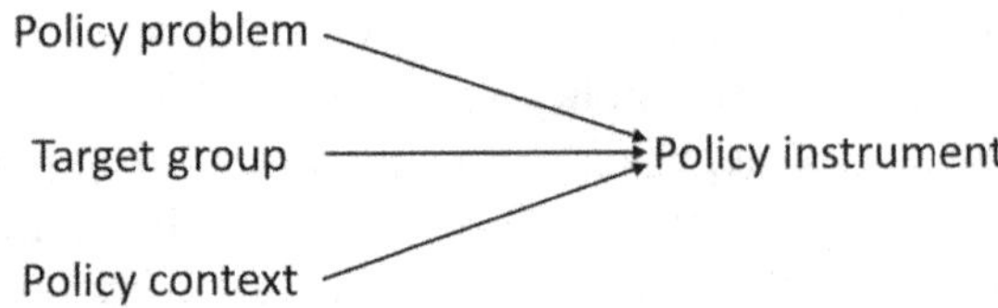

Figure 1. Elements of Policy Design, Author's Description Based on Schneider, 2015.

populations or benefit groups; (3) instruments and rationales, (4) policy context (Schneider, 2015, p. 223). Figure 1 depicts this model.[8]

The central question of this paper relates to discussions of target group constructions within policies and their impact on the design of policies (Schneider & Ingram, 1993). This is especially relevant, as "[. . ..] the social construction of target populations [. . .] shapes both the policy agenda and the actual design of policy" (Schneider & Ingram, 1993, p. 334). In regard to sustainable consumption policy, the way consumers are perceived might influence the choice of policy instruments. The goal of sustainable consumption concepts is to change people's behavior and push them toward more sustainable ways of consumption. This relates to the debate about behavioral assumptions of policy tools[9] (Schneider & Ingram, 1990) and behavioral governance research (Strassheim & Korinek, 2015; Thaler & Sunstein, 2009). Policy tools deal with different expectations about target populations or the general public. They can provide authority or incentives and try to force or persuade citizens of certain behavior (Schneider & Ingram, 1990, p. 514; Vedung, 2007, p. 29–30). Thus, assumptions about consumers and their behavior might impact the use of policy instruments. Schneider calls this "underlying behavioral assumptions" (2015, p. 225) that do not have to be explicitly laid out in policy documents to impact the design of a policy.

The second relevant element of policy design is the policy context. I focus on the role of policy legacies or inheritance described by Rose (1990) who, with a focus on public spending policy, argues that decisions once made impact policy-making for long durations of time and programs once introduced are only in a very few cases terminated. I adopt Rose's perspective to discuss why certain policy instruments dominate the area of sustainable consumption policy in the EU. Therefore, I do not resume Rose's concept and methods entirely but rather use the idea of long-term effects of policy decisions. The paper focuses on empirically and analytically on the role of target group construction and the relevance of the policy context.

The policy problem in this research is the relevance of sustainability and is seen as a given problem on which I do not further elaborate. The introduction to this paper described the basics.

Research Design and Methods

Empirically, this paper focuses on three central agendas formulated by the EU Commission. These documents were selected because they outline and deal with the broad ideas of sustainable consumption policy and set the course for more detailed policies and the favored policy instruments in this area. Following Howlett's multi-level policy design perspective, the selected documents can be characterized as rather abstract documents describing general aims of policies and political programs than "operationalized specific on the ground measures" (Howlett, 2009, p. 75). Thus, the documents provide the frame and context for more detailed policies—including characterizations of target groups and the interpretation of the concept sustainable consumption. Furthermore, the three initiatives were formulated and adopted within a time frame of 10 years (2003, 2008, 2013), which might show either continuity or changes in the way sustainable consumption is dealt with and consumers are perceived. The paper offers an empirical analysis investigating how consumer perceptions and the interpretation of the concepts of sustainable development and sustainable consumption impact on instrument choices.

Methodically, this analysis builds on the literature on interpretative policy analysis (Fischer, 2007). Following Yanow (2000), this paper investigates the beliefs and perceptions regarding consumers in policymaking and how they are linked to instrument choices. It is based on the assumption that the political (and thus discursive) construction of *the consumer* is relevant for the choice of policy instruments and goals linked to these instruments. The construction of the problem (e.g., unsustainable development) and its solution (in this case: ways of changing of consumer choices) are relevant steps in the process of policymaking (Hajer, 2008). Thus, a post-positivist policy analysis perspective can help explain how interpretations of problems or target groups influence policy design.

The analysis in this paper is executed in two steps. First, based on the different aspects of consumption and consumer policy described above, the analysis focuses on (1) the role assigned to consumers for sustainable development, (2) the characterization of consumers, and (3) and the perspectives on sustainable consumption in general. The second step covers the choice of policy instruments and concentrates on the construction of policy addressees.

My assumption is based on the ideal type and conceptual features described before and the relevance of target group characterization for policy design. A dominance of the average-rational consumer type and a weak sustainable consumption perspective promote the usage of non-coercive policy instruments, since far-reaching market interventions are not the objective in these perspectives. Rather, they aim at gradual changes within existing market-logics and consumption patterns. On the other hand, a dominance of a weak-vulnerable consumer characterization combined with strong sustainable consumption objectives would suggest more coercive instrument choices following objectives like changing consumption patterns and reducing overall consumption. Therefore, a dominance of one perspective that is discursively matched in the documents to the assumed preference for policy instrument types can substantiate the assumed relevance of target group characterization for the choice of policy instruments. Furthermore, a dominance of an average-rational consumer type explains the EU's focus on non-coercive tools to change consumer behavior. Thus, the concentration on soft policy instruments within the area of sustainable consumption policy in the EU can be explained.

To investigate the research question, I conducted a qualitative content analysis (Mayring, 2008) in the three central policies on sustainable consumption: The Integrated Product Policy (COM/2003/302), The Sustainable Consumption and Production Action Plan (COM/2008/397) and The Single Market for Green Products Agenda (COM/2013/196). These agendas are the fundament for further policies dealing with sustainable consumption (and production) and set the course, e.g., for eco-labeling schemes, because they formulate a frame enabling a certain set of policies and limiting political options for other policies.

I coded the documents using MAXQDA and grouped three thematic dimensions. For each dimension, I formulated ideal-type features based on the literature on sustainable consumption discussed in this paper. The pillars are:

1. Role assigned to (individual) consumption

   I coded text elements that address (directly and indirectly) individual consumption and perceive it explicitly or implicitly as relevant for a sustainable development and put individual consumption into the context of sustainable development.

2. Consumer Type (average-rational or vulnerable-weak)

   For the *average-rational consumer,* I coded text passages that describe consumers as information seeking and assign relevance to policy to foster information for consumers in order to promote sustainable consumption choices and the uptake of green products in the market.

   For the *vulnerable-weak consumer,* I coded text passages that describe a vulnerable consumer that can be deceived, e.g., by wrongful product advertisement, and is influenced by social aspects or (purchasing) routines.

3. Sustainable Consumption Perspective (weak or strong)

   For the *weak sustainable consumption perspective,* I coded text passages that address (eco-) innovations to improve the efficiency in resource usage and the relevance of purchasing those efficient products (or services) to improve individual and general environmental balance, while maintaining existing patterns of consumption.

   For the *strong sustainable consumption perspective,* I coded passages that address the need of a change in consumption patterns and levels to reach a state of reduced consumption or longer use-phases of products. Additionally, I searched for a citizen perspective on consumers.

Analyzing EU Policy on Sustainable Consumption

The following sections present the results of the text analysis regarding the role assigned to consumers, the perception of consumers and the perspectives on sustainable consumption. To get a general idea of the relevance of consumer perceptions and the role EU policy assigns to them in regard to sustainable development, I compiled an overview of the number of coded sections in all three policy documents (Fig. 2). The mere number of coded passages in the text does not imply relevance. But it does hint at general trends in the documents and the way sustainable consumption is addressed and consumers are perceived.

What becomes quite clear is the dominance of an average-rational consumer characterization in the documents. Generally, the EU perceives their consumption behavior as reasonable and based on (product) information. Furthermore, consumption and the goal of sustainable development are combined in a weak sustainable consumption perspective. The IPP very marginally addresses the idea of a broader inclusion of consumption choices into the objective of sustainable development. The SCP refers more detailed to an overall conceptual inclusion of individual consumption in regard to sustainable development. The SMGP addresses the relevance of consumption for a sustainable development but to a lesser extent compared to the SCP.

Role Assigned to Consumption for Sustainable Development

The extent to which consumers are explicitly addressed and the way their behavior is linked to a more sustainable development varies throughout the three documents.

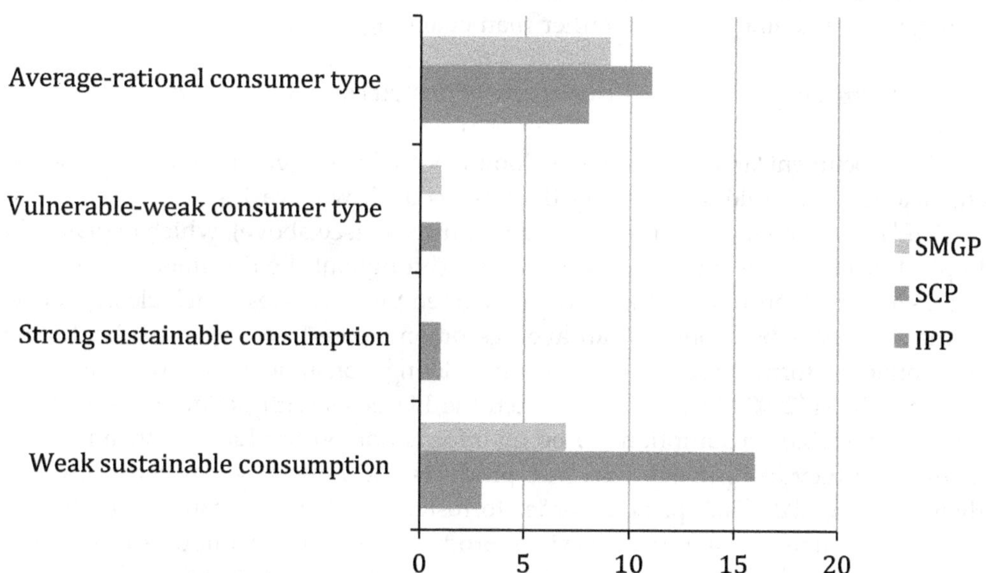

Figure 2. Number of Coded Sections in the Analyzed Documents.

The IPP clearly puts a focus on the link of environmentally friendly products and sustainable development but it does not explicitly link individual consumption to this goal. Nevertheless, the document does capture a consumer-perspective indirectly in regard to product usage and includes a life-cycle-perspective: "the product can be designed perfectly, but inappropriate use and disposal will cause significant environmental impacts" (COM/2003/302, p. 4). Overall, the EU expects consumers to contribute to sustainable development by "[p]urchasing greener products" (COM/2003/302, p. 23).

The SCP also addresses the objective of sustainable development but links this goal clearly to a consumption perspective: "The challenges [of sustainable development] are directly linked to our way of life. [. . .] The impacts of consumption in the EU are felt globally [. . .]" (COM/2008/397, p. 1). Most importantly, the relevance of everyday consumption choices is used as a justification for the policy agenda and its objectives. In regard to the role of consumers in the market, the SCP uses the same approach as the IPP and focuses on increasing the proliferation of green products by: "[fostering] their uptake by consumers" (COM/2008/397, p. 3).

The SMGP does not address consumption patterns or approaches to change them and rather concentrates on the effects of environmentally friendly products: "[The] higher market uptake of such products combines societal benefits of reduced environmental damage with higher satisfaction of consumers as well as potential economic benefits for producers and consumers through more efficient use of natural resources" (COM/2013/196, p. 3).

To summarize these findings: (1) The IPP only indirectly addresses the relevance of consumption choices, (2) the SCP intensively relates to individual consumption as a relevant factor to reach the goal of a sustainable development, (3) the SMGP does so to a lower extent and is more similar to the IPP in this regard. However, the SCP seems to be an intermittent document while there is continuity in regard to greening products rather than changing lifestyles.

Perception of Consumers—Dominance of the "Average-Rational Consumer"

The document analysis shows a dominance of the average-rational consumer characterization while the intensity the topic is dealt with varies.

The IPP addresses consumption rather indirectly (see above), which explains the implicit dealing with consumer perceptions. Throughout the document, consumers are defined by their role for the increase in green product sales which clearly relates to the ideal type perception of an average-rational consumer. Most explicitly, this perception is formulated in the section "Giving consumers the information to decide" (COM/2003/302, p. 12) in which the EU deals with policy instruments to foster sustainable consumption. Based on information on products, "consumers can assess how they can purchase greener products and how they can better use [. . .] them" (COM/2003/302, p. 5). In order to foster sustainable consumption, the EU defines consumer awareness regarding product labels as an important aspect to increase the market share of green products, because a higher "level of consumer awareness [is] necessary for [consumers] to play their full part in greening products"

(COM/2003/302, p. 12). In one instance, the EU addresses the possibility that wrongful consumer information might "reduce the overall confidence in environmental product information" (COM/2003/302, p. 14), which relates to the weak consumer type because the document acknowledges that consumers might be manipulated by unjust advertisements. Nevertheless, the overall importance of this passage is marginal.

The SCP perceives consumers exclusively as rational and expects them to make the right decisions (in this context: green consumption choices) based on the provided information (COM/2008/397, p. 4). In line with the overall focus of this document, the EU also focuses an increase in the level of consumer awareness and a "more coherent and simplified labeling" scheme (COM/2008/397, p. 4) to inform consumers about their choices and "increase their proactive role" for sustainable development (COM/2008/397, p. 5). The agenda intensively addresses the relevance of "consistent information" (COM/2008/397, p. 7) given to consumers and deals especially with the EU Eco-Label and its function as a "label of excellence to signal to consumers [...]" those products that are environmentally friendly (COM/2008/397, p. 7).

The SMGP deals with consumers in a similar way. In the document, the EU focuses on the relevance of well-functioning market mechanisms: "There are barriers for both producers and consumers to supply and purchase [environmentally friendly] products, many of them stemming from the ambiguity of what constitutes truly a 'green' product [...]" (COM/2013/196, p. 2). This perspective relates to the necessity of complete information for consumers to make the 'right' decision. Here, a rational cost–benefit calculation by individual consumers is implied and constitutes the vantage point for legislative approaches. The SMGP also mentions risks of wrongful information in regard to consumer choices: "Inadequate communication can confuse or mislead recipients, obstruct decision making and undermine the trust in environmental claims" (COM/2013/196, p. 11). This passage can also be tied to an average-rational consumer type since undermined trust in environmental claims might interfere with the rational process of decision making.

Perspectives on Sustainable Consumption

The analysis of the three documents shows the dominance of a weak sustainable consumption perspective in all agendas. The IPP, SCP, and the SMGP focus an increase in resource efficiency and the positive effects of (eco-) innovations on the preservation of the environment. While the IPP rather implicitly addresses the idea of a broader concept capturing the interdependent effects of product supply and consumer demand, the SCP more directly relates to a weak sustainable consumption perspective. It focuses on "[...] products that have significant potential for reducing environmental impacts [...]" and their uptake by consumers (COM/2008/397, p. 4).

The SMGP captures the idea to address and empower consumers as citizens: "The EU consumer policy can provide the market tools to empower citizens, as consumers, to make sustainable environmental choices" (COM/2013/196, p. 9). In these cases, I would argue, the EU still reasons from a position that relates to the average-rational consumer ideal type but incorporates aspects of a strong sustainable consumptions approach without aiming for fundamental changes in consumption patterns.

This analysis shows clearly that the EU extensively uses a perspective on consumers that can be tied to an average-rational consumer ideal type and focuses ways to protect the environment and foster sustainable development that relate to a weak sustainable consumption perspective.

The Impact of Target Group Characterization on Policy Instrument Choice

The analysis of central EU agendas shows a dominance of an average-rational consumer characterization and a dominance of a weak sustainable consumption perspective.

Analytically, this paper concentrates on the role of target group characterizations for the choice of policy instruments. I assumed that the characterization of consumers is the vantage point for the design and formulation of policies and the usage of policy tools. How does the interpretation of consumers and assumption about their behavior promote the choice of policy instruments?

As Schneider and Ingram (1990) argue, the addressees of policies are indeed a relevant factor impacting policy design and instrument choice. The analysis shows clearly a linkage between an average-rational consumer characterization and the choice of soft policy instruments. As cited earlier, the goal of sustainable consumption policies is to help "consumers make better choices" (COM/2008/397, p. 4). Better choices here points at purchasing eco-friendly products. Policy instruments are supposed to provide information (e.g., through product label) to facilitate these informed consumption decisions. Because consumers are expected to be eager to consider product information for their consumption behavior, information instruments are sufficient to reach the goal of more sustainable consumption and the choice of these instruments is a logical decision seen from within the EU's assumptions about consumers. The EU expects consumers to make the right (ecologically friendly) choices based on a calculation of costs and benefits.[10] Furthermore, the EU supposes consumers to incorporate a common good perspective in their purchasing behavior and value environmental protection and sustainability. Thus, the EU focuses on a consumer policy that contributes to improving the availability of clear, reliable and comparable information on the environmental performance of products" (COM/2013/196, p. 7). Within this policy, actions "to increase consumers' awareness" are essential for the EU (COM/2008/397, p. 9). Additionally, since a weak sustainable consumption perspective (emphasizing increases in efficiency and proliferation of eco-innovations) is dominant in the documents and within EU policy, extensive legislation to reduce consumption levels (and thus promote goals linked to a strong sustainable consumption perspective) seems uncalled-for and would have no basis in the existing policy agendas. Thus, the assumptions regarding target group behavior and the translation of the concept of sustainable consumption into policy are highly relevant for the choice of soft policy instruments.

Furthermore, the analyzed documents neither provide hints at other policy instruments than information or education to promote sustainable consumption and persuade consumers of more sustainable choices nor links to nudging approaches or ways to manipulate consumers toward a behavioral change marking a departure from previous policy objectives.

This result can be linked to the concept of incremental change in policy. Policymakers do rarely aim at far-reaching change but prefer less controversial and more efficient solutions for adaption (Lindblom, 1959). This is especially relevant in the light of increased trust in the market that has been deeply anchored in the institutional construction of the EU (Streeck & Thelen, 2005; Schmidt & Thatcher, 2014). The prospect of a reduced consumption or a political intervention in the market to limit consumption (see Di Guilio & Fuchs, 2014) and thus contribute to a reduction of recourse usage seems unlikely against this background. The argument of incremental change is linked to the impact of the policy context on instrument choices I discuss in the next section.

Relevance of Policy Context

Despite the target group characterization, the policy context impacts policy design. My argument is the following: Accompanying target group construction the institutional frame of EU's environmental policy presupposes the usage of soft policy instruments in the area of sustainable consumption policy. The course for soft policy instruments was set with the turn toward new environmental policy instruments and the "substantial shift in the dominant regulatory philosophy of the Commission" with the Fifth Environmental Action Programme in 1992 (Jordan et al., 2003, p. 563). Additionally, European environmental policy was "primarily a policy flanking the common market" (Knill & Liefferink, 2013, p. 14).

The policies analyzed in this paper are linked to the creation and potentially refinement of the common market, which is especially clear in regard to the *Single Market* for Green Products Agenda (SMGP) formulated in 2013 but holds also true for the other two agendas. In regard to the EU Eco-Label, the IPP addresses this label "as the best available label [...] covering the whole EU market" (COM/2003/302, p. 13). The SCP includes a single market perspective, too. It aims at setting standards for environmentally friendly products "throughout the Internal Market" and values the Common Market as the most important arena for "reinforcing information to consumers through a more coherent [...] labeling framework" (COM/2008/397, p. 2f.). Finally, the SMGP explicitly puts sustainable consumption policy and its instruments in the context of the internal market. The formulated agenda is designed to ensure "that the normal functioning of the internal market is enhanced" aiming at an increased uptake of green products throughout the EU (COM/2013/196, p. 2).

The relevance of soft policy instruments in this area can be linked to the turn of the EU toward new environmental policy instruments and a focus toward de-regulation (Holzinger, Knill & Lenschow, 2009, p. 49–50; Jordan, Benson, Wurzel & Zito, 2013). The prominence of soft policy instruments is based mainly on two factors. First, EU member states tried to preserve their national "long-established and successful national eco-label schemes" (Jordan et al., 2013, p. 314). Second, against the background of a complex decision making procedure on the supranational level in regard to binding top-down legislation and before mentioned national interests, the Commission increasingly relied on soft policy instruments and the harmonization of standards to be able to formulate policies in contested areas (Holzinger et al., 2009, p. 50). Thus, the institutional context of EU environmental policy favoring new and soft policy instruments impacts the choice of policy tools in the area of sustainable consumption. Especially, since the nature of soft policy instruments is to "activate rather than regulate" (Holzinger et al., 2009, p. 50). In this regard, the IPP can be considered a cornerstone of sustainable consumption policy in the EU since it has set the course for following agendas. The policy features the consumption perspective and assigns consumers the task of: "Purchasing greener Products" (COM/2003/302, p. 23). The document introduces two important aspects: (1) the prospect of a rational consumer and (2) the idea that a larger market share of green products contributes to sustainable development and environmental protection (linked to a weak sustainable consumption perspective). Thus, it is linked to the objectives and basics of general consumer policy in the Union. The two following policies, SCP and SMGP, use these perspectives and build on the IPP. Therefore, subsequent agendas dealing with the topic inherited the once defined perspective on consumers, their behavior and qualities as average-rational individuals, and the concentration on a rather reformatory weak sustainability approach impact (see section on theoretical background).

Furthermore, the EU's superior policy goals affect environmental and therefore also sustainable consumption policy. Within the analyzed documents, one global goal is economic growth. Economic objectives are important as a reason for an increased sustainable consumption and promotion of green products. The EU argues in favor of "improving the resource efficiency of EU economies [...]" that might lead to "[...] the creation of up to 2.8 million jobs by 2020" (COM/2013/196, p. 4). In this regard, the SCP puts sustainable consumption into the context of economic growth. The document starts with the description of the status quo: "Over six million jobs have been created in the last two years [...]. European industry is globally competitive [...]" (COM/2008/397, p. 1).[11] Following this introduction, the EU Commission focuses on the challenge of integrating sustainability-related aspects into this overall context of continuing economic growth. The framing of sustainable consumption with economic objectives does contribute to the choice of soft instruments. As the functioning of the internal market is an overall goal of European policy, the use of hard policy instruments or economic instruments (like eco-taxes on unsustainable products) seems rather unlikely. Additionally, because the domestic consumption is an important variable of economic growth, chances are low that policymakers consider measures that reduce the overall consumption (Ludvigson, 2004). In regard to conventional understandings of economic growth, buying more is usually better. Thus, sustainable consumption policies are consistent with the general objectives of EU environmental policy. Again, with the Fifth Environmental Action Program, the EU focused on bridging the goal of sustainable development and economic growth (Holzinger et al., 2009, p. 49). Furthermore, under the header of a green economy, the combination of both policy objectives is discussed and tends to favor a rather weak approach to sustainable consumption (Borel-Saladin & Turok, 2013; a critical assessment of the concept provides Brand, 2012). In the aftermath of the economic crisis of 2008 even the EU's environmental frontrunner states (e.g., Scandinavian member states, Germany, Netherlands), as well as the Commission and the majority of the European Parliament accepted the urgency for short-term economic agendas impacting not only environmental policy but other areas linked to sustainability as well (see Falkner, 2016; Pollex & Lenschow, 2016). Thus, a change in policy priorities occurred toward economic growth and pushed the concept of a green economy (Slominskis, 2016, p. 349, 351).

Analytically and empirically, this paper concentrated on the characterization of policy target groups and its impact on the choice of policy instruments. The analysis shows that the policy context must be considered. In the section on the theoretical background (p. 5) this paper discussed a basic analytical model to capture the elements policy problem, policy context and target group. Considering the empirical evidence in this paper, the relation of the three elements must be reconsidered. Figure 3 represents the connection between policy context and target group construction.

Especially, the policy context of an increased usage of new environmental instruments and the goal to activate and inform citizens and consumers (Holzinger et al., 2009; Jantke, Lottermoser, Reinhardt, Rothe & Stöver, 2016) effects the target group characterization. Because sustainable development and economic growth are seen as complementary, the role of individual consumption must be "fitted" into this context. With regard to the empirical analysis in this paper, I could show that consumers are seen as elements of the market and that sustainable consumption is interpreted as a complementary aspect to economic growth. Additionally, EU's general consumer policy supports an average-rational consumer characterization and the focus on non-coercive policy tools. Therefore, I argue that the target group construction is a crucial element for designing policy and choosing instruments and is also impacted by a policy context. Thus, different policy contexts (e.g., dominant interpretations within policy fields or differences in national policy areas) might also lead to different target group characterizations and roles assigned to them effecting in varying policy tools.

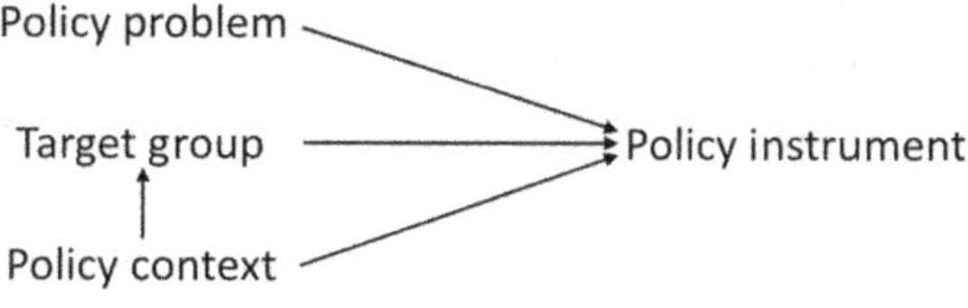

Figure 3. Relation of Policy Design Elements.

Conclusion

This paper raised the question why the European Union relies nearly exclusively on soft policy instruments in the area of sustainable consumption policy despite scientific and also societal requests for a more ambitious legislation to promote sustainable development. Consumer-focused policies merely try to persuade individuals of more sustainable behavior while the usage of coercion or manipulation (e.g., nudging) is neglected. To answer this question, the paper followed the assumption that the target group characterization heavily impacts the policy design. Looking at central policy documents, the paper shows the construction of a target group to be a key factor to affect instrument choices. Furthermore, the policy context seems to be of central importance for the description of a target group. Within the analyzed documents, the features of a green economy perspective entail an average-rational consumer characterization. Additionally, the overall context of environmental policy in the EU affects this consumer-perspective, too. The turn toward policies focusing on activating individuals rather than limiting options builds on a rational addressee characterization. Especially, the perspective on EU citizens as sovereign and competent actors in the market rather calls for policies to provide more information than to restrict individual freedom regarding consumption.

This result has implications for the three research strands I used to develop the paper's research question. First, in regard to research on the role of consumption for sustainable development: The European Union elaborates on the role of consumers for sustainability but only one of the analyzed documents provides a thorough examination of this topic. On the whole, the relevance assigned to consumers seems secondary. Especially with the economic crisis in the Union in 2008, policymakers focused on the cardinal objective of economic growth and prosperity. Sustainability is interpreted as a way to support this goal rather than being the primary focus. Thus, consumers—as average-rational individuals—become an integral part of the Union's green growth agenda and their role is fitted into these market-driven objectives. Second, in regard to expected ambitious policy goals in the area of sustainable consumption: The prospects of far-reaching legislation to support more environmentally friendly individual behavior or even limit consumption levels are slight. The turn toward individuals and consumers in policy is rather non-specific. Based on varying perceptions on consumers and their behavior—and thus on how to influence it—policies and research addressing individuals place diverse emphasis on the use of policy instruments. The relevance of consumption for sustainable development seems contested and calls for more intense research. Overall, the dominant focus in policy is regulating production instead of consumption. Third, although a turn toward consumers as well as toward behavioral aspects can be identified within political and environmental science, the approaches' impacts seem to be limited. This paper therefore calls for a deeper investigation of how new instruments and approaches are applied in policy and what conditions promote or limit their application. However, these instruments might be more relevant in some member states and other policy areas.

Lastly, the turn toward consumers and their role for sustainability is embedded into two "meta-frames." Frame one captures the focuses on a free and growth-oriented market and frame two deals with individual liberties. Both frames limit perspectives on sustainable consumption to the proliferation of green products and green growth. However, there are policy areas coined by different frames. For example, within health policy the protection of citizens' health "allows" policymakers to at least restrict options. The EU's policy on tobacco products might represent one interesting case for a deeper analysis and comparison. Thus, the understanding and analysis of these differences in policies and frames impacting policy areas is a challenge for policy analysis.

Jan Pollex is a Ph.D. candidate at the chair of European Integration and Policy at Osnabrueck University. His research interests include Policy Analysis, EU Environmental and Sustainability Policy, and Local Politics and Government.

Notes

I thank the anonymous reviewers for their helpful comments. Especially, I would like to thank Andrea Lenschow for her helpful feedback and support and the participants of the 2016 ECPR General Conference's Panel P130, European Environmental Politics' for their helpful comments on an earlier version of this paper. This work is part of the project "Sustainable Consumption of Information and Communication Technology in the Digital Society—Dialogue and Transformation through Open Innovation". The project is funded by the Ministry for Science and Culture of Lower Saxony and the Volkswagen Foundation (VolkswagenStiftung) through the "Niedersächsisches Vorab" grant programme (grant number VWZN3037).

1. Some researchers argue that a fundamental change in consumption patterns to reach a sustainable development requires a change in lifestyles since they impact individual perceptions of personal needs (e.g., Gilg, Barr & Ford, 2005). I cannot discuss these questions in this paper adequately and can only hint at research discussing these matters, e.g., Di Guilio and Fuchs put forward the idea of consumption corridors (2014); Seyfang (2006) links sustainable consumption to ethical aspects and the role of consumers as (ecological) citizens.
2. The Eco-Design directive is one example for this distinction. It aims at "greening" all products and thus addresses the production of goods and services. Thus, it addresses consumers only indirectly and does not aim at changing their behavior directly.
3. These approaches and concepts relate to rather reformatory ones like ecological modernization and more fundamental ones like degrowth, see: Lorek & Fuchs, 2011; Demaria, Schneider, Sekulova & Martinez-Alier, 2013. An insightful discussion of the effects of efficiency gains in products (e.g., rebound effect) is provided by Fuchs et al., 2016. I cannot include a more detailed discussion in this paper as it focuses on sustainable consumption policies.
4. The world summit on sustainable development marks only one milestone in the discussion of sustainable development. The idea of incorporating individual behavior into environmental protection was already discussed in Meadows, Meadows & Behrens, 1972.
5. These ideal type considerations are used as an analytical perspective on the documents investigated in this paper. A more in-depth discussion cannot be provided in this paper, for a deeper analysis see e.g., Geels et al., 2015.
6. Following Vedung (2007, p. 29–35) the paper understands soft policy instruments as tools using no coercion to change behavior. They differ from economic tools or regulations since they try to rationally convince addressees of a behavior change without forcing them to comply.

7. This focus on soft policy instruments must also be put into the context of the post-Maastricht era in which the EU concentrated on improving efficiency of regulation. I cannot discuss this in more detail in this paper. But see e.g., Jordan et al., 2003, p. 564.
8. The premise for using this simple model is some degree of rationality in the process of policymaking. I do not imply this rationality but use this model to clarify what is reason and what is effect.
9. I use policy instruments and policy tool as synonyms in this paper.
10. There might be a link to a sociological argumentation and analysis regarding the role of social norms and the relevance information can play for individuals trying to follow these norms. I cannot address this topic in this paper.
11. This is the first sentence of the document, which underlines the importance assigned to economic objectives.

References

Albers, M. 2016. "Staatliche Verbraucherinformation: Gewinn für Konsumentenentscheidungen oder Gängelei?" In *Nachhaltiger Konsum. Institutionen, Instrumente, Initiativen*, ed. K. Jantke, F. Lottermoser, J. Reinhardt, D. Rothe, and J. Stöver. Baden-Baden: Nomos, 167–94.

Beland, D., and M. Howlett. 2016. "How Solutions Chase Problems. Instrumental Constituencies in the Policy Process." *Governance: An International Journal of Policy, Administration and Institutions* 29 (3): 393–409.

Borel-Saladin, J. M., and I. N. Turok. 2013. "The Green Economy. Incremental Change or Transformation." *Environmental Policy and Governance* 23: 209–220.

Brand, U. 2012. "Green Economy—The Next Oxymoron?" *GAIA* 21: 28–32.

COM/2003/302. Integrated Product Policy. Building in Environmental Life-Cycle Thinking. Brussels. http://eur-lex.europa.eu/legal-content/EN/TXT/PDF/?uri=CELEX:52003DC0302&from=DE. Accessed June 18, 2003.

COM/2008/397. Sustainable Consumption and Production and Sustainable Industrial Policy Action Plan. Brussels. http://eur-lex.europa.eu/legal-content/EN/TXT/PDF/?uri=CELEX:52008DC0397&from=en. Accessed July 16, 2008.

COM/2013/196. Building the Single Market for Green Products. Brussels. http://eur-lex.europa.eu/legal-content/EN/TXT/PDF/?uri=CELEX:52013DC0196&from=DE. Accessed April 09, 2013.

Cseres, K. 2005. *Competition Law and Consumer Protection*. The Hague: Kluwer Law International.

Demaria, F., F. Schneider, F. Sekulova, and J. Martinez-Alier. 2013. "What is Degrowth? From an Activist Slogan to a Social Movement." *Environmental Values* 22: 191–215.

Di Guilio, A., and D. Fuchs. 2014. "Sustainable Consumption Corridors. Concepts, Objections and Responses." *GAIA* 23 (S1): 148–92.

Falkner, G. 2016. "The EU's Current Crisis and its Policy Effects: Research Design and Comparative Findings." *Journal of European Integration* 38: 219–35.

Fifth Environmental Action Programme. 1993. Towards Sustainability. A European Community programme of policy and action in relation to the environment and sustainable development, Official Journal of the European Communities No. C 138/5. May 05, 1993.

Fischer, F. 2007. "Deliberative Policy Analysis as Practical Reason: Integrating Empirical and Normative Arguments." In *Handbook of Public Policy Analysis. Theory, Politics, and Methods*, ed. Frank Fischer, Gerald J. Miller, and Mara S. Sidney (Hrsg.). Boca Raton, London, New York: CRC Press, 223–36.

Fuchs, D., A. Di Guilio, K. Glaab, S. Lorek, M. Maniates, T. Princen, and I. Ropke. 2016. "Power: The Missing Element in Sustainable Consumption and Absolute Reductions Research and Action." *Journal of Cleaner Production* 132: 298–307.

Geels, F. W., A. McMeekin, J. Mylan, and D. Southerton. 2015. "A Critical Appraisal of Sustainable Consumption and Production Research: The Reformist, Revolutionary and Reconfiguration Position." *Global Environmental Change* 34: 1–12.

Gilg, A., S. Barr, and N. Ford. 2005. "Green Consumption or Sustainable Lifestyles? Identifying the Sustainable Consumer." *Futures* 37 (6): 481–504.

Goldsmith, B. E., and S. Piscopo. 2014. "Advances in Consumer Education: European Initiatives." *International Journal of Consumer Studies* 38: 52–61.

Hajer, M. 2008. "Diskursanalyse in der Praxis: Koalitionen, Praktiken und Bedeutungen." In *Die Zukunft der Policy-Forschung*, ed. Frank Janning and Katrin Toens. Wiesbaden: Springer VS, 211–22.

Hoekstra, A. Y., and T. O. Wiedmann. 2014. "Humanity's Unsustainable Environmental Footprint." *Science* 344 (6188): 1114–7.

Holzinger, K., C. Knill, and A. Lenschow. 2009. "Governance in EU Environmental Policy." In *Innovative Governance in the European Union. The Politics of Multilevel Policymaking*, ed. I. Tömme, and A. Verdun. Lynne: Rienner Publisher, 45–62.

Howlett, M. 2009. "Governance Modes, Policy Regimes and Operational Plans: A Multi-level Nested Model of Policy Instrument Choice and Policy Design." *Policy Sciences* 42: 73–89.

Howlett, M., and R. P. Lejano. 2013. Tales from the crypt. The rise and fall (and Rebirth) of policy design. *Administration & Society*, 45 (3): 357–81.

Jantke, K., F. Lottermoser, J. Reinhardt, D. Rothe, and J. Stöver, eds. 2016. "Shoppen gehen im Anthropozän. Nachhaltiger Konsum als institutionelle Herausforderung." In *Nachhaltiger Konsum. Institutionen, Instrumente, Initiativen*, Baden-Baden: Nomos, 9–45.

Joerges, C. 1979. "Zielsetzungen und Instrumentarien der europäischen Verbraucherrechtspolitik: Eine Analyse von Entwicklungen im Bereich des Zivilrechts." *Zeitschrift für Verbraucherpolitik* 3 (4): 213–27.

John, R., M. Jaeger-Erben, and J. Rückert-John. 2016. "Elusive Practices: Considerations on Limits and Possibilities of Environmental Policy for Sustainable Consumption." *Environmental Policy and Governance* 26: 129–40.

Jordan, A., and C. Adelle. 2013. "EU Environmental Policy. Contexts, Actors and Policy Dynamics." In *Environmental Policy in the EU. Actors, Institutions and Processes*, 3rd ed., ed. Andrew Joran, and Adella Camilla. London: Routledge, 1–11.

Jordan, A., D. Benson, R. Wurzel, and A. Zito. 2013. "Governing with multiple policy instruments?" In *Environmental Policy in the EU*, 3rd ed., ed. A. Jordan, and C. Adelle. London: Routledge, 309–25.

Jordan, A., R. Wurzel, A. R. Zito, and L. Bruecker. 2003. "European Governance and the Transfer of New Environmental Instruments (NEPIs) in the European Union." *Public Administration* 81 (3): 555–74.

———. 2009. "Consumer Responsibility-Taking and Eco-Labelling Schemes in Europe." In *Politics, Products and Markets. Exploring Political Consumerism Past and Present*, ed. Michele Micheletti, Dietlind Stolle, and Andreas Follesdal. New Brunswick: Transaction, 161–80.

Knill, C., and D. Liefferink. 2013. "The Establishment of EU Environmental Policy." In *Environmental Policy in the EU. Actors, Institutions and Processes*, 3rd ed., ed. Andrew Joran, and Adelle Camilla. London: Routledge, 13–31.

Lindblom, Charles E. 1959. "The Science of 'Muddling Through'." *Public Administration Review* 19 (2): 79–88.

Lorek, S., and D. Fuchs. 2011. "Strong Sustainable Consumption Governance—Precondition for a Degrowth Path?" *Journal of Cleaner Production* 38: 36–43.

Ludvigson, S. C. 2004. "Consumer Confidence and Consumer Spending." *Journal of Economic Perspectives* 18 (2): 29–50.

Mayring, P. 2008. *Qualitative Inhaltsanalyse*. Weinheim: Deutscher Studien Verlag.

Meadows, D. H., D. L. Meadows, and J. R. W. Behrens. 1972. *The Limits to Growth. A Report for the Lub of Rome's Project on the Predicament of Mankind*. New York: Universe Books.

Murphy, J. 2001. "From Production to Consumption: Environmental Policy in the European Union." In *Exploring Sustainable Consumption. Environmental Policy and the Social Sciences*, ed. Maurie J. Cohen, and Joseph Murphy. Amsterdam: Elsevier Science & Technology, 39–58.

Norwegian Ministry for the Environment. 1994. *Symposium on Sustainable Consumption.* Oslo, Norway: Norwegian Ministry for the Environment.

Pollex, J., and A. Lenschow. 2016. "Surrendering to Growth? European Union's Goals for Research and Technology in the Horizon 2020 Framework." *Journal of Cleaner Production Special Issue on Degrowth and Technology.* doi:10.1016/j.jclepro.2016.10.195.

Rauh, C. 2016. *A Responsive Technocracy? EU Politicisation and the Consumer Policies of the European Commission.* Colchester: ECPR Press.

Rose, Richard. 1990. "Inheritance Before Choice in Public Policy." *Journal of Theoretical Politics* 2 (3): 263–91.

Schmidt, V. A., and M. Thatcher. 2014. "Why Neoliberal Ideas so Resilient in Europe's Political Economy?" *Critical Policy Studies* 8 (3): 340–7.

Schneider, A. 2015. "Policy Design and Transfer." In *Routledge Handbook of Public Policy*, ed. E. Aral, S. Fritzen, M. Howlett, M. Ramesh, and X. Wu. London: Routledge, 217–28.

Schneider, A., and H. Ingram. 1990. "Behavioural Assumptions of Policy Tools." *The Journal of Politics* 52 (2): 510–29.

———. 1993. "Social Construction of Target Populations: Implications for Politics and Policy." *The American Political Science Review* 87 (2): 334–47.

Scholl, G., F. Rubik, H. Kalimo, K. Biedenkopf, and O. Söebech. 2010. "Policies to Promote Sustainable Consumption. Innovative Approaches in Europe." *Natural Resources Forum* 34: 39–50.

Seyfang, G. 2006. "Ecological Citizenship and Sustainable Consumption: Examining Local Organic Food Networks." *Journal of Rural Studies* 22: 383–95.

Slominskis, P. 2016. "Energy and Climate Policy. Does the Competitiveness Narrative Prevail in Times of Crisis?" *Journal of European Integration* 38 (3): 343–57.

Spaargaren, G., and A. P. J. Mol. 2008. "Greening Global Consumption: Redefining Politics and Authority." *Global Environmental Change* 18: 350–9.

Strassheim, H., and R-L. Korinek. 2015. "Behavioural Governance in Europe." In *Future Directions for Scientific Advice in Europe*, ed. James Wilsdon, and Robert Doubleday. Cambridge: Creative Commons, 155–62.

Streeck, W., and K. Thelen. 2005. "Introduction. Institutional Change in Advanced Political Economies." In *Beyond Continuity. Institutional Change in Advanced Political Economies*, ed. Wolfgang Streeck, and Kathleen Thelen. Oxford: Oxford University Press, 1–39.

Thaler, Richard H., and Cass R. Sunstein. 2009. *Nudge. Improving Decisions About Health, Wealth and Happiness.* London: Penguin.

Vedung, E. 2007. Policy Instruments: Typologies and Theories. In *Carrots, Sticks & Sermons. Policy Instruments & their Evaluation*, ed. Marie-Louise Bemelmans-Videc, Ray C. Rist, and Evert Vedung. New Brunswick, London: Transaction Publishers, 21–58.

WBGU: Wissenschaftlicher Beirat der Bundesregierung Globale Umweltveränderungen, Hauptgutachten. 2011. *Welt im Wandel: Gesellschaftsvertrag für eine Große Transformation.* Berlin: Wissenschaftlicher Beirat der Bundesregierung Globale Umweltveränderungen.

Weatherill, S. 2013. *EU Consumer Law and Policy.* Cheltenham: Edward Elgar.

Yanow, D. 2000. *Conducting Interpretive Policy Analysis*, vol. 47. Thousand Oaks, CA: Sage.

Why You Should Read My Book

Nikolaos Zahariadis (ed.) 2016: Handbook of Public Policy Agenda Setting. Cheltenham, UK and Northampton, MA: Edward Elgar. ISBN 978-1-78471-591-5.

It is the first nearly exhaustive guide to the study of agenda setting from its origins to the present day and beyond. It introduces the most important theories and concepts such as multiple streams or punctuated equilibrium, paying attention to institutions such as the media or policy entrepreneurs, and comparatively applying theories to different issues in a variety of empirical settings, such as the US federal government, the European Union, natural disasters, and others. Aside from expanding the debate and charting likely future research agendas, the book also includes chapters on agenda setting's "founding fathers"—Cobb, Elder, and Kingdon—providing context to individual scholarship in order to gain a better sense of why and how the field was created.

Nikolaos Zahariadis
Rhodes College, Memphis, TN, USA

doi: 10.1002/epa2.1011

Nikolaos Zahariadis (ed.) 2014: Frameworks of the European Union's Policy Process: Competition and Complementarity across the Theoretical Divide. London and New York: Routledge. ISBN 9780415719230.

The book aims to build better theoretical frameworks of the European Union's policy process. In a single volume, chapters written by proponents of promising policy lenses—punctuated equilibrium, multiple streams, normative power Europe, constructivism, advocacy coalitions, policy learning, and multilevel governance—specify the assumptions, logic, and hypotheses of each lens, assess theoretical strengths and limitations, and develop a research agenda utilizing the lenses both as competing and as complementary explanations. The book's significance rests on outlining a research design that explains which lenses to use and when, based on the filters of institutional and issue complexity.

Nikolaos Zahariadis
Rhodes College, Memphis, TN, USA

doi: 10.1002/epa2.1012

Michael Hill and Frédéric Varone (eds.) 2017: The Public Policy Process. London and New York: Routledge. Seventh edition. ISBN 978-1-138-90950-2, www.routledge.com/9781138909502.

This textbook is essential reading for anyone trying to understand the complexities inherent in policy processes. It gives a thorough analysis of the various actors involved in policy-making, namely politicians, pressure groups, civil servants, publicly employed professionals, academic experts, journalists, and even sometimes those who see themselves as the passive recipients of policy. Its discussion of the policy process is grounded in an extensive consideration of the nature of power in society and in the state. The book provides a rich and accessible overview of relevant policy process theories: e.g., pluralism, neo-corporatism, Marxism, rational choice, policy networks, advocacy coalitions, punctuated equilibrium, policy narratives, street-level bureaucracy, or the policy process at the age of governance and accountability. Illustrative examples from a diverse set of policy issues and countries show how these theories can be applied. In addition, an extensive chapter is dedicated to the design of comparative policy studies. This book thus offers a firm foundation for new students, experienced scholars, and practitioners for understanding, studying and influencing policy processes.

Michael Hill[1] and Frédéric Varone[2]
[1]*University of Newcastle and* [2]*Département de Science Politique et Relations Internationales, Université de Genève*

doi: 10.1002/epa2.1009

Sabine Kuhlmann and Geert Bouckaert (eds.) 2016: Local Public Sector Reforms in Times of Crisis: National Trajectories and International Comparison. Governance and Public Management Series; Palgrave Macmillan. ISBN 978-1-137-52548-2.

Our book compares the trajectories and effects of local public sector reforms in Europe and fills a research gap that has existed so far in comparative public administration and local government studies. Based on the results of the COST

Action entitled, "Local Public Sector Reforms: an International Comparison," the volume is a unique synthesis of local-level reforms covering 28 countries on key issues that will shape the future of local government in the next decades, questioning the impact of New Public Management, and revealing the diversity of reform paths. It is the first time that territorial, functional, managerial, and political reforms of the local public sector are considered jointly at such a scale. The book brings together the most renowned local government scholars in Europe and presents an extensive, and at the same time nuanced, analysis of modernization movements in various countries. The contributions provide the reader with insights into specific reform processes, as well as with middle-range theories and broader views on general trends of reforms from a trans-European perspective. The analyses of the tensions and trajectories are sharp and the implications for practitioners are prescient. Reading our book will be an enrichment to all those who study and teach public administration and local government from a comparative perspective as well as to practitioners interested in current reform trends and impacts.

Geert Bouckaert[1] and Sabine Kuhlmann[2]
[1]*Public Governance Institute, KU Leuven and* [2]*University Potsdam*

doi: 10.1002/epa2.1010

Michael W. Bauer, Christoph Knill and Steffen Eckhard (eds.) 2017: International Bureaucracy: Challenges and Lessons for Public Administration Research (Public Sector Organizations Series) London: Palgrave MacMillan. ISBN 978-1-349-94977-9.

You may be interested in this book for three reasons. First, you agree that comparing constitutes the heart of systematic understanding in public administration (PA). Second, you are convinced that a prime challenge for PA lies in reconnecting our discipline with the ongoing transformation of the nation states into international orders. Third, you wonder whether our classical analytical concepts for understanding bureaucratic behavior and administrative impact on policy making are still valid in multilevel and international constellations. If any of these points are of interest to you, "international bureaucracy" might make a good read. We apply established PA concepts such as influence, authority, administrative styles, autonomy, budgeting, and multilevel administration to the study of international bureaucracies. By doing so, we learn how international public administrations function and whether international bureaucracies are actually "special." The short answer is they are not in terms of pure bureaucratic organization, but they are in view of their competences as well as of their institutional and political environment—and this has consequences. International public administrations, so our main thesis, do spearhead developments likely to gain importance also for national administrative governance. If anything, our volume shows how important it is to take the challenges posed by bureaucratic internationalization (more) seriously.

Michael W. Bauer
German University of Administrative Sciences Speyer

doi: 10.1002/epa2.1008

www.ingramcontent.com/pod-product-compliance
Lightning Source LLC
Chambersburg PA
CBHW081646270326
41933CB00018B/3366
* 9 7 8 1 6 3 3 9 1 6 0 4 3 *